DARE *TO BE* SPIRITUAL

PATRICK MOONEY

authorHOUSE®

AuthorHouse™ UK
1663 Liberty Drive
Bloomington, IN 47403 USA
www.authorhouse.co.uk
Phone: UK TFN: 0800 0148641 (Toll Free inside the UK)
       UK Local: 02036 956322 (+44 20 3695 6322 from outside the UK)

Published by AuthorHouse 06/23/2021

ISBN: 978-1-6655-9098-3 (sc)
ISBN: 978-1-6655-9099-0 (hc)
ISBN: 978-1-6655-9100-3 (e)

There is a world of difference between "nothing" and "no thing". Initially this may seem but a nuance of the English language. In fact, it involves the most fundamental of all questions on earth: "Is life meaningful, or is it absurd?"

How we answer this question determines our existence. It has become alarmingly clear that the overriding paradigm of atheistic materialism, which has so captivated the attention of the human mind, is leading to our destruction. Our world is deteriorating at an alarming rate. The paradigm of materialism is not working. Assured by the aggressive claims of atheistic science, we have opted for absurdity. We entered the battle on warhorses, but now we are returning, bedraggled and weary, on crutches. Atheistic materialism is killing us. Humanity needs a new paradigm.

Infidelity to the status quo must become our new orthodoxy.

We impose excessively the temporary on the eternal.

We have forfeited our heritage for a bunch of empty promises.

Wonder has lost its sense of mystery. The lowest common denominator has become the measure of our success and potential excellence. Violence and decadence have become the prevailing patrimony of Western culture. We have forfeited art to insidious entertainment and vulgar amusement. We are a people distracted from our own dignity.

The masterpiece we have been called to create has been covered over by peeling paint.

We are but a celluloid copy of our true reality. Idiot laughter claps like thunder and steals all our attention and meditation. The voice of conscience has been shoved to the perimeter of our human experience. We live like dummies.

The flowers we grow in our garden have plastic roots. We have lost our sense of the one, the true, and the beautiful. Profit and competition matter much more than cooperation. Matter itself has outstripped what matters.

An apocalypse of catastrophic proportions awaits civilized humanity unless we change to a new paradigm.

Quite simply, according to atheistic enlightenment, we have, through natural selection, arrived at a full-stop conclusion in our evolutionary journey. We are taught to believe that our consciousness of being conscious is the full complement of human existence. Humanity is its own conclusion. Consciousness has nothing further into which it can proceed. We are no

1

longer of the future. We have no possibility. Because of this full-stop conclusion, which atheism promotes, the human race has been hijacked from a more benign potency.

For the past three thousand years, since the Iron Age, the human race has become more and more violent. Our ploughshares have been turned into swords, and our swords into nuclear bombs. Never has the story of humanity needed a sense of morality more. The domination of atheistic materialism is so cleverly subversive that in our dumbed-down culture, we no longer are aware of its rampant ensnarement and enslavement.

Indeed, we seem to relish it.

Insisting that the purpose of evolution involves only man's ingenuity and creativity, with no great nonlocal Intelligence to guide it, is like saying that the creation of nuclear warfare is so far our greatest achievement, and that violence and aggression define us. Evil always triumphs when morality is missing. We fail to become aware that atheistic materialism is subversive. The signs of our times indicate this. We are decadent. Atheism promotes the manufacture of lethal machines, which return obscene profits to their makers.

In such a world, horror and terror become our acceptable insanities.

This makes the waging of war appealing. The West has become expert in invasion and the creation of war—not because of threat to the home front, but merely for the exploitation of natural resources which do not belong to us. If we do not balance our grasping arrogance as the world's masters, then the natural world will in time get rid of us. It is time for the Christian West, through nonviolent resistance, to heed the prophetic voice of its courageous Founder. The time has come for individual Christians to fire their consciences instead of guns. We make a difference one by one.

One book, One pen,
One child, One teacher can save the world.
—Malala Yousafzai

A passion of conscience is the only rational way to subvert our national differences. The time is here for a new style of stock exchange. Christ has told us that we find by giving away. We become more by giving ourselves to one another.

The spirituality of nonviolent resistance is urgently needed to change our controlling ways. We have tried too much violence already, and it has not made us happy. We may prove our might through our murdering and conquering ways, but eventually each of us will die alone, when no state is capable of salving our consciences.

A materialistic society is driven by an attitude of self-entitlement. We in the West are very good at demanding civil rights be respected in foreign nations, but we forget that privileges are coupled with obligations. We in the West have huge obligations towards poorer nations because of all the goods we have stolen from them through our imperialism. We can only accept ourselves as being civilized and enlightened to the extent that we live connected lives with nations that suffer from poverty and deprivation.

If we do not awaken to our responsibility, Mother Nature will get rid of us. We think of invasion and war as always happening in other nations, but astoundingly, we have scarcely realized terrorism far worse than that perpetrated by ISIS is working right here in our homes. Its mission is to destabilize our Christianity and turn us into slaves to serve an atheistic agenda. A bunch of self-appointed psychopaths, called the illuminati or elites, direct destructive missiles towards us, but we are so placated with trivia that we continue to remain somnambulant and indifferent. Passivity promotes decadence and a zombie existence. When we die to the one, the true, and the beautiful, we die to all that is best about us. We exchange our wonder and our worth for a fistful of fiat money that is not worth the paper it is printed on. This is the reality we are living in. Our minds have been more murdered than our bodies.

Wolves in sheep's clothing crawl along the corridors of our minds, but we have become so passive that we see feet instead of claws. We have been lullabied into complacency to such a degree that we now live as nicely behaved zombies. We have become what the pathological elites want us to be: obedient servants to their system of slavery. We have become so incrementally brainwashed by the dream of a false utopia that the needs of our egos have become primary. We are taught that satiation of the ego is our only purpose. Contrary to natural law, the profit motive has become the driving force of our lives.

We believe material goods are our one and only sufficiency.

The crisis facing our planet is not between materialism and religion. It is not between the nanotechnological wizardry of man versus the irrational claim of organized religion's pie-in-the-sky divinity. The crisis stems from our failure to differentiate between religion and spirituality on the one hand, and religion and politics on the other. Social inequality arises exactly because we have failed to balance the relationship between materiality and spirituality.

Atheistic materiality can never bring peace to our planet. The fact that we are now on the nuclear level of our so-called material progress is in itself a siren warning: materialism alone as the essence of our definition will destroy us. Natural law is always unitive. The human body has no meaning or purpose without its spiritual dimension. Inequality keeps spiralling upward because of this imbalance, to the point that sixty rich people now own more wealth than half the earth's human population. The exploitation of the egotistical, atheistic few has reduced most of the human race to slavery.

Not only have we separated the interconnection between materialism (immanence) and spirituality (transcendence), but even more confusedly, we identify religion with spirituality. We have failed to separate spirituality from religion. We think they are synonymous, whereas in fact they are as distinct from each other as spirituality is from politics. Spirituality's concern is transcendence. It involves the inner journey. It connects the outer to the inner. Spirituality is about the story of life as a continuum. It is about the holiness and sanctity of the ordinary. Its process is from the I to the thou. It forgets the self for the sake of the beloved. Spirituality is the journey of selfishness into selflessness. Spirituality teaches that we are most ourselves when we give ourselves away truly, as Jesus said, "We find by losing … we receive by giving away."

Nothing that you have not given away will ever really be yours.

—C. S. Lewis

Spirituality in its purest form has always taught that forgetfulness of the ego is the greatest healing we can offer to the world. Religion, on the other hand, politicizes spirituality. Religion robs spirituality of its purity. Religion involves itself much more with the ego than it does with selfless love.

Atheistic materialism and religion are strange bedfellows. They both mongrelize spirituality. They both feign goodness in their prescriptions for the human race, but underneath they are whitened sepulchres and lechers.

The self, the ego, is the god of materialistic atheism. Its prevailing philosophy is selfishness. Its only concern is its own self-interest. It dismisses the idea of transcendence in favour of bodily satiation.

Atheistic science, from the so-called period of the Enlightenment, and especially since the publication of Darwin's theory of evolution, insists that life came about by mere chance. It is a random act. Natural selection remains the only purpose of the evolutionary push. This theory is taught in all secular schools, to the exclusion of ideas of God. It totally contradicts the existence of a spiritual dimension to human existence. With this frame of reference, and in order to strengthen its own self-interest, scientific atheism dismisses religion as unenlightened and superstitious. To believe in a benign God is poppycock. If this is the case, why on earth make any step to walk in the direction of a dead-end street? There can be no journey without a destiny! Why suffer if there is no mystery to live? Better to get it over and done with. A Mercedes-Benz cannot make the journey more ultimately enjoyable.

It doesn't seem reasonable that the chaos born from the big bang should end in natural selection, as atheistic materialists claim. Atheists rage against a belief in a benign God, deeming it but a childish search for security. Freud calls it "opium". Modern psychology, stripped of a spiritual dimension, suggests other opiates to enable us to get rid of our anxiety. No cure, however, seems to fully satisfy our human search for meaning without integrating mind and body. Atheistic psychology, bereft of a spiritual component, turns the human race into cosmic orphans.

It is the atheistic demand for reasonable evidence which is itself unreasonable. Proof comes through a higher discipline than the flatland of mathematics. It is illogical to demand the discipline and expertise of one regime or sphere from another. The farm work of a labouring man is of a different vintage than the neuroscience of a doctor. The huge expanse of an elephant cannot be measured by the tiny circumference of a mosquito which may have landed on it.

Truth comes through our capacity to imagine it. Evidence is mystical. It comes through our practice of it. It cannot be realized without its subjective application. Atheism cannot understand this because it separates the spiritual component of the imagination from what it deems logical.

We will never know what the accepting smile on another's face can do to us unless we ourselves have experienced it and responded to it. A smile is its own rational evidence.

When atheism debunks the spiritual dimension in our search for truth, it thereby debunks all the potentiality of our five senses. How can atheists possibly tell us anything about seeing when it lives in blindness? Atheism, which demands reasonableness, is itself totally unreasonable.

There can be no operation without a spiritual dimension. Without a taste for life, there is no reason to taste it. Why should we practise and sacrifice for a marathon without a reason to run in it? When what is natural is closed to our desires, we become like aborted foetuses, never knowing the light of day.

It does not seem reasonable that nature can have an evil intention. Why should we have an unquenchable longing for something more without any possibility of appeasement and closure?

> I find within myself a desire which no experience in
> the world can satisfy, the most probable explanation
> is that I was made for another world.
>
> —C. S. Lewis

Why achieve if we cannot create? Creativity gives us our greatest impulse.

Without spirit, we turn our Davids and Pietàs into blocks of marble and our great paintings into blank canvases. The elan of humanity loses all its meaning and purpose without direction. The absence of creativity in any civilized society is the greatest proof that it needs therapy. The murder and mayhem now raging in the West exists because the domain of humanity's spiritual impulse is notoriously squashed to pieces.

Creativity arises out of a clash of opposites. When God is excluded from human society, imbalance sets in. Evil becomes rampant. The spiritual realm is always within us. It is up to each one of us to send it an invitation to appear at our banquet.

Atheism, on the other hand, totally lacks imagination. Unlike Michelangelo, atheism looks at a block of marble and declares to the world that it is impossible for a David to come out of it. David is not there! End of message! Atheism teaches that children, looking for the comfort of parents, want him to be there for the sake of security. It is impossible for something to come out of nothing. Thus ends their doctrine. The creativity of spiritual imagining tells a more benign story.

Western civilization without a guiding principle is like a shoal of fish in a devouring sea, with no comprehension of its immensity. The absurdity which atheism promotes is the most tragic flaw in our evolutionary flow of complexity consciousness. Why study cerebrally without opening it to a more profound complexity? To give a conclusion before even studying another possibility insults our intelligence. It is the most absurd profanity of all.

Insidiously, atheism has stopped the fullest expression of complexity consciousness in midtrack. To deny as absurd humanity's inbred urge for a spiritual resolution to the human journey, atheism keeps the human race on the purely egoic level. While admitting survival of the fittest, it denies the triumph of good over evil. On the purely egoic level, it accepts the material gain which survival of the fittest brings, but dismisses the capacity for good which compassion and love offer humanity through spirituality. Atheism is incalculably more divisive than any of the culturally religious expressions of God.

In comparison to the earth's fifteen billion years, the evolution of the human species is but four billion years old. The story of humanity's appearance is comparatively recent. In terms of all the accumulated wisdom of the earth, atheism is of recent vintage. It is a newcomer to the block of complexity consciousness and by far its most dangerous enemy. Never before in the history of humanity has such an outrageous attack been levelled against divinity and transcendence. Despite its more recent incarnation, atheism arrogantly attempts to replace the wisdom of the ages with its own dogmatic thinking.

The intention of atheism is malevolent. Through mind control, it aborts the soul of humanity, leaving the human race with naught but the skeleton of the body. So successful has its mission been in Western society that citizens, without a murmur, have become the sheep and the atheistic elites the herder. As herders, their aim is to slaughter rather than shepherd. The Atlanta Guide Stone makes this evident.

Atheism introduces, self-admittedly, the diabolical and the occult as the dominant force in in determining a new world order. Paradoxically the most atheistic secret societies, such as the illuminati, have no problem in accepting the Devil, while at the same time, they deny the existence of God. The Devil has no tolerance for compassion. An evil man considers love a curse. That is why the cult of the elites is so dangerous. This club has no sense of faithfulness to anyone outside their brotherhood.

Theists believe complexity consciousness continues after natural selection atheists disagree. Complexity consciousness means that consciousness grows more complex as it evolves from one species to a higher one. Thus the mind of man is more complex than that of an animal. To be conscious is to know there is nothing after the chance nothingness of atheism. The amazing complexity involved in the evolutionary push, according to atheists, has no purpose except to introduce atheism.

Theists who believe in a benign prospect see that earth is magnificently fine-tuned. Not even the human imagination can capture the ineffability of its structure. The big bang already had the human person in mind when it first exploded. All the chemicals and minerals necessary for our appearance were congealed and churned in that first clash. We have been concocted from stardust.

Could such a stardust clash have been designed to process us with rising complexity, only to make us conscious of being conscious? Is this the end of our story? So the atheistic doctrine of the West declares. In essence, atheism tells us that to be conscious of being conscious is all there is to life. We have been brought through the complexity of evolution for this reason, and it all happened by mere chance.

Most of Western society, because it is so caught up in the ego, doesn't remotely realize that the atheistic agenda is now in control of our minds. Like cattle to slaughter, we take the twisted route of atheism's herding without even suspecting the looming slaughterhouse around the corner. Atheism, through its insistence that the story of evolution ends in natural selection, arrests the growth of complexity consciousness and demands that we stay on the level of the animal. Atheism proposes that from now on, we can solve our problems through the material and the mathematical.

The West now lives in the clutch of atheism. Humanity accepts its insidious grip on the human mind as progressive, modern, and enlightened.

Modern society is very sick. Contemporary society recognizes this, but continues to support its butchers without a murmur.

We are falling apart psychologically. Family life has been degraded because the pressure to pay the mortgage compels both parents to work outside the home. Many of us seek therapy to relieve stress. Rarely do we make a connection between our planet's sickness and atheism.

We are ill at ease with ourselves. We feel dis-eased. We fail to realize we are as commodified as the offerings on shop shelves. We have become as marketable as any other commodity and are viewed as objects to increase profit. Atheism has made us into things.

Atheism dehumanizes. We fail to realize what it has done to the human race. Because it saturates our mentality and dominates all our forums, we accept it as normal. Like fish in water, we fail to see the immensity of the sea. Like a delinquent cell in the body, atheism snowballs with such intensity that we fail to detect the cancer it is causing. Atheism brings disease with it.

The time is already here when we must start a revolution against atheism. It is time to enter a new paradigm, in which matter and spirit are joined together and never again permitted to be separate. Complexity consciousness must be allowed to continue on its unique journey to unity, where parts are connected to each other and become one in the one whole.

The moment we cross over the threshold between good and evil, we decide whether the devil or the saint dwells within us. The decision is not partial. Because of that choice, we decide between evil and good, meaning and absurdity.

Western civilization, so dumbed-down spiritually because of the aggression of materialistic atheism, has scarcely realized how our basic instincts for the good have been coerced and prostituted towards evil and its results. Evolution, as presented in public education, is only partial and not full. It creates more evil than good in its thwarted pedagogy. As such it again suggests the triumph of evil over good, which remarkably suits the atheistic agenda.

No money or profit is involved when spirituality abounds. God is a threat in the marketplace of atheistic materialism. Atheists do not want divinity to invade their space. Atheism must surely feel confident and triumphant in removing complexity consciousness from public education and also from Washington, Wall Street, and the European Union.

One day for sure, if and when public consciousness awakens, the idolatry of atheism will be toppled, and the human race will be integrated with its spiritual dimension. Nature dooms us to continue the way towards a singularity and unity of consciousness. Spirituality will have the final say.

Evil triumphs when the one, the true, and the beautiful are taken out of the equation. When we invade, occupy, wage war, murder, maim, and exploit, evil triumphs. Corruption is never impartial in the vicious way it carries out its consequences. Humanity designates itself by its actions. The rest is hyperbole and hypocrisy.

Cultural religious differences necessarily create tensions. However, these tensions are caused by man and are not intrinsic to the process of consciousness complexity. That is why it is absurd to teach but half of our evolutionary journey and its complexity consciousness to students in public schools. The rendition given in public education is only half the story. It refuses to teach the possibility of a future for consciousness. This is tantamount to the state promoting the atheism of nihilism.

In the interest of parity, the full story of complexity consciousness in evolution should be taught, rather than the partial one which best suits the atheistic agenda.

The problem with the atheistic rendition of evolution is that it stops with humanity without any further process. Human civilization and refinement are ongoing phenomena, despite what atheistic materialism proclaims.

The unquenchable longing stamped by nature in the mind of every person is readily recognisable. We accept the insufficiency involved in all that is materially available. This admission indicates that there is something or someone outside natural selection who will give an answer to our cosmic yearning. The answer which materialistic atheism presents is not enough.

The atheistic rendition solidifies the onward push of complexity consciousness precisely at its halfway point. It denies the human species any further growth of complexity into a higher experience of reality. Complexity growth cannot be measured by the grasping of money, weapons, or the deceit of Wall Street. Atheism measures progress and growth precisely on this principle.

All the decimating barbarism we experience on earth today stems precisely from the half-told story of our evolution. Without truly realizing it, humanity has retarded complexity consciousness by catering to our egoic needs without an impulse to attend the needs of our spirits. We have grown spiritually illiterate simply because we have allowed our unquenchable appetite for something more to be almost entirely smothered by the lust of our egos. Atheistic materialism has usurped complexity consciousness from evolving into something greater, which is our inbred need to grow ethically and morally stronger.

Human society, in order to become stronger and more civilized, needs refinement if it is to take on the mantle of complexity consciousness. If, as atheists declare in their half-told story, complexity has ceased with the appearance of the humanoid, then the process of evolution becomes a closed book. We are born only to disappear.

If such is the case, why has nature been so cruel? It has given us a clue through our unquenchable longing for something greater, only to throw vomit over it when we have tried to believe in immortality. The half-told story of growing complexity is the very foundation for all Western institutions. Rather than being progressive, it retards our growth. There cannot be true development or progress without a further growth into complexity consciousness. A spiritual dimension is needed to define us. We have not reached the end of our human journey yet. Complexity consciousness still continues.

A half-told story can create more damage than it resolves. Atheism insists on the separation of church and state—rightly so, simply because cultural religious differences, if taught in a public forum, would surely cause problems between one religious group and another. But complexity consciousness is not a religious issue. Complexity consciousness is in total harmony with the idea of a cosmotheandric God. Without the baggage of our religious cultural differences, most spiritually inclined people agree that we all have the same God. A cosmotheandric God is the God that best addresses the unquenchable longing of the human spirit for something more. A cosmotheandric God rises beyond our universe and is the one God who, despite our religious cultural differences, is accessible to the whole cosmos.

Our evolutionary journey from the big bang forward has always been driven by complexity consciousness. The central truth in our dynamic journey has been compromised and stultified by the atheistic agenda. Evolution from its very beginning has been driven by complexity consciousness enlarging our vision. Atheists dogmatize that natural selection is the end of the human evolutionary process. But the unquenchable longing of the human spirit for something more is not addressed when atheists insist the parts are the whole. Quantum physics determines this to be atheistic science's greatest blunder. Evolution instead thunders on, in a spirit of complexity consciousness, into its unity with its cosmotheandric God.

Evolution through complexity consciousness joins humanity to a higher reality. Evolution of the spirit carries on. Complexity consciousness now centres itself in the human mind.

To grow into a higher complexity demands that ethical and moral behaviour enter into the equation, else we stay on the purely biological animal level. If we do not grow in complexity, then we retard the evolutionary flow. The only way we can enter into a higher plane is through our carved-out spirituality.

The gift of self-awareness introduces the next step in our complexity consciousness push. Our Olympian journey continues into something higher. We have now been introduced to the reality of our spirituality. We can remain fixated, as atheism imposes, or we can decide to refine ourselves into a greater complexity of consciousness. From now on we must cooperate with the evolutionary process. Atheism insists we stay put on the purely natural selection level. It is a dead-end street. A spiritually centred reality views natural selection as a crossroads instead of a dead-end street.

We have the freedom to choose retardation and minimization, or we can opt for ecstasy in and through our human journey.

To impose the atheistic view on the human mind is to promote but half of the human evolutionary journey. This is tantamount to the state promoting atheism. The complexity of consciousness, which has always been the dynamo driving the evolutionary process forward, has not ended with the appearance of the humanoid. Thus far we have arrived in a state where we are conscious of being conscious. But why must the dynamic radial pull to refine the species into more complexity stay on the level of the human mind?

Atheism, which is the dominant paradigm of Western society, will not tolerate a greater understanding of complexity consciousness to be entertained in any public forum, be it the public education system or political institutions. As a consequence of this state of affairs, morality and ethics become more and more compromised in the interest of atheism. When hedonism becomes the norm, morality flies out the window. Contrary to the dominant paradigm of atheism, if the full evolutionary story of complexity consciousness were to prevail, morality and ethics would necessarily enter the public forum. If this were to happen, as indeed it must, atheistic materialism would lose its monopolistic grasp on the human mind.

The greatest flaw prevalent in Western society is that the construct of Darwin's evolutionary story ends with natural selection. Darwin acknowledges complexity but says nothing about consciousness. But why may we not say that evolution still continues on a road to higher complexity? Why close it off to new possibilities? When matter becomes consciousness, as quantum physics teaches, spirituality becomes a possibility.

Why can there not be something beyond physical death in store for us? Why must the irreducibility of the atom be destructive instead of constructive? Why is no thing the end? Is it not possible that a mystical nothingness provides the answer to our complexity? Consciousness has the potential to carry us into an even greater complexity. Evolution is not over and done with yet.

13

Why must natural selection stay stuck? If the evolutionary journey is process, then surely it is future-orientated. If that is so, a spiritual dimension can logically enter with ethics and morality to guide us. Atheists claim ethics and morality belong on the ordinary plane of our everyday lives. But once they say this, atheism goes out the window. Life has a purpose when it becomes moral. If that is so, then the very evidence of divinity's presence has entered into the human condition. The moral code indicates some absolute. But atheism denies an absolute.

Without ever recognizing it, atheists who live morally and ethically—despite their protestations—are agnostics at least, and no longer disclaim the possibility of God with rational evidence. To live according to a moral code is to admit the possibility of God. Atheism is a non sequitur. We need spirituality in our public forum. Otherwise evolution will get rid of us.

Atheism only begets its own death and absurdity.

To know is to learn that we do not know very much. The more we learn from our searching, the more we uncover miraculous balance and fine-tuning in the cosmos. The more miraculous happenings we uncover, the more we realize they are embedded with even more complexity.

To search and remain curious mothers vitality, and its pregnancy is endless.

Atheistic materialism is the very antithesis of gestation and pregnancy. It aborts the elan of life before it is ever experienced. It is the most soul-destroying thought process to ever have befallen humanity's urge to procreate. Yet modern society fails to recognize atheism's total colonization of our minds. For the sake of its posterity, it promotes its own egotistical security while incarcerating humanity's search for meaning and purpose.

It is absurd to say, as atheists do, that evolution ends with natural selection. Evolution is genesis. It is process. It is an ongoing phenomenon. Human beings are the only conscious sentient reality in this world. We are the first beings who can personalize and give witness to our own existence. We are the first to say "I" or "we" about ourselves.

Atheism, despite its smothering power over Western civilization, cannot answer nor control humanity's unquenchable longing for something more.

Nuclear weapons are not the answer to satisfy our yearning. They terrify us rather than inspire us. Instead of serenity, they carry a sword of destruction with them. Some other force beyond our capacity to fully know is needed to satisfy us. A spiritual ombudsman, however, is continuously excluded in our tedious, warring negotiations, while self-interested corporate chiefs keep all discussion on a purely secular and profitable plane.

Our material success has mostly brought comfort to the rich, leaving the rest of humanity switched off. Beyond its unequal distribution, atheistic materialism is also guilty in the production of destruction. Its so-called successes have become our atrocities. The more we generate monstrous success stories, the more our humanity becomes atrocious. Evil is its own begetter, and atheism is its driver. If nuclear terror does not deter us from pursuing the evil which atheistic materialism brings with it, then how will we humans cope with the potential for much more evil being unleashed upon the human race through transhumanism, transgenetics, and the hydron collider in Cern?

Why must the atheistic indoctrination of our evolutionary process be favoured in our public forum, to the detriment of the full story of complexity consciousness? It would appear that Western civilization, having turned its face from divine purposes, has now canonized the material and egoic world with divinity. Matter alone has become our hero. Why does the West continue with this prostituted solution, when in fact it produces much more lethal evil and suffering than all of the civilisations which preceded it? Could it not be through the exclusion of our fundamental spirituality, the needs of the ego take centre stage? Matter triumphs. The egoic rather than the mystical defines us.

With this atheistic, overriding paradigm now in place, the economy—the enterprise of buying and selling—becomes our only reason for living.

Some atheists claim the same scenario has been prevalent throughout the ages. That indeed may be the case, but society until now always had a devil's advocate who brought balance to the conundrum of good and evil. Our world today faces a much more threatening crisis than ever before, with nuclear warfare and the power of transhumanism. Materialistic atheism has become the perpetrator and the devil's advocate over society at the same time. As though there were not enough evil in our world already, atheistic science daily continues to add new instruments of torture to an already oversupplied stockpile of murderous and destructive machinery.

The powerful countries in the West monotonously attempt to mechanically solve humanity's social problems. We constantly hear of their heroic efforts as negotiators through the mind-controlling messages on mass media. Self-appointed "specialness" gives them the autocratic right to negotiate and mediate. When morality and ethics are removed from negotiation, the hubristic claim of specialness becomes a curse rather than a blessing.

The drone of drones still continues in the hypocritical solutions which the West proposes. Foreign ministers rush about ambitiously, camouflaged as peace negotiators, while at the same time their homelands manufacture the supplies which keep murder and mayhem in perpetual motion in far-flung territories.

The only possible way to end all unjust invasions and occupations is through reverting to the demands of nature. The natural world instructs us to continuously keep a balance between matter and spirituality. Atheistic materialism, with is prevailing doctrine of nihilism and psychopathic aggressiveness, has saturated Western society to such a degree that otherwise good men and women have become passive and silent slaves. We are terrified of sounding unintelligent or ignorant because of the atheistic demand for rational evidence of God's existence. It is of course as impossible to give such evidence as it is to prove that a lamb is a lion. We cannot prove a lion's prowess or a lamb's meekness by just scrutinizing their dead bodies. Immanence and transcendence cannot be separated.

To demand rational evidence within one reality without its connection to a higher one is an impossibility. A coherent answer is only possible when the realms are joined. The fallacious demand of atheism in requesting rational evidence for God's existence can be justifiably turned around by asking materialistic atheists to give rational evidence for God's nonexistence. Their usual answer is to debunk God for the sins of organized religion. Richard Dawkins's book *The God Delusion* relentlessly dismisses the notion of a Creator because of his creature's sins. Suffice it to say that it is important to realize that the good in life is far more revelatory than the bad. Despite atheism's pernicious flaw, the good and the beautiful can yet be experienced. The heroism of one great soul impresses and inspires far more than the malevolence of ten thousand cowards.

We observe that the words "good" and "God" are remarkably similar.

Organized religion, like scientific atheism, has concocted its own thesis. Organized religion's dogmatism concerning God is as destructive as the stopgap measure of atheistic materialism. Both systems, when confronted by honest questions, are totally inadequate to give authentic answers. Atheism dismisses the question rather arrogantly, and organized religion refuses to profess agnosticism. Both the elites of atheistic materialism and the hierarchy of organized religion are propagandists. They are equally culpable in promulgating laws to suit their own self-interests.

The only true church is the one that receives its authority from the divine truth which conscientiously lives inside each one of us. God works universally and not according to the individual mindset of a select few. Hierarchy is necessary for order but not for domination. When the hierarchal teachings are contrary to a *sensus fidelium*, then it is time for authority figures to become the students and their followers to become their professors. Promotion and self-interest are inconsistent with spirituality. God invites but does not compel.

In our times, atheistic materialism has gained the West's allegiance especially because organized religion no longer inspires or intelligently stirs our imagination. Atheistic science appeals to the ego by promising heaven on earth. However, through its covert agenda, it is even now turning earth into hell. Profit alone is its motive. Scientific atheism is much more lethal than the terrorism of ISIS.

Those who proclaim exceptionalism mistake nationality for patriotism.

A cowboy bully-boy mentality scorches the soul of humility and brands it with brutality. The United States and Europe are indifferent at best to the mayhem and murder they initiate through invasion. Western media has become so contaminated with lies that the crisis which its governments have caused has turned consequence into cause. Invaders and occupiers have been turned into heroes, while the murder and mayhem inflicted on victims has been reduced to insignificance by the euphemism "collateral damage".

Bereft of spirituality, the golden rule of life has been tarnished. The West has hammered it into leaden bullets and bombs. We camouflage our immorality by the charity of our offerings to feed the hungry of a world in which we have initially caused bloodshed. We are good at bandaging the wounds we have caused. The West's salve for the screams of a wounded world is a feigned concern. Its aid is a trickle of poison—and sometimes depends on the reciprocation of an arms deal. It is sheer hypocrisy.

Whether we admit it or not, the human race, like all living things, is doomed to be spiritual. We must remain in consonance with natural law. We in the secular West have strayed from our original ground and are almost totally out of tune with the harmony of the universe. Like Adam and Eve in the garden of Eden, we have haughtily proclaimed our independence from the jurisdiction of divinity. We have foreclosed and suspended the natural law which connects and relates all life in an interdependent way.

Without a spiritual dimension, the lure of rampant consumerism and the profits gained from war is far more appealing and satisfying to the ego than the Golden Rule. Those who have been exposed most to the propaganda produced by the powerful elites are among the most spiritually impoverished people on earth. They are deprived of truth. The solitary voice which said, "Do unto others as you would have them do unto you", also said, "The truth shall set you free". We have refused to learn that freedom bears responsibility. We have been propagandized to believe we can be free while others suffer. We benefit by exploiting their labour. We remain unfree because those who control us imprison us with lies and dishonest information.

Atheistic materialism manufactures its own truth inside of us. Like a parasite, it chews all that is vital out of us. We no longer believe we are made in the image of God. Parallel psychology turns us into monsters. Propaganda increasingly obliterates truth in the so-called lands of the free. Total control of the media operates in the West. Western media's only agenda is to crush the mindset of those who are spiritually unawakened. The elites who control the message turn the masses into dumbed-down receptors of mediocrity.

Consumerism makes us miserable. It only addresses what is external. It neglects the world of our feelings and interiority. We see the results of our spirituality exploding at an alarming rate in modern society. The pain is so great that a huge percentage of people in the West can only survive with the help of opiates. The number of young people with deep psychological problems has doubled during the past twenty years. The disjunct between the interior life and the external world is causing unparalleled anxiety.

We soon grow tired of all the stuff we think we need to make us happy. Yet we continue to endorse a materialist, atheistic culture which has proven itself to be valueless and divisive. Our minds have been colonized. We passively accept the pit into which our monetized system has dumped us. Atheistic materialism will destroy us if we allow it to encroach any further on our Christian Western culture.

Murder documents are blueprinted and designed in foreign lands, far from the atrocities of their enactment. Nations interested in exploitation and money set the scene for disturbance through the infiltration of their agents. Then, hypocritically, the West pretends to be an agent of diplomacy and arbitration. In the meantime, the wounded, the maimed, the slaughtered, and the pillaged are blamed from afar for the horror and terror which essentially was seeded by the empire of the West.

The madness behind the horror of war is not the reaction of the conquered and the terrorized, but the obscenity of hypocritical operatives who scheme behind closed doors. Devils more than saints parade the corridors of Western power.

Defence is consequent upon offense. In the West, offense has been twisted to mean defence. Those who defend are not the offenders. Scientific materialism encourages murder and mayhem for the sake of profit. Its only concern is money. The gross national product is its end game. Nothing else matters. Economy is all.

As we grow more and more secular, we robotize ourselves to such a degree that life will eventually become all head with no heart. We are sowing weeds instead of flowers.

Dance and music are muscled out of life. The testosterone grasp of domineering patriarchs squeezes all tenderness, warmth, and security out of our mother's cry to cradle us. The one-way monolith of secular, materialistic atheism denies life's essential sexuality. Creativity comes out of agony and ecstasy. Contraries are complementary. Privileges bear responsibility. A life of material comfort does not, despite what the ads tell us, answer the deepest yearning in our psyches for something more. We must work to find the pearl of greatest price.

What is needs its opposite to live. There cannot be a prize without a contest.

Spirituality only lives in us to the extent we make the effort to cultivate it.

Power, if it is to be exercised with equanimity, must be both male and female. One without the other creates imbalance. We cannot be if we are not yin and yang. Secularity cannot be unless it is coupled with spirituality. Materialism challenges and hones our spirituality. Secular materialism only holds promise insofar as it is a continuum.

The sacred is already in the now. But the exaggerated needs of our materialistic culture do not recognize it. The real terror of the age we live in is that the West has almost totally moved into that new world where spirituality has been abolished and demolished. More and more, material things talk to us like people, while our growing tolerance for dumbness makes us less capable of speaking plainly. There cannot be any new birth in this world without secularism and spirituality spawning us together. We as body-mind are a continuum.

Crops cannot mature without photosynthesis. A body without spirit is like a plant without the sun. We may gestate, but in the end we will be stillborn. The natural world tells us all we need to know about life. Metaphorically, it teaches us everything.

The truly spiritual person is the real patriot. One has definition when home and destiny mean the same. To the truly spiritual person, the sale of one's soul in the name of xenophobia is not negotiable. It is anathema. It takes great courage to be a whistle-blower. We think we are true patriots when we agree with the political dogma of our nation. But what if our nation is not engendered by compassion and defined by divinity? To say we trust in God is pure hypocrisy when by our actions we perform the opposite.

The greatest citizens of any nation are its whistle-blowers. They are the men and women who, by their own courage and heroism, call their country to moral responsibility. Men and women who defy the mind control and propaganda of their own nation are its greatest heroes and ambassadors. They stand apart and defy the hypocrisy and lies which their nation pumps out in praise of its own purity and superiority.

Great heroism and courage do not come easily. It is much easier to find security and comfort through a herd mentality. To lose one's own convictions for the sake of a nation is to collude with the enemy of your soul. To wave a flag in consort with the main populace of one's nation is a woeful act of collusion, contrivance, and convenience when it is done in blindness to the fact that one's nation has committed war crimes.

Patriotism erupts out of love. However, like all that is important in this world, a flag is an emblem which not only represents the comfort of the homeland but also the challenge to live up to its moral responsibility. Love is not possible without sacrifice. Privileges carry with them obligations. When exercised with love, criticism of one's nation can be the most heroic of testaments.

To nonviolently resist our place of birth when it has perverted the majesty of human life is the sign of the true hero. Conformity is easy. It is more convenient and less noticeable to stand in the middle than on the periphery. The man or woman who does this is the real traitor. It takes a courageous and heroic soul to stand alone and defy the contrivances and evil intentions of one's nation when all of one's fellow citizens spit at one and label one "unpatriotic".

To say "I can't do anything about it. I have enough to do to take care of my family" is a cowardly cop-out. When your house is burning, you had better wake up and get out of it.

The one person who stands apart from the crowd and refuses to wave a flag which represents not only home but also moral cowardice will be remembered long after all the listless flag-wavers have left our planet. Such is the power of courage and witness that the voice of one heroic citizen will drown out the mediocrity of a million flag-wavers.

Patriotism means unqualified and unwavering love which implies
not uncritical eagerness to serve, not support for unjust claims, but
frank assessment of its vices and sins, and penitence for them.
—Aleksandr Solzhenitsyn

When we in the West start to live with the same passion for authentic living as did this great Russian hero, who modelled his life on Jesus Christ, then for the first time our civilization will survive without overabundant bloodshed. Aleksandr Solzhenitsyn, through his suffering and courageous criticism, almost single-handedly toppled the whole Soviet Union. One person has the possibility within themselves to transform a whole nation.

When the centre no longer holds, deceit smothers truth with a pillow full of pillage. The true hero is the citizen who empties the pillage out of the pillow and names the festering rot smothering his nation. Ken O'Keefe is such a man. As an ex-marine, he has demonstrated the courage of his convictions. He defies the atrocities committed by his own nation and its propensity for violence. He truly is a Christ figure in our modern understanding of crucifixion as a necessary ingredient for courage and heroism.

Muslims are my brothers and sisters.
—Ken O'Keefe

Thesis is tested by antithesis. There cannot be consensus without this battle. The West has become so destroyed by its own comfortable, convenient lifestyle that is has forsaken the battle. A clash of opposites is essential for any improvement. The West has forsaken the inward, disciplined battle demanded for authentic growth. We want our privileges without obligations or responsibility. We believe we are entitled to everything. We love thesis but despise antithesis. We admire our paradigm of materialistic atheism. We have become dumbed-down to such an extent that we no longer cognitively recognize that crucifixion is necessary for creativity.

It is not the level of our prosperity that makes for happiness but the kinship of heart to heart and the way we look at the world.
—Aleksandr Solzhenitsyn

At this juncture of Western civilization, the world of science and technology has captured the mind and the spirit of humanity to such a degree that the idea of God has been guillotined from the mystery of our being. We are the beneficiaries of scientific exploration and accomplishments, but this fact alone does not address all the unfulfilled dreams and aspirations of our restlessness. Many of the scientific community's discoveries have had their birth through the intellectual genius of man, to the detriment of any transcendent value. Many life-enhancing medicines and technological wonders have helped our bodies but neglected the restless ache of our hearts.

Some of science's inventions have led to a deeper severance from the self rather than an enlargement of love and hope in our everyday lives. In an age when the atheistic paradigm reigns, the human race has been so horrifically mind-controlled and propagandized that it has become a house divided from itself. We live in rooms on a foundation of shifting sands. We have severed ourselves from the deeper consciousness of our higher being. Science, at best, has only given us partial answers since the Enlightenment of the eighteenth century. Because of its success in the physical sphere, science has arrogantly denied the need for a more holistic approach. With a deeper understanding of the atom through quantum physics, science is now beginning to tolerate the idea that there is indeed an interconnection between matter and spirit. We no longer can put matter on a pedestal to the exclusion of the spiritual. The human person is an integrated whole of matter and spirit. Quantum physics has finally given us this insight. Consciousness which is no thing is the foundation for "thingness".

We live in total contradiction with the way of true spirituality. Matter is only the surface of what is deepest about us. Consciousness is the cornerstone of our reality. It is not a thing. It exists beyond and behind time and space. Our biological roots can only be found in nothingness. Yet we live dismissively, as though our origin and future only have relevance in terms of our thingness.

The Ancient Egyptians lived life in the completely opposite way. The underworld was but a pure shadow of the overworld. Life should be lived with this primordial outlook. This is the way to bring harmony into human existence.

Science is beginning to admit our process does not end with the materiality of natural selection. We go from now-here into no-where. This is a huge breakthrough which connects matter to spirit. Transcendence defines us.

Materialistic science, without the heart of compassion and love, is merely robotic. A spiritual component must always enter into our human constructions; otherwise our science and technology will turn almost certainly into something lethal and destructive. Science without the balance of spirituality creates a monstrous reality. Science endowed with spirituality brings balance into our world.

Nations which manufacture and sell arms for the sake of profit, no matter their religiosity, are the true murderers and terrorists of this world. Because of the insidious subtlety of mind-control and propaganda from the victors, the innocent are slaughtered in the name of democracy. Because of atheistic materialism, countless die mutilated and convulsed in suffering, while their elitist murderers luxuriate in their distant estates of entitlement and grandeur. If the United States spent half of its military budget on solving world poverty, then all the hunger in the world would be instantly eradicated.

Western civilization can be justly proud of its creative accomplishments, but it is the so-called civilized West which also created the most atrocious machinery for the annihilation of humanity. We have collected and stored enough nuclear bombs to blow the planet into smithereens more than a thousand times over.

Humanity's greatest victory in any war is never to have started it!

The greatest crisis facing humanity is spiritual.

May we truthfully claim that the demise of our planet and its growing acceptance of calculated immoral standards is due primarily to the promoters of atheistic materialism? May we claim that a religious interpretation of reality is the only antidote to a world that is on the verge of collapsing?

The answer to both of these questions is a definite no.

Religion before the Enlightenment had its own field day of horrific wars, murder, mayhem, intolerance, prejudice, corruption, exploitation, and plunder. To make matters more hypocritical still, all this brutality was acted out under the banner of the wrong God. That God was not the God of spirituality.

Apart from these external acts of physical corruption and abuse, organized religion even more insidiously shackled the minds of its followers with theological dogmas and teachings which were incomprehensible to the point of absurdity. Is it any wonder that atheists such as Richard Dawkins should unapologetically dismiss the teachings of religion as irrational and harmful to humanity? Just as with atheistic materialism, organized religion has done awful damage to the advancement and progress of the human prospect.

Atheism and religion equally use mind control and incrementally hoodwink the masses to accept the propaganda metered out to them. If we as a species are to advance, we will have to awaken to the fact that neither atheistic secularism nor the teaching of organized religion will answer the dilemma of the human predicament.

The foremost question facing reality is the fundamental option—namely, is life meaningful or absurd? Atheism opts for the latter, but religion infallibly claims to be the dispenser of transcendence.

Both organized religion and atheistic materialism are anathema to natural law. Both systems sever our interrelationship with the overarching nonlocal Intelligence which pervades the universe.

No system of philosophy, no theology, and no atheistic scientist can declare who or what God is. All we can do is make a feeble stab at a definition. We do not define divinity. Divinity defines us.

Both organized religion and atheistic materialism are infected by "meism". Both systems cater to the ego and its lust for power. Both systems have twisted the truth for their own self-interest. Both systems have led to war and murder.

Organized religion now hangs as a tassel on a cloth of faded glory. So also will the lunacy of atheistic materialism one day lose its fanatical grip on the soul of humanity. The smouldering wick of Armageddon, which fundamentalist Christians so self-righteously predict, will only burst into flame if humanity itself causes it. God does not will our destruction. Armageddon may come because of our misuse of nuclear technology. If it happens, it will be because of man's stupidity rather than God's vengeance.

The real Antichrist will be ourselves. Biblical prophecy creates balloons full of lead. We make our own Armageddon.

The prevailing mistake in Western church culture is that humanity has failed to make the distinction between religion and spirituality. Mention religion to an atheist and he scoffs at it. Mention religion to a theist and he thinks about rules, regulations, or church attendance. Christians who are now almost totally mind-controlled by atheistic materialism think of religion as an inconvenience and an invader of their privacy. Except for the major events in their lives, such as birth, marriage, and death, religion does not interest them. Like every other convenience on offer in the supermarket, religion has become commodified. Catholics still buy cards for spiritual favours.

Most of the mental tensions and worries of our contemporary lives ensue from problems created by atheistic manipulation, in which the body is everything and the soul is nothing. But tell clients their problem is a spiritual one, and they immediately interpret it as an inconvenience imposed by the observance of laws they cannot understand. Or perhaps the issue is dogmas decreed by a church which insults rational thinking. Christians cannot make the distinction between spirituality and religion.

This is the underlying cause of humanity's problem in contemporary Western society. Spirituality has been turned into an obligation and a decree. Christians and atheists treat it as a joke and of no relevance.

Most of our sickness comes from the fact that we have separated ourselves from the natural world. We fail to realize that our story of life and death is the same as that of all other sentient creatures. We may curl our hair and varnish our nails, but in spite of our death-denying attempts to smother our essential truth, we are a part of the natural world, not apart from it. Curls are straightened by humidity and paint eventually peels. Our sickness comes from our avoidance. Atheistic materialism at all costs wants us to live in a way disconnected from the rhythm of the seasons and the call of an all-absorbing universal Consciousness.

Spirituality is endemic in all that moves and lives in this world. It invades all life. It is the fire in the heart of things. It surrounds us and is inside of each one of us, whether we are in our kitchens, our toilets, or our bedrooms. As Patrick Kavanagh, the Irish poet, said, "God comes to us in common statement" and "God is a pearl necklace worn around the neck of poverty."

Healing and wholeness come to us when we learn to live in a manner consonant with our human nature. Dogmas, supernatural teachings, and laws which are unrelated to our human experience are hindrances to holiness. They are dualistic. They divide our humanity from our spirituality and disrupt the flow of healing and wholeness in our bodies. Atheism is not holistic. It separates. So does organized religion. It also is dualistic.

Quantum physics calls upon both religion and medicine to change to a new paradigm. Spirituality is about what is real. It is holistic. It is about now. It is about the mystery of the ordinary. It is about walking in muck and looking up at the stars. It is about cleaning the smelly bottom of our newborn child. Spirituality is about making a nutritious dinner to feed our children. Spirituality is about waiting in anticipation for the return of a spouse or a loved one. It is about thanksgiving for the fruits and the wheat of the earth. Spirituality is about the awakening of our conscience to the fact that we are conscious. We humans are the only creatures so blessed with the full benefit of what it means to be conscious.

Spirituality is applied theology. It must be relevant to humanity's present experience.

Spirituality interpenetrates every petal of our being as colour interpenetrates the flower.

What use is a Christ to us who was born two thousand years ago? If his story does not interpenetrate the story of our contemporary lives, then it serves no purpose. Spirituality is an ongoing, everyday reality.

There is no sense in running off to church unless we bring the interiority of God there with us. Serenity and freedom cannot come as long as we remain addicted to slavery. Both organized religion and atheistic materialism are systems of slavery. They squeeze what is deepest about us out of us. They abort the primordial flow of what the natural law intends for us. Both systems are an insult to our human intelligence. They destroy our awareness that we in fact are infinite wisdom living through a limited human experience. We live a veiled existence. Like curtains, we experience our lives as coloured cloth blowing in the wind. But we refuse to recognize the Source of the blowing and indeed what lies beyond the windowpane.

27

As Saint-Exupéry said in *The Little Prince*, "Only the children know what they are looking for. Only the children keep their noses glued to the window pane."

Hubristically, organized religion and atheistic materialism have missed the salient flow running through our daily routine. It is time to overthrow them! Both systems have failed to recognize the chlorophyll gurgling through the leaves on our tree.

It seems ironic to claim that atheism serves spirituality much better than religion. Religion is mediocre and stands in the middle—a body on earth but disjoined from Intelligence. Atheism and spirituality stand as thesis and antithesis. Opposites purify and challenge each other. Without this clash, newness cannot dawn. Shocks, if they do not petrify, surely purify. Dawn comes through the clash of night with day. Consciousness comes when matter no longer matters. Paradox is the creator of mystery. A tear can flow from both laughing and crying. Nothing is as it seems. There is always shadow in substance. A candle casts a more mellow light than a neon glare. It generates possibility and stimulates imagination. As Edmund Burke said, "Imagination is the greatest evidence of God."

Both atheism and religion are addicted to definition. Haughtily, they proclaim the answer to the mystery lies in their domain exclusively. Spirituality speaks differently. Wisdom teaches the awakened person that life on this planet is a mystery to be lived and not a problem to be solved. Religion and atheism, fortress-like, remain intransigent on the validity of their own truth.

One might validly ask the atheist, "How can the reality of truth exist if life is due to mere happenstance?" Life without the reality of transcendence is meaningless. If one's immanence does not proceed into transcendence, then what is the purpose of the Olympics? A life without the possibility of transcendence turns human beings into automatons with no desire for growth or improvement. Passive, like a dormant seed untouched by the warmth of the sun and the cool spring rain, life is no more than an endurance test. It is a hindrance to love and universal consciousness. Atheistic materialism is intolerant of both the sun and the rain. It produces an autumn of stunts instead of stalks.

The true purpose of life is not self-actualization, as atheistic materialism teaches, but self-transcendence. To be holy is to be holistic, joining heaven and earth together. The full realization of the now is to recognize we are already in eternity. We atrophy when we fail to recognize that our end takes us back to where we started from.

Our now-here becomes our no-where. Our constant urge is to anthropomorphize the possibility of limitlessness to the confines of our own configuration. "Nothing" is calculated by the atheist as "absence", but to the mystic it means the fullness of presence. Experience, rather than a mathematical explanation, is lateral much more than it is literal. Atheistic science, like Christian fundamentalism, reduces matter to special location. According to Christian fundamentalism, the Bible alone gives all the answers. It is God's Word to man instead of man's word to God.

Fundamentalist Christians, just like atheistic materialists, study life through the microscope or telescope of their study. They do this under special location. But how can we find a reasonable understanding of a bird if we only study its carcass? What if we rob the earth of the sight of migrating birds, flying with such determination to an environment best suited for survival? What if humanity is never again to hear the unending song of benediction which the skylark pours down upon us?

That precisely is what fundamentalist Christians and atheistic materialists do to our planet. They rob us of flight and they rob us of song. They do the exact opposite of what Jesus commanded. Look to the birds of the air ... look to the lilies of the field."

Life is much more metaphorical than it is literal. That is why this world needs poets and mystics. They deal with the unexplainable. They live outside of evidence and the cold world of statistics. When we objectify and decry the subjective in any study, we crucify and codify rather than elucidate or enlighten.

Biblical studies and prayer ceremonies held in centres of power are anathema to the ear of that unique man from Nazareth who lived and died in the name of nonviolence. Despite all the controversy surrounding his life, his birth, and his miracles, the central message of his mission remains still the greatest challenge and benign hope ever to reach the ear of humanity. Whether this world accepts him as God's only begotten Son or just a son like other men, such a concern is but the plumage on the bird that sings, "Do unto others as you would have them do unto you."

The thesis which atheistic science and religion propose is the exact opposite. Both rob the skylark of its song and only study its carcass. However, atheism does serve a purpose. In the legitimacy of enquiry, it questions the absurdity and pomposity of organized religion. The church has always stressed the hereafter to the detriment to the here and now, while atheism stresses the body to the detriment of the spirit.

Both systems play themselves out with horrific consequences. Spirituality, on the other hand, joins heaven and earth together harmoniously. When we truly become aware that a universal consciousness interpenetrates and connects all life, then we shall know how much religion has indoctrinated us with sensationalism. When the natural law is invaded, one has a very justifiable reason to become sceptical. Adherence to sensational supernatural miracles as a proof for the existence of God provides farcical fodder to the critical atheistic mind. Oscar Wilde said, "Mystery is in the seen, not the unseen."

But mind-controlled religious minds do not understand this. They cannot understand that lovemaking can be a divine experience. Spirituality invades the ordinary experiences of our everyday lives. All experiences become holy and sacred when we direct them to God. When we connect the ordinary experiences of our everyday world with the miracles that explode naturally and effortlessly within and without our bodies, then we will feel integrated and happy. The human body alone is a minefield of unexplored wonders and miracles.

We crave for God to intercede for us. We terrify ourselves with the biblical stories of Armageddon, while at the same time we disconnect from the responsibility of becoming careful stewards of the earth. As Edmund Burke, the Irish parliamentarian, said, "For evil to prevail in this world, the only thing necessary is for good men to do nothing."

Spirituality concerns itself more with ecology than it does with theophanies. Spirituality is much more about a hands-on approach to life than God suspending the natural law and interfering supernaturally.

Western science and technology are growing exponentially without an accompanying moral compass. A Frankenstein reality crawls ever closer to our doorstep. Many of the signs are already here. If we do not bring the spirituality of consciousness into the equation, then for sure consciousness will abandon us. God will not stay near us without our cooperation.

Whether we like it or not, consciousness will have the last word, because it is the whole which embraces the parts. If the parts depart, then God can no longer cooperate. We neglect our spiritual dimension to the detriment of our humanity. Without the overarching spiritual component of our reality, there can be no balance in the politics of world governments. Without consciousness, the world becomes a tented city of the Devil.

It is ironic that the atheistic elites—who are so vociferous and determined to deny the possibility of a benign Being holding the universe together—are the same people who indulge in satanic rituals and worship. We lust for transcendence of some kind, it would seem. Even Devil worship indicates our lust for transcendence. How is it possible to believe in the Devil but not in God? The occult and Devil-worshippers cannot have it both ways. Can it be that Lucifer best meets the selfish greed of the elites?

The bad and the good exist potentially in everyone. Either reality has the potential to have dominion over any one of us and the world, as we will it. Matter and antimatter coexist. Human life becomes a contest as a consequence. We determine Armageddon to the extent that we refuse awakening to the universal Consciousness dwelling within us. We in fact are our own saviours. God's work has to become our own.

The saint and the devil lurk inside of each one of us. Without consciousness, corruption conquers hearts and minds, which have been created for the noble purpose of love. Atheistic materialism gobbles up the moral fibre of the land. It creates a tension within each one of us. We no longer feel at home with ourselves. We are stuffed with stuff, but the mind and the heart have never felt so empty. We are out of tune. With no moral compass to guide us, we grow more depressed, stressed, and fractious.

To be conscious is to be aware. To be conscious makes a human being an inherent participator in the one great Consciousness which envelops and embraces the earth. But the one great universal Consciousness cannot dwell within us if, as individuals, we allow ourselves to become egotistically enslaved.

We have the power within us to disengage or detach from our true identity or to grow aware of our higher destiny. Consciousness calls us to our higher selves. In contemporary parlance, we can allow God to go to hell, or we can let go of all that retards our flow into divinity. Atheistic materialism thrives on the egoic self and is oxygenated by the false utopia with which consumerism lures us. Through subtle propaganda and mind control, the lure of consumerism bombards us daily. More and more, Western civilization passively and unconsciously absorbs the message of the media. As we inhale the toxic indoctrination of atheistic materialism, shopping malls become our new cathedrals.

We have kicked the God of consciousness out of town.

The controlled mass media in the West, especially the American version, demeans and debunks our humanity. Through its focus on murder, corruption, and violence, it proposes blood thirst, vengeance, and aggression as the normal way of life. Profit comes from competition rather than cooperation. Fulfilment and happiness come through toughness. "Devour or you will be devoured" is its motto. To the contemporary mind, the gun—or any other war machine—elicits far more excitement and enthusiasm than the sight of beautiful golden wheat fields blowing in the wind. Ugliness prevails as the consummate mark of our appreciation. The design of a car triggers euphoria, whereas the design of a flower withers with our indifference.

Atheistic materialism promotes use but never value. Its intention is to keep humanity on a lower level of consciousness. It considers *Homo sapiens* as residing on the evolutionary level of the chimpanzee. Dumbing humanity down to this evolutionary level, mass media reverses the evolutionary process. It ignores the fact that humanity has been genetically ordered to be conscious of being conscious, and that consciousness is an ongoing process. This is the differentiating point between humanity and the rest of the sentient world.

The chimpanzee is conscious but not aware that it is conscious. We, by our consciousness of being conscious, have moved into the realm of the metaphysical and the spiritual. The science of atheistic materialism—the science of the ego—does not want us to realize this. Instead of being aware that we are made for more and that the best is yet to be, atheistic materialism insists that what we immediately experience is all there is. There is no other "isness". There is no Yahweh! Atheistic materialism wants humanity to think that it is only this world which matters. It is stupid to believe in an afterlife—the ego is all, with its own purpose. Life came about by mere chance. Only oblivion and annihilation await us.

To be conscious, on the other hand, is to realize that we as human beings are a threshold people. We have one foot in the immediacy of matter and the ego, and the other in the metaphysical reality of our consciousness. We are a mixture of matter and spirit.

Immanence is in transcendence, and transcendence is in imminence. It is all one continuum. Incarnation and eschatology are the one reality. Everything is sacred; nothing is secular. We walk on holy ground. We are the custodians of a sacred place set in time. When we approach life with this sensitivity, then matter matters because it is holy. Everything is touched with a spark of divinity.

If we want to find God the Creator, we need to discover the God who lives within us and all around us. We will not find God unless we work to bring consciousness home to live with us. Go to sleep with it and wake up with it. Believe that God invades all that is natural and flowing in our everyday lives. We do this by realizing all the interconnecting silk threads which join at the centre. If the core is not there to support us, the ropes on the troubled bridge of human existence will unravel and strangle us. An axial turn towards consciousness is the only antibiotic which will cure the disease of atheistic materialism.

To make such a turn, we start by investing ourselves in our own homes, harrowing the ground of selflessness and accommodating consciousness instead of egotistical selfishness. Paradoxically, we feel much better about ourselves when we give rather than take. Smiles cannot be bought on supermarket shelves, and banks do not sell compassion. The greatest treasures of all lie on the shelves of the human heart, and we all can afford to share and give them away, especially to those who most need them.

Now, more than ever in our culture, we are obligated to become counterculture.

Consciousness is teaching us that infinite growth cannot fit into a finite earth. Future generations will have to forego a sense of egotistical entitlement.

The self-generating energy of the earth expresses itself copiously through cosmic consciousness and is truly present for all of us who wish to avail ourselves of it.

Atheistic materialism is destructive. It has to die. It depletes the soul and smothers the underlying meaning of human existence. We are surrounded by invisibility, but atheistic materialism will not accept this. It drains humanity of direction. We are obsessed by the glitz of electronic technology. With no moral compass to guide us, we are out of tune with our deepest yearning. As a consequence, we are always pining. Atheism demands rational evidence and because of this, as the poet Emerson noticed, "Things are in the saddle and ride mankind." Everything is turned upside down.

Atheistic science continues to bring the demand for objective verification into an arena where material objects do not exist. The evidence it demands cannot be shown in an objective, rational way. Proof of God's existence cannot be demonstrated visibly because the spiritual domain is invisible. It is not touchable, it is not local, it is not placeable. Its only demonstrability is its results.

Consciousness demonstrates the affairs of the heart rather than the things of mathematical equations. More and more, scientific materialistic atheism tries to exploit and obliterate consciousness from the study of humanity, to such a degree that whoever believes in an afterlife or a Creator is considered quite stupid. It is not fashionable to believe in God any longer.

Unabashedly atheistic science denies the unifying field of all reality. It squashes and squeezes the final particle to answer that atheism is its final disclosure. Atheists, who believe there is no future for the atom, cannot abide the thought that matter and consciousness are interconnected in an immeasurable and indestructible way.

At the moment of death, the shackles of humanity's physicality cease. The material departs, but the spirit lives on. Spiritual consciousness teaches this.

The unifying force underlying all that is real must be brought into consideration for an honest debate about humanity's presence here on earth. The existence of God can no longer be considered a mere proposition to be pondered but a necessity for holistic living. Our need for God is far greater than our banter concerning the existence of the divine.

Spirituality is not an option. The soul dimension connected inextricably to our bodies is not negotiable.

The time has come for the reality of consciousness to be brought into consideration in all of humanity's deliberations. Peace and harmony are not possible without it.

HISTORY OF THE CHURCH
TO THE REFORMATION

Roman Catholicism became the state religion of the empire under Constantine in the fourth century AD. From that time, religion became organized and turned into a politically engineered institution rather than a messenger of transcendence. Its adherence was more to the state than to God. It muddled the gospel mandate and directed it towards its own grandeur rather than concerning itself with the spirituality of transcendence.

As a result, the Holy Roman Catholic Church and its consequent fracturing through Protestantism became more Roman than holy.

The problem, unfortunately, remains the same to this day. Scandals continue to erupt in a church which insists that it alone is the *vox Dei*, when instead it was called to become the *vox fidelium*. Consciousness as our unifying field threatens all authority figures who want to maintain their own sense of luxury and security.

The decree of papal infallibility is a hubristic attempt to replace the authority of God with the authority of a politicized human person. Life is an ongoing journey into the unknown. What we believe today may, through study, not be credible tomorrow. This is as true in the arena of the transcendent as it is in halls of rational study. No one can say "forever".

Contrary to the holiness by which the church names itself, organized religion, like all institutions, continues to this day to be composed of a mixture of devils and saints. Its ministers are no different than the rest of us. They have no special odour of sanctity automatically hanging around them. Christ would spit at the opulence displayed in the Vatican. Golden staffs and diamond rings are a far cry from the tattered unadornment of his peasant class.

Those who, at the cost of their own egos, bring compassion, understanding, and healing to others are the saints in this world. This is the only church Christ came to establish. Its faithful transcend the awful boundaries which bickering men have imposed on it.

Those who politicize their own consciences are the evil ones in our midst.

The disposition of the human heart and our response to Christ's message entitle us to call ourselves Christian. Love alone is what matters most in this world. The God within us, but for our unawakened consciousness, will disband our oppression and loneliness. That is the promise, if we will only allow divinity enter in.

Infatuated by the worldly power bestowed upon it by the Emperor Constantine, the church turned itself into judge and jury in all matters of intelligent enquiry. It had the final say in all matters of dispute: *"Roma locutu est. Causa finite est."* With this attitude, the church arrogantly proclaimed its doctrines to suit itself. Only the Roman Curia possessed enough power to define divinity. The ineffable, inscrutable, unknowable whole of the parts could, it seemed, at last be defined through the small outline of a penny catechism. As always, though, the God defined in that Roman treatise smacked more of canon law than compassionate love.

The Roman church and its offspring are growing more and more irrelevant and unappealing to a modern atheistic world, which is growing ever more irreverent and intolerant. Atheism attempts to erase religion from the face of the earth, scarcely ever attempting to pass the same scrutiny on itself. Contemporary atheistic science, with its chance theory of a material evolution, has left us as wandering orphans in the dark.

While science and technology attempt to appease our bodily cravings, we become in the end, according to this system of indoctrination, a can of worms created to feed on itself. Through the Enlightenment, the church became less of a player in the political realm. The Papal States were seized back from it. Its stopgap conclusions and saccharine, cliché answers made little sense to scientific minds, which were growing ever more sophisticated.

Challenged by Luther, the Vatican did not have the humility to admit that it had strayed from the teachings of its Founder. The Council of Trent built an apartheid wall to keep out legitimate questions. Men like Martin Luther asked about moneymaking indulgences and nailed theses to the door. Christianity split as a consequence. The Council of Trent turned the Vatican into a fortress of orthodoxy, hubristically proclaiming papal infallibility.

More and more, the church lost its control over the minds of questioning scientists, who insisted on objective evidence as proof of God's existence. More and more, objective science severed its ties with religion, assessing it as little more than a drug to soothe the masses into submission.

The so-called Enlightenment of the eighteenth century stripped religion of its credibility. Men like Freud thought of religion as an opiate to smother the dread of annihilation. He wrote of it as an unresolved father-child issue. Nietzsche, with the concept of nihilism, introduced death of God theology. The final hammer blow was ushered in through Darwin's theory of evolution. With each new discovery, science became more assured of its own superiority. Necessarily, the idea of God the Creator was dismissed as a superstitious myth. From the time of the Enlightenment, science became the true diviner and avatar of humanity.

Every new discovery, especially in the field of medicine, and every new invention which lessened the burden of human toil strengthened the conviction that objective material science could solve all human problems. It would prove the steady-state theory, which existed before the big bang theory with no need for a creator. Life came about by mere chance. It came out of nothing and became more complex due the chance meeting of chemicals that eventually, through an evolutionary process, determined *Homo sapiens*. Adaptation of the fittest and natural selection determined humanity. Our story, according to atheistic science, is a story of materiality. It proclaims there is no evidence for God's existence. The microscope and the telescope teach all we need to know.

As we have already noted, atheism, despite its pejorative connotation, does play a vital role in the refinement of a religious vision. Good and evil exist in everything. It is only through the combination of both forces that we find completion. Good and evil are not dualistic but unitive. One purifies the other. We cannot appreciate nor give reverence to one thing without the harangue of its opposite. Knowledge advances through the discovery of a mistaken identity.

Atheistic science has challenged imperialistic organized religion to its very core. With each new scientific discovery, superstitious beliefs of the prescientific world had to be forfeited and abandoned. Science, to this very day, serves to clarify what was previously held as sacrosanct. If the church is to become relevant, then it must readjust its teaching to keep pace with scientific discovery. Theology, while maintaining its central core of spirituality, must always stay in tune with and embrace the furtherance of knowledge which science gives us.

God has to be freed from the narrow, parochial confines within which the imperialist church has placed him. God grows along with us. God is not static. God is dynamic. Atheism, despite its claim to progress, is closed to a final solution. Spirituality is always open to the imagination.

Spirituality preoccupies itself with the telling of a good news story. The God of the Old Testament is a God of wrath and punishment. The story changes utterly with the introduction of the Christ figure. Through Jesus, we are reminded of our true worth and dignity. Christ peppers man's relationship with God with the message of compassion. If the message of Jesus were to be reduced to one word, it would be "love".

In modern seminaries, students are brainwashed to learn all the tedious distinctions and meaningless psychobabble of dogma, moral law, and canon law. In a world of social disrepair and indeed despair, humanity needs to learn what Jesus taught—that Godness lives inside each one of us.

The primary duty of religion is to live and preach the truth of God's availability living inside of us. No one has a monopoly on this truth. God comes to us commonly. Religion must come down from its throne of hypocrisy and mediocrity and live as Jesus did, in the midst of social inequality. The church needs to become a community of concerned laity, freed of the unenlightened oligarchy which still dominates it. Instead of future ministers concentrating their minds on propaganda, a clergy of the laity must be trained.

This broken world needs wounded healers much more than autocratic politicians or religious leaders who seem so out of touch with the explosive inequality surrounding the poor of the world. Instead of protecting the status quo of their own hierarchy, a future church must prepare itself by inculcating its ministers with the principles of excellence found in the grammar of sociology, psychology, cosmology, and the arts in general. Future, inspired ministers must learn to love great art and literature, for therein lies the one, the true, and the beautiful.

Instead of submerging young priest's minds in the rigors of canon law and dogma, the church, if it is ever to be viable, will necessarily have to direct its ministers more to the caring professions. A church true to the ideals of the Christ-Man, instead of concentrating on canon law, should train its ministers to become secular lawyers who render their services free of charge. The same professionalism should be maintained in all similar levels of the caring profession. In a world which often requires such aid, healing and social solutions should be offered free of charge. Such administration becomes a possibility with the assistance of a minister's awakened sensitivity and conscience. The peace of harmony will come, irrespective of our cultural religious differences, when Christians learn to live less egotistically.

When we get out of the glass bottles of our egos and escape, like squirrels slipping out of cages and getting into the forests again, we shall shiver with cold and fright—but things will happen to us, so that we don't know ourselves.

Cool unlieing life will rush in, and passions will
make our bodies taut with power.
We shall stamp our feet with new power and old things will fall down.
We shall laugh and institutions will curl up like burnt paper.

—D. H. Lawrence

Since the vast majority of lay people today are preoccupied with the ordinary pressures of putting food on the table and keeping the bankers happy, there is little time left to ponder the purpose of human existence. Our leisure time becomes lost in the robotized land of crass entertainment. Atheistic materialism thrives on the dumbing down of our consciences.

Conspicuous consumption is all that matters in a paradigm which only caters to the ego.

The paradigm which now rules the West is atheistic. Since, atheism implies, life on our planet has evolved to this point by mere chance, we have no purpose but to eat, drink, and be merry. There is nothing after material life ends. The true purpose of life has become self-actualization. Self-transcendence is pure nonsense—it is only the ego that matters, according to the culture of the West.

Atheistic materialism found its initial impulse from religion. In the beginning, the church initiated investigative curiosity, never dreaming that the findings of science would more and more contradict the biblical account of creation. The historical truth of the Bible could not be taken literally. Science, through Copernicus and the observations of Galileo, proved the earth was not in fact the centre of the universe but moved as a planet around the sun. The church became so threatened by this new information that it increased its tactics of torture and murder to silence the findings of the scientists. Bruno, an Italian monk, was burned at the stake for his scientific views.

The rivalry between science and religion grew ever more heated, until finally science and religion separated. It is here, for the first time in the world's history, that man was separated from his spirit. Science, in its own doctrinaire way, insisted that the study of the body is all. The spirit could not be proven because there was no objectivity to it. Only that which could be objectively verified should be accepted as truth. With this stance, materialistic atheism subsumed the mind of the scientific world. Faith in God became anathema. The parts without the whole became the totality of scientific scrutiny. The hologram of spirit and matter was forsaken, to such a degree that medicine considers only the sick parts of the body, to the exclusion of the total person.

Likewise, in the field of education, students are prepared to become trained zealots instead of participators in human consciousness. Education is what atheistic materialism pumps into young minds, preparing them to become automatons instead integrated human persons. Instead of dumbing down, education should draw out from students all that is original and best about them.

Western culture, with the power of mass media, spreads its degenerative and decadent message throughout the world, contaminating and conditioning the innocent minds of future generations to a life of slavery. When egos are placated with softness and selfishness, a society becomes incapable of judging rightly. It can neither discriminate nor appreciate. Without spirituality, excellence, honour, decency, and honesty become reduced to their lowest common denominator. The paradigm of atheistic materialism has brought Western humanity to precisely this level. As James Joyce said in respect to his native land, "We are an old sow who eats her farrow."

In this threatening nuclear age, we seem defenceless. Is there anything we can do about it? This is the most vital question facing humanity. Much to the contrary of men's outlandish passion for a football outcome, the result of the nuclear game is the most important one in town.

There are fifty trillion cells in the human body. Each cell is an exact replica of the other. Each cell is a complete individual in itself, carrying all the DNA of the others. If the fifty trillion cells in our body can work together to express our unity, then so also can we come together to offset the division and slavery of atheistic materialism. Such is the divine power within each one of us that, when we tap into it consciously, we immediately connect to the one great Consciousness which infiltrates and fuses together all the parts into the whole.

In many ways we are living in the worst of times but also in the best of times. We have arrived at a juncture where we recognize our world is falling apart. We feel insecure, bored, weary, and depressed. Life seems more and more to have lost its sense of innocence and joy. The fear of terrorism has subjugated us to such an extent that our human rights are incrementally being compromised and taken from us. We don't seem to be aware of it. The masters of materialistic atheism are calculating that they are already in control because of their devious efforts to sedate us.

The more submissive we become, the sooner our slavery. The more the atheistic illuminati create an atmosphere of fear, the more we huddle together like sheep for the slaughter. Bereft of human feeling, these psychopaths think nothing of slaughtering others. Murder is normal in their scheme of reality. Elimination of the nonproductive and inefficient is their overall strategy. There are much too many of us already.

Thankfully, in the midst of this terrifying reality, the menacing truth of the elites' plan for genocide has begun to be discovered. Until recently, information given by the mass media was totally controlled by the establishment. But now, through the alternative media beyond the control of the elites, a spiritual awakening and renaissance is beginning to dawn. People are realizing the autocratic, genocidal plan of the elitist psychopaths. A new understanding and a new day has dawned for us.

The shadow government which controls the world's riches can and will be kicked out of town, but only through our awakening spirituality. This force alone will conquer evil. Whenever or wherever spirituality is quashed by atheistic autocrats and all portals seem closed to its recurrence, it again appears with a more passionate resurgence. The unquenchable longing of the human spirit for something more can never be destroyed or obliterated. The more atheistic materialism gives us to further our quiescence, the more we become restless and anxious. All the machines which give us convenience are useless unless we have a family home where we can enjoy the comfort. Affirmation and understanding are far more important in any home than a telephone. A smile is the greatest of all medicine cabinets.

Psychological pain erupts through a castigation of the spiritual. The human heart becomes harrowed when acceptance is not treasured. The pain and confusion which atheistic materialism has dumped on humanity can become the fertilizer for a new spring—if we allow it.

We learn through suffering.

QUANTUM PHYSICS

R eligion and atheistic materialism have failed to satisfy the human quest for purpose and meaning. Neither paradigm seems to offer a satisfactory answer. We still lack at-oneness with nature and home. We look for more. Surely there exists somewhere a justification for our searching?

For the first time in the annals of human history, a reconciliation between body and spirit has become possible. The Enlightenment of the eighteenth century has given way to an acceptance that the human person cannot be understood except holistically. Life has to be understood as a hologram. Matter and spirit are all one. Quantum physics teaches this. There is always a subject as well as an object involved in all scientific study, in spite of what atheistic scientists tell us.

Evidence can never be objective without a mind which declares it. This involves the subjective. Quantum physics has forced scientific atheism to include the subjective. An object is changed by the way we look at it.

The two great tools used in scientific discovery are of course the microscope and the telescope. These tools provide us with a greater view than that of the human eye. One is micro and the other macro. The scientific study of the universe through the telescope is called astrophysics. It looks outward. The exact opposite direction of study is taken by the microscope. It looks inward and is called quantum physics.

Quantum physics, which breaks matter into atoms, descends through ever-smaller particles like quarks until finally matter disappears into what quantum physics calls consciousness. It is at this level that the material body is left behind and the realm of Consciousness reigns supreme and eternal. This is the realm outside of space and time. It is no place; it is no thing. The laws of physical nature no longer apply. This is the realm of pure being. It is the underpinning and the overarching energy behind life. It is the all-encompassing envelope of all that is. It is isness. It is the drop in the ocean and the ocean in the drop. It is the original ground and the unifying field of all that is. It makes the cosmos one, joining everything on earth with eternity. Through consciousness, the here and now mutates into the hereafter with no reference to chronological time. Immanence is stretched into transcendence. The shackles of matter are left behind, and we are free at last to live eternally.

Ironic as it sounds, it is science rather than religion which has introduced a rational possibility for an afterlife. Quantum physics has opened the door to exciting new possibilities. Unlike the fundamentalism of atheistic science, objective evidence is no longer absolutely needed. Quantum physics takes us into an arena where the material and the body become post-functional. The rational measurements of things past do not preclude the possibility of a future which is beyond the visible. Quantum physics, without defining it, names its possibility. The birth of the metaphysical begins when science loses its grip on the fullness of reality.

The science of materiality knows nothing about the affairs of the heart nor the experience of the spiritual. Atheistic materialism and its avowed mission to bring utopia to the ego guillotines all that is noble and civilized about humanity's unquenchable longing for something greater. Only the spirituality of consciousness can address what is deepest about us.

Civilization, as it contemporarily expresses itself in the West, has been greatly shaped by Judeo-Christian influences. Before Judaism, the pagan people of the world worshipped many gods, each one emerging from the needs and fears of a simple tribal society. A cry for the assistance of some higher Power can be found in all the multitudinous tribes of humankind. The presence of an evil force also rustled concomitantly through the primitive understanding.

Throughout the history of the human race, men and women have always reached out transcendently for meaning and significance. There seems to be a universal and primordial cry of the heart written into the very soul of humanity. All humankind, whether affluent or not, still cries out for more. The fact that humanity for the past four billion years has always reached beyond itself for attention is a testament to the fact that the material world does not complete our story.

As if by intuition, we have always believed quite simply in a god or gods—until recently. As science has become more rational, we have abandoned our old securities, to the point that we have kicked the divine to the perimeter or even debunked it completely. God no longer lives nor is considered an integral part of the decisions we make on our high streets. The twenty-first century version of God is a bankrupt Santa Claus.

Scientific atheism has ushered in a new world of unbridled egoism, to the detriment of our evolution into an earth full of selfless love. Atheistic science espouses itself as the only rational way to view life. As a few drops congealed together, it declared itself the totality of water.

No matter what we have accrued in terms of material stuff, we still want something more. We struggle to accumulate, and when we receive what we desire, we become bored and the search starts all over again. We know internally something is missing. We recognize the insufficiency of materiality. Whether atheist or theist, we share in the desire for something greater. We never seem satisfied. Insufficiency is our greatest insanity.

The search of the human mind and heart among primitive people is the same cry which haunts contemporary society today. In the modern world of the West, our bellies may be full, but our consciousness lies in ruins. We have become spiritual illiterates. We have learned to walk among the trees without even remotely praising them for the blessings they give us. Sanitized and plasticized against connectivity with all that the natural world gives us, we romp around distractedly, oblivious to our dependency. Blessing, gratefulness, and reverence have been deleted from our lexicon.

Through our nanotechnology, we are much more impressed with the configurations of the human brain than the great Intelligence behind it. Consumed with a sense of our technological wizardry, we are not only disconnected from God but also from each other. We remain the only species on earth who live outside the exclusion zone of the natural world.

Oxygen and carbon are partners. The natural law performed their wedding ceremony in the big bang. The greed which atheistic materialism causes rapes and separates this principal bond of life on earth. Metaphorically it asphyxiates the overwhelming majority of humanity. Wood means profit to the rich and slavery to the cutter. Each becomes as separated from the other as carbon from oxygen. The poor cutter is blamed for the visible, unconscionable slaughter, while the grasping elitist stays at home in his mansion with inlaid floors of mahogany and other rare timber.

In this upside-down world of atheistic materialism, the elites live lives of obscene luxury, while the poor woodcutter is reduced to penury. In a world of atheistic materialism, everything is turned inside out. The transcendent aspect of every human act can no longer be contemplated.

A people who have been dumbed down by seductive entertainment and propaganda scarcely have the capacity to be aware of the spiritual dimension to their decisions and acts. When only the body matters, as atheism insists, then life becomes nothing but a game of plunder.

Primitive society lived life in a totally contrary way. We, with all our scientific sophistication, dismiss what we consider the ignorance and superstition of savage tribes, who before they cut down a tree say a prayer to its spirit and gently ask its forgiveness. We in the West now enter the woods of these primitive tribes and laugh at the bareness of their backsides. With the savagery of our almighty saws, we hack to death towering temples of praise and beauty which for the past three hundred years have drunk in the poison of carbon from our lungs and replenished our asphyxiation with oxygen.

Our world, so bent on the destruction of the environment for the sake of profit, has forfeited the wisdom of the so-called primitive tribes of the Amazon Basin in favour of our own so-called enlightened sophistry. A culture bent on materialism has forgotten its heritage and the interdependence of all sentient life. Ultimately our grasping will only lead to unsustainability.

A primordial wisdom in respect to God as the essence of life erupts in cultures far removed from each other. These illiterate tribes all sing the one song of praise to the Great Spirit. They thank God for their sustenance. Who is the more ignorant savage—the person who believes in the consciousness of trees or the criminal who cuts them down for profit?

We have become so out of touch with the natural law that many of our children think milk is born on a supermarket shelf. Atheistic materialism, under the guise of comfort and convenience, has softened us to such a degree that we pick the fruit but curse the tree. We have become so lobotomized that we no longer know the elemental flow through the food that sustains us, nor the purifying sand that sieves the water which revives and renews us.

We are out of tune. We relinquish our attention to what must be primary and replace it with a lust for what the moth eats and the rust corrodes. Why or how has the West become so decadent and out of tune?

We still pride ourselves on our Judeo-Christian heritage. But Judaism was not content to leave primitive tribes with their idea of a polygamy of gods. Instead they preached a monotheistic God. The Christian and Islamic worlds shaped their views with the same foundational theism: there is only one God and one truth. He alone must we worship.

Following the God of Abraham, Isaac, and Jacob, the Jews of the centuries before Christ saw themselves as a people specially chosen. They lived lives of slavery and persecution under the dictatorship of the Roman Empire, and stayed with a faith that gave them a distinct cultural identity. Their relationship with their God was often thorny, sometimes obedient and sometimes rebellious. The God of their testament was often harsh and retributive. But through the wisdom gained from this relationship, the Torah became the message of their identity and their liturgy of worship.

Orthodox Jews follow the Torah in all of its original purity. The Talmudic Jews, however, carved out of the Torah their own sense of theism and identity. The Talmud is more a record of the Jewish people as they adapted and changed their identity. It is the Talmud rather than the Torah which is the root cause of a smouldering anti-Semitism in our world today. It is peppered with awful anti-Christian slogans and rhetoric.

Semitic Jews are very much opposed to Zionism, which initiated and supports the State of Israel. Semitic rabbis insists that the Torah predestines the Jewish race to be a people in exile rather than an overpowering occupier.

European Jews or Ashkenazis disdain this biblical interpretation and mix politics with religion, much like Constantine and the Christian religion. Through the Balfour Declaration during the First World War, Zionists carved the land of Israel out of Palestine and declared it the future homeland for displaced European Jews. Zionism, with its obscenity of wealth gained from the Federal Reserve in the United States, based its claims on the Holy Land from teachings found in the Talmud and not the Torah.

The Talmudic Jews in Israel are not Semitic at all. They are European in origin and Ashkenazi rather than Semitic. So the use of the phrase "anti-Semitic" is a misnomer. The Semitic Jews and Palestinians are both Semitic and lived together in peace and harmony for centuries before Palestine became an occupied land.

The original story of the Jewish ordeal in establishing and solidifying its concept of God is sometimes brutal and unforgiving, sometimes faithful and pleasing, and just as often conflicting. A recall of the birth pangs of this new religion is recounted in what is called the Pentateuch, which is composed of the first five books of the Old Testament.

The psalms and the writings of the great prophets, like Isaiah and Jeremiah, continue to inspire all people of goodwill. Like all great literature, these writings are treasure troves of wisdom, balancing the relation between immanence and transcendence through worship and reverence. As in all great art, there is the ring of the eternal in them. Handel was so inspired that he created his masterpiece, *The Messiah*, from the beauty of the psalms.

Art must first be filtered through a personality. The prophets of the Old Testament were just ordinary people like you and me. They lived in a three-dimensional world with the same five senses deciphering human experience. They lived according to the visible light given to them, not knowing that physically, the full spectrum of the universe's light was not available to them. Yet they intuitively recognized the deeper dimension of transcendence galloping through the psalms' language. It is only through the recognition of the invisible and the transcendent that great art is possible. That is why the magnificent language of the Old Testament psalms continues to inspire humanity to this day.

Sadly, though, contemporary society has become grossly saturated with crassness and vulgarity. We have forfeited our divine heritage. We have been warned by the more contemporary Russian prophet, Dostoevsky, who wrote, "Beauty shall save the world."

In our modern world, spiritual transcendency has become suspect, even to the point of derision and ridicule. Much of modern Bible and biology scholarship is conducted by atheistic minds who are hell-bent on proving the absence of a great Intelligence at work in the world.

Of course there is a possibility that we are just cosmic orphans wandering in the dark, but as the natural world teaches, the story of all observable phenomena indicates a drop can still be called water even when it is drowned by the sea. Life seems geared more towards transcendency than a descent into oblivion.

The electrical flow we notice everywhere seems to be more constructive than destructive. An overwhelming agent of intelligence seems to be at work in everything. As Walt Whitman once said, "I believe the egg of the wren is a chef d'ouver for a five star restaurant ... the narrowest hinge in my hand puts to scorn all machinery ... a mouse is a miracle enough to stagger sixtillions of infidels."

Even the most hardened atheist must surely admit that the good in this world is far more revelatory than evil.

Some biblical scholars, in their efforts to demythologize the Old Testament, now claim that Abraham and Isaac, rather than being historical, are figures based on Egyptian myth. Abraham is claimed to be an Egyptian pharaoh. The story of Moses being found in a basket on a river's edge is also thought to be of Egyptian origin. Biblical scholars suggest that King David is also is a mythological figure, thereby denying the modern Jewish claim to Palestine.

Christians considers Christianity a tributary, as it were, of the Jewish river, but in its flow, it has been enlarged by other tributaries.

The Jews of the Old Testament waited in expectancy for their messiah to come. He would address all their earthly needs and reward them with a kingdom on this earth, free at last from the overlordship of the Roman Empire. It is precisely at this point that the expected messiah of the Jews became the existential Messiah of Christianity.

Jesus as the Messiah was already in the Jews' midst, but he did not live up to their earthly expectations. Although he was one of them, they rejected him. He wasn't of very much use to them. They considered him a blasphemer for comparing himself to God. He also talked to women in public. This was a tremendous taboo in the Semitic world. To make it worse, he talked to Samaritan women. The Samaritans were the most despised people in the Middle East of that time.

The scribes and Pharisees hated him. He was an upstart who challenged the injustice of their domination, which forced the poor to live like slaves to enrich their own devious way of living. Jesus had a strange way of teaching and did not immerse himself in quotations from the Torah. His lessons were mostly original and taught in provocative stories, which could be easily understood by his illiterate followers. His inspiration and passion seemed to come from a sense of his own interiority. His followers recognized some Presence within him which deeply enlarged him. He was different. He preached unconventionally an iconic message.

The peasant crowd were shocked when they heard him call God by a pet name, "Abba", which means "Daddy" in English. This kind of familiar language had never before been used to refer to the ineffable God. This reference alone indicates the spirit of an original and unique man. The word "Abba" was instrumental in bringing the God of the heavens down to earth. The Father of Jesus became a God involved in human occurrences. Jesus made God available and approachable No one had ever spoke to the Jewish people in such a manner.

As the poet Patrick Kavanagh wrote, "God comes to us in common statement … a kiss here and a smile again … God whispers in the argument of a churning and in the streets where village boys are lurching." We find God, as the poet says, wherever life pours ordinary plenty. Jesus lived his life in this very ordinary, penetrating way.

To the contemporary ear, the word "Daddy" conjures up the idea of a father figure who lives to protect, guide, and take care of us. Daddy is a man who is totally concerned about our welfare. When Jesus used this precise word in reference to God the Father, he absolutely changed the Semitic understanding of God as a harsh, jealous, and vindictive God. The *evangelia* which Jesus preached was indeed the good news. The God of Jesus was a loving and caring father figure: "Come to me all you who sorrow and I will refresh you."

The Father that Jesus spoke of was not a distant, disinterested deity who, in a primordial moment, created time and space through the big bang and then let chemistry run the show. That might be the Aristotelian version of God, but it is not the God of Jesus. No! Jesus saw God as the Father of the universe, who from the very beginning intended the appearance of the humanoid to spiritualize. The energy and coagulated chemistry which operates in the production of mass has followed a precise creative strategy.

The God of Jesus lived in the midst of the ordinary while remaining extraordinary. The God of Jesus resides so close to us that he lives inside of us.

Jesus informed us that God is a continuum who was, still is, and will proceed into the eternity of what is to be. It is divinity which defines our isness. "The Father and I are One. As the father is in me and I in the Father … so also is the kingdom of God inside of you."

No one in the Middle Eastern world had ever spoken like this before. God had always been "out there". No prophet had ever suggested that God is so close that the supreme Creator sits on his throne inside of us.

Jesus told us divinity resides inside and awaits our awakening. God invites cooperation. God does not compel like a strategic commander. When it comes to the laws of nature, God is not omnipotent. He goes with the flow of his tender creation. Even divinity must work in accordance with the construction of the earth which God initially created. Without our cooperation and consent, God is helpless.

To intervene supernaturally, as the televangelists and fundamental Christians claim, only lends to the destruction of the natural law. God cannot overpower the creative law of the universe. It has been perfect in every respect from the beginning. It is eternally written and cannot be changed one iota. God would become a contradiction should this happen. The only dogma that must be changed is our own attitude towards creation. Original sin is an absurdity. The natural law would never tolerate such an atrocity. To introduce the man Jesus as Saviour and Redeemer of the world, as the Christian church does, is to deny divinity the primordial energy in creativity.

The natural law does not lie or change. It is now as it always was. This planet, with all its incredible miraculousness, does not need a saviour to redeem it. What is necessary for its redemption is our own willingness not to sin against our evolutionary flow into the unifying field of consciousness. Jesus did not come to redeem us. He is not a scapegoat, but an ordinary man like any of us. He had the courage of his convictions, for which he sacrificed his life.

This planet has been incredibly created. Humanity has desecrated its own nest, and it is up to each one of us to clean it up. Jesus has shown us the way to accomplish this. Jesus was a visionary much more than a redeemer or a wonder-worker. To introduce Jesus as a saviour is to deny the primordial plan of creativity.

It is like saying divinity made a mistake when it initiated the big bang. The process worked perfectly for eleven billion years until humans, through sin, arrogantly objected to the earth's creative design. But not even God can withdraw from the drawing board his own design.

Atheists object to the Christ story as a fantastical tale, not to be taken seriously. The sensational and miraculous details of Christ's life are what open the atheistic mind to ridicule and reject him.

Biblical and demythologizing scholars dismiss these details as nonessential. They are but literary devices to add to the attractiveness of the Jesus message. Unfortunately, through a lack of true developmental theology, the sensational and miraculous details of the life of Jesus have taken the central place in his authoritative teaching. Usually it is the external which invites a chemical reaction, and this is where most of humanity chooses to stay, as Edward Bernays so insightfully noticed.

Thus began the capital foundation for the material. Packages tied up in beautiful ribbons became more tantalizing than the gifts within them. Spirituality tells a much more profound story. It is always the with-in-ness that gives the full import and significance to the message.

Christ was a man of huge interiority. It was not his Semitic looks or the fanfare of his sensational accomplishments which gave credence to his authenticity, but the passionate conviction that the eternal God lives within each one of us. Apart from the sensational entrapments of his birth, death, and resurrection, his central message continues to be, two thousand years hence, the greatest challenge to all of humanity's accomplishments.

There is an enduring and profound wisdom in all of Jesus's teachings, so much so that none of us yet, not even Shakespeare, has been more accomplished. A music deeper than Mozart or Beethoven runs through all his lessons. If humanity were to listen intensely enough, then surely our ordinary streets would fill with singing instead of crying.

To tame his magnificent and wild articulation into numbers of chapters and verses, as the fundamentalist Christians do, must make Christ turn his face. Music does not come equationally. For a profound experience, we need to hear the full score.

Despite the anger of fundamentalist Christians against such a thesis, our understanding of divinity cannot remain static and literal. It can only exist dynamically. It expands and changes when we, with faithful scrutiny and careful understanding of cosmology, allow it to grow. The allied sciences also assist in the discovery of eternal truth. Science has a crucial role to play in the development of an authentic spirituality.

What often appears to us as supernatural intervention has more to do with the embrace of our fractional frequency in available light. Outlandish things may seem to happen, but they are illusory. It is impossible for God to separate divinity from the ordained, natural flow of things. Supernatural acts, defined as when the natural law becomes suspended, are a contradiction in terms. They necessarily imply that the Creator in the beginning could well have improved on the natural process. When the natural law appears to be suspended by an external force, healing is occurring from the compassionate natural energy surrounding the body. That is why prayer is so important—it whips up compassionate energy. Healing does not come through a suspension of the natural law. It comes from the divine energy inside each one of us.

Healing not only comes from the application of medicine, but just as importantly from our will to accomplish it. The more we open ourselves to the full spectrum of light, the more we spiritualize our existence. When we cooperate with the God of interiority, miracles erupt naturally. The urge to adore the Creator of earth brings healing to our minds and also to our wounded earth. Miracles come from humanity staying naturally integrated with its original ground and not the other way around.

The primary mission of Jesus was to awaken the Godness within us. The miracle is to stay faithful. The option facing us is Christ or Hiroshima.

The incident of Jesus calling his Father "Daddy" is a detail of immense value to biblical scholars. Such familiar language in respect to God is totally alien to the Jewish mind. The scholars who attempt to demythologize fiction from fact in their search for the historical Jesus cite this detail as having huge significance. Cultural anthropology is one of the main tools used to discover the truth about historical figures. The fact that Jesus called God the Father "Abba" was so countercultural and unthinkable that it is considered an authentic echo of his preaching.

Most of us are remembered not for our sameness but for our differences. Jesus was different in that he was fully alive and awakened to God living inside him and inside each one of us. He lived like few men on earth, in terms of the potential we possess for compassion. Without knowing the science of quantum physics, he intuited the unifying field of consciousness. He consciously lived that inner intuition which makes the human family interrelated, interconnected, and interdependent.

Quantum physics teaches that the cosmos is one. We are all one family. "Come home to your deepest self" is the message of Jesus. The beatitudes of the shepherd man and of quantum physics agree with each other.

We already have the energy of God within us. If the desert blossoms, it is because we ourselves have watered it. God is the reservoir, and we the falling drops of moisture. Cooperation rather than competition is the seed which roots everything. Consciousness has to become part of us through cooperation. God's work has to become our own. If the cherry blossom is to appear on the tree, an awakening spring must first induce its vitality. We are the ones who invite the trees into blossom.

We will discuss the life of Jesus and his impact on Western civilization more deeply in a later chapter. Suffice it to say here that the story of Jesus in the history of monotheistic religion is remarkable and impressive. Possibly every person on earth, whether or not they are part of the multitude who follow him, has heard his name. No one apart from this man has so vividly explained divinity to humanity. No one has ever cloaked God so proximately. Every one of us, despite the fact that we may follow the divine according to our own cultural identities, must surely agree with the centrality of his message. His convictions remain authentic, compelling, and enlarging, despite what the Christian church has done to them. His message remains of immense evolutionary importance, despite the details which surround the Bible story.

We have given a brief outline of the Jewish and Christian synthesis, and now we move on to the third monotheistic expression of religious faith which emanated from the Middle East. Like Judaism and Christianity, Islam traces its roots back to Abraham, Isaac, and Jacob.

All three monotheistic religions are Jewish in foundation. All three believe in the one God. How this God is understood and proclaimed differs according to cultural interpretation. Judaism expects the Messiah, but a worldly one who will immanently save them from their earthly troubles. Christianity believes the Messiah has already come in the person of Jesus. The Messiah of Christianity is concerned primarily with the transcendent and preaches a future kingdom.

Islam was founded by Muhammad some six hundred years after Jesus. Islam believes in a God they call Allah, and their main tenet is "there is no God but God".

Muslims believe Islam is the latest revelation from God to humankind. They believe it is final revelation and humanity should follow this latest communication between God and the human race.

Islam believes that Muhammad is the latest and last in a string of prophets, Jesus among them. Islam differs from Christianity in that Christ is considered but a prophet like Muhammad. He cannot be God's only begotten Son. He is no more God than Muhammad is. God is one. God cannot be fractured by the appearance of a Son of God. God cannot be split in two. There is no God but God, and his name is Allah. Jesus, like the rest of us, is of divine origin, but merely human.

Like all three monotheistic religions, the constitution of Islam's belief system has been stenographically recorded in a book called the Koran. This holy book contains all the disclosures from Allah to Muhammad, as the final revelation. Islam considers the revelation of God to humanity, as testified by Muhammad, to be the most all-encompassing revelation of divinity to the human race.

Muhammad was illiterate. He could not read or write. The divine revelations in the Koran were remembered and later transcribed.

There remains one great, glaring difference between Islam and Christianity, and that is the acceptance of Jesus as a mere prophet rather than the only begotten Son of God. This book, *Dare to Be Spiritual*, substantially agrees with this thesis, but as always, the centrality of a cosmotheandric God, who holds the web of all life together, begins to take on new pressures learned from various cultural experiences.

Religious wars stem from cultural differences, which are at best only fringe concerns. They are of secondary importance in comparison to our common belief in a cosmotheandric God, who has created us according to unifying field of consciousness. It is only when this spiritual understanding of life prevails among us that peace shall prevail on earth.

We are all one. A cosmotheandric God glues us together. The chemistry in the stardust of our beginning was not discriminating. It all swelled up from the same pot of creativity. God does not curse any one of us. Look at life in an astrophysical or quantum way, and it relays the wonder involved in the commonality and sameness of our human journey. Ours is an invitation to savour our spiritual sameness.

All monotheistic faiths have much in common. Instead of diverting so much attention and energy to our cultural religious differences, a new industry of spirituality must now be encouraged to blossom on the positive stance of our commonality and sameness. The religious wars of the past have had their day. They are now passé. The unifying field of consciousness displaces tribalism, with the primary mandate to become one. Difference, of course, brings a spectrum of glory to our human habitat and must be celebrated to take the monotony of the mundane out of our tired and jaded experiences. But fundamentally we all stand on the same original ground, and our foundational identity cannot be attacked. On this level, the monotheistic faiths basically agree.

In respect to Christianity, the central message of Jesus is consistent with all the noble wisdom garnered through the centuries from various traditions. However, Jesus learned his wisdom from his own lived experience. He lived his message before he preached it. He authenticated the problem of human suffering through his own experience before he ever talked about it. He lived inwardly before he spoke outwardly. He befriended himself with his own integrity. He hammered out spirituality on the anvil of his own personality. He never yielded a gun or a bomb; he remains the greatest nonviolent revolutionary in human history. He taught the world that a true sense of insecurity is our greatest asset. A smile given to a stranger costs nothing but enhances civilization when done in love.

The aphorisms of Jesus and his remarkable parables still resonate today with a profound authenticity. They truly represent the historicity of one of the most profound wisdom teachers who ever lived. The testimony of Jesus is first-hand. Jesus is the author of his own testimony. Even though his message was later recorded mythologically, he lived what he preached. He knew first-hand that suffering and sacrifice purify wisdom.

Islam is filtered through Muhammad's personality. Unlike Jesus and the Bible, the Koran was filtered through Muhammad rather than by him. It is second-hand. Jesus lived his message. Muhammad is a proxy. This represents the second great difference between Islam and Christianity.

This is the religious history of Western and Middle Eastern religion. Despite their common foundation, these three approaches to God have never reconciled. The Judeo-Christian rendition was driven out of the Middle East by the Islamic Ottoman Empire. Constantinople became Istanbul. Hagia Sophia, the magnificent Byzantine church whose dome is considered one of the greatest achievements in architecture, was turned into a mosque.

No matter the irreconcilable differences, the fact remains that the idea of God remained central to all three monotheistic religions. This remained the case in the West until the Enlightenment of the eighteenth century. Through scientific discovery and the new information which it afforded, many death blows were thrown at Christianity, which weakened it terribly.

In the Middle East, however, Islam grew ever stronger. God was the centre and content of the Islamic world. No endeavour or project could commence without first calling on the holy name of Allah. God became central in the Islamic bloodstream, invading every corner of their world. Muslim family life was based upon the rules which their holy prophet Muhammad had directed in the Koran. This religious perspective so intimately infiltrated Islamic life that it has been at the core of their world view for the past fifteen hundred years.

The holy name of God has remained central in all of Islam's public speaking, whether religious or political. Islam has fixated on the literalism of the Koran, its adherents, zombie-like, submitting their lives obediently to the teachings of their mullah overlords. The Islamic world has held on to a slavish interpretation of consciousness. Their embrace, however, contains enough reverence for God as their original ground that it remains much more spiritual than the heathen West.

The atheistic West, in all of its deliberations, has consciously thrown the God of consciousness right out of the picture, deeming divinity but a fairy tale. The West now uses the name of God more as a curse than a blessing.

The leaders of the Islamic world have not developed an expanding theology. Islam stands still with a medieval theological perspective. It has not embraced the expansive understanding which the God of consciousness brings. It is not tolerant of the idea that theology, rather than being a closed book, is instead capable of eternally expanding. The human perception of God is continuously challenged to change and grow according to the new, authentic information given to it. God is not finished with humanity yet. Medieval perceptions do not fit into a technological and scientific world very readily.

The problem with the modern world is that the imperialistic West, consumed with pride, has thrown God out of the garden of Eden, whereas the Islamic God hasn't grown much since the story of Adam and Eve was first told.

THE ILLUMINATI CHAPTER

The West is governed by a bunch of psychopaths called the elites, whose only concern is the accumulation of wealth and the mind control of the masses.

More and more through the control of mass media and the chemical poisoning of our air, food, and water, our nutritional needs are covertly and incrementally being depleted. This psychopathic bunch of bankers are utterly corrupt, devoid of any human decency or compassion. Instead of Western governments controlling them, the illuminati control the body and soul of the West. Ultimately they start the wars. They sell and manufacture the arms of the military complex, making huge profit. They impose interest rates on fiat paper money which is not backed by gold. Through debt, they enslave the middle and lower classes in a life of indentured servitude. The greater the debt, the greater the profit which pours into their pockets. They are the richest two percent of people in the world, controlling the wealth of the world.

In 1910 on Jenkyll Island, which is a small piece of land off the coast of Georgia, a secret group of obscenely rich men set up what is called the Federal Reserve of the United States. It was set up in such a clandestine way that it was neither federal nor a reserve. They themselves became the recipients of all the profit at the end of a gushing faucet.

This so-called group of illuminati think they are at the top of the evolutionary peak, much more clever than the rest of humanity. They view themselves as the most enlightened group of men on earth. The big bang or the steady state intended them from the beginning. Full-spectrum light makes available to humanity but a small slice of its whole. The elites, through the control of their bloodlines, live on the light and information given to them on a higher level. This is their mantra. The rest of humanity are less evolved.

The elites consider other humans to be little more than a herd of cattle for corralling and controlling. They consider themselves genetically different from the rest of us. They chemically preserve sperm for the continuation of their purity and superiority. Their genetic make-up is deficient in empathy. They lack compassion, and honour the bloodletting and sacrifice practised in ancient religion. Zionist Jews, the royal families of Europe, the pope, and the presidents of the United States are counted among elite membership. As the possessors of 98 per cent of the world's wealth, they buy and infiltrate their way into all powerful human societies. They are in fact the shadow government of the world.

After the First World War, under British colonial rule, they created the land of Israel as a homeland for the displaced Jews of Europe. This is known as the Balfour Declaration.

Considering themselves to be men of superior intelligence, they chose the destruction which war engenders as a way to gather more and more money. War is good for the economy.

Psychopathic by nature, they show no compassion for the planet. Their hidden agenda is to reduce the world's population by five billion, so that the earth will become more pristine for them.

Jewish Zionists are adamant that the Holy Land belongs to them. They claim their roots as the chosen people go back to the time of King David. This is a false claim, since most of the Jews in the Holy Land are of European extraction, known as the Ashkenazis. They are not Semites, although they claim to be so. The true Jewish Semites have lived in peace with their Semite Palestinian brothers and sisters for hundreds of years. They did so before the European Jews, who are converts to Judaism, ever set foot in Palestine. Jewish Zionism, mostly composed of wealthy bloodlines, is purely secular. It is dismissive of the very religion which they claim gives them the right to the land of Palestine. Had they been faithful to the voice of their Jewish prophets, the global prospect would be far more peaceful.

At their very core, Jewish Zionists grow ever more exploitative. They ignore the warning of Jeremiah, the Jewish prophet:

> Woe to him, who builds his house by unrighteousness and his upper rooms by injustice, who makes his neighbors work for nothing.
> Did not your father eat and drink and do justice and righteousness?
> Then it was well with him.
> He judged the call of the poor and the needy.
> Then it was well.
> Is not this to know me? Says the Lord
> But your eyes and heart are only on your dishonest gain for shedding innocent blood and for practising oppression and violence. (Jeremiah 22:13–17)

It is Jewish Zionism itself which is anti-Semitic.

The question must now be asked, "Who is the real terrorist?"

It is important to understand that a psychopath is a person with abnormal sensitivity, bereft of any capacity for compassion. He looks on other human beings as mere fodder to be engineered for profit. The human person, to the psychopath, is but a beast of burden to be whipped into passive obedience.

This group of psychopaths give themselves the right to play God, deciding who shall live and who shall die. They own 98 per cent of the world's wealth, thereby empowering themselves to buy or sell whatever they want. Their plan is to control the planet and all humans on it through the indoctrination of atheism. They already own most of the media in America and Europe. Through this monopoly, they contaminate the Western mind and its magnificent heritage expressed through Christianity. These men covertly broadcast entertainment and dumb humour to distract the media audience from the elites' aim to overthrow whatever remains Christian in Western culture. This vision is called *the new world order*.

As the lords of the manor, they are even now carving out a future when the earth will be depopulated, leaving only two classes: the rich and the slaves who serve them.

When Ted Turner, the media mogul behind CNN and now an amazingly wealthy landowner, was asked what his goal was for the population of the world, he answered, "I think two billion is about right."

Henry Kissinger told the NCC, "Depopulation should be the highest priority of US foreign policy towards "The Third World."

The US economy will require large and increasing amounts of minerals from abroad, especially from less developed countries ... Population is relevant to the supplies and the economic interests of the US."

Secretary of Defense Donald Rumsfeld proposed developing very toxic weapons, the likes of which would poison thousands if hit with even one bacteria.

The United States government, under the control of the illuminati, has already spread Agent Orange over Vietnam and depleted uranium over the Middle East. That uranium is right now destroying the genetic future of people who are still living there. Henry Kissinger, who is responsible for the slaughter of millions in Cambodia and Vietnam, was awarded the Nobel Peace Prize. Everything has been turned upside down.

In order for a nation to afford the ferocity and atrociousness which war involves, a huge amount of money is needed. In the case of the United States of America, the most powerful nation in the world, the money needed to wage war is not supplied from its savings but by the Federal Reserve, which is its central bank. This bank is privately owned by the illuminati.

Once agreed upon and initiated, the Federal Reserve loans billions of dollars—with interest added to it—to the American government. The higher the debt, the more the illuminati like it. If there is not enough paper money to pay for the war, the Federal Reserve, through quantitative easing, prints more. Since the illuminati agenda is morally atheistic, wars are started to make profit rather than peace.

The Federal Reserve of America, manned as it is by Zionist illuminati, loves war. It cannot live without war. Debt is its only value. Debt turns the illuminati into billionaires. Their tactics are diabolical. All of our most recent horrors have covertly been initiated through them. Through their propaganda and deceit, they have become so powerful that they buy even hate.

We cooperate with them by our silence. This is what these psychopathic men love most about us.

Permit me to issue and control the money of a
nation and I care not who makes its laws.
—Amschel Rothschild

I care not what puppet is placed upon the throne of England
to save the Empire on which the sun never sets. The man
who controls Britain's money supply, controls the British
Empire, and I control the British money supply.
—Nathan Rothschild

Woodrow Wilson, after he had supported the elites initially, later declared, "Our great industrial nation is controlled by its system of credit. Therefore all our activities are in the hands of a small group of men who chill and check true economic freedom. We have come to be one of the most ruled, completely controlled and dominated governments in the world. No longer a government of the majority but a government of the opinion and duress of a small group of men."

I sincerely believe the banking institution having the issuing power
of money are more dangerous to liberty than standing armies.
—Thomas Jefferson

Since this small, elite group of psychopaths own 98 per cent of the world's riches, they control all the professions, which carry out their wishes.

Even the president of the United States is tutored and controlled by them. The president is selected and not elected.

The Zionist illuminati totally control the mass media, only allowing the message of their avowed agenda to be broadcast. With no moral compass to guide humanity, the Western world has been turned upside down and left standing on its head. The media only broadcasts its own lies.

None are so helplessly enslaved as those who think they are free.

—Goethe

The so-called democratic nations of the West, which constantly preach to the rest of the world about freedom, are in fact the most unfree people on earth. With all the release from drudgery which our robotic machinery affords us, women are forced to put their babies in crèches and fathers are forced to work at two jobs just to keep the bank gurus from barking on their telephones. Stress is a growing phenomenon. Suicide, in many cases, is the option people choose to escape their burdens. The cornerstone for true happiness and self-fulfilment has been chipped away so ferociously that the experience of family love and integration has been seriously undermined and almost bulldozed out of existence.

All of the social problems in this world are due to our lack of spirituality. The atheism which the illuminati imposes has a direct impact on social cohesion. The so-called Christian West has been covertly converted into an at-one-ment with the psychopathic elites. We have lost our Christian heritage.

The Christian West has been propagandized to death by the atheistic illuminati. Christians have become spiritually illiterate. Yet we think we are the most blessed and free people on the face of the earth. If a nation talks atheism and lives atheism, then it is atheistic. Any nation which lives atheistically while hypocritically proclaiming God, and while still killing others through war, is an abomination on the face of the earth.

A Christian individual must find at-one-ment within the self before finding at-one-ment with his or her nation. When a person finds their own centre, therein lies the key to the threshold of peace on earth. Spiritual integration with the self is the seed which will sprout into freedom on earth.

It can be clearly observed that Western civilization is in decline. Obscenity and decadence of the most salacious kind are now our trademarks. We have become exactly what the atheistic illuminati want us to be. We are soulless slaves to serve their atheistic agenda. There is scarcely one politician on either a national or the world stage who dares to bring the holy name of God into deliberations. Atheism has so conquered the human mindset that the idea of divinity is no longer tolerated. To mention a higher Intelligence is forbidden as the epitome of ignorance. The sad truth is that even if atheists could prove there is no God (which they can't), the human race would be far better served with divinity present. Atheism only assists the elites. It brainwashes and dehumanizes the rest of us. It is time to introduce divinity into our legislature.

Look at us now! Everything is turned upside down: Hospitals destroy medicine, lawyers destroy justice. Universities destroy knowledge.

—Michael Ellner

The gullible and unsuspecting public of the West has become subconsciously trained zealots who do the illuminati's bidding. Western Europe and the United States are a global village. The umbilical cord that binds them together is the central bank of each country, which in turn is linked to the behemoth, the Federal Reserve of America The world is scarcely aware that all the interest paid on mortgages reaches its final glory hole in the pockets of the elites who own the Federal Reserve.

Debt is the exploitative means of working the poor to death and the rich into obscene luxury.

Contemporary citizens of the Western world have become diseased to such a degree that we no longer realize how our consciousness has been drugged. We walk around like cyborgs instead of human beings. We talk more to machines than we do to people. Our phones are our constant companions. To lose a phone causes more hysteria than the death of a loved one. It is through our phones that we find self-esteem and feel redeemed. We spend many more hours with machines than we do with our spouses and children. We use phones as our psychological counsellors. Phone voices may laugh because a laugh is audible, but they cannot smile because a smile is invisible. Voices do not have eyes. They cannot see. They have ears, of course, but those ears are hardware.

Uplifting human encounter has become as redundant as those obsolescent refrigerators and stoves we throw away. So what is the purpose of being human? We seem to have forgotten the answer. Ah, but what the hell—it makes no difference so long as we keep calling each other!

The sickness of the West is that we have become so decadent and removed from the real that we have separated ourselves even from what is intrinsic about the self. The self-thou relationship is no more. It is as extinct as the dinosaur.

Justice is infected to such a degree that the rich and the criminal go free while the innocent and the needy are incarcerated. Everything has been turned upside down and inside out. The spiritual dimension of our identity has been obliterated in favour of cannibalistic hardware.

Humanity has an aching need for beauty and truth. Will the controlled media of the West ever address this need? Certainly not.

Citizens of the West live corralled lives. We have been beaten into submission by an elitist 2 per cent who hold 98 per cent of the world's wealth. Even the power of the president of the United States is bought by the money of these oligarchs.

The loans which banks tender are an illusion. The money does not exist in reality, but the interest on it does—which can only be paid back by the hard work of slaves. Slavery is the only incubator of honest money. The rest is fiat.

Presidents of the United States are elected in the hope that they will bring peace and social justice to reign not only in North America, but throughout the world. Although the United States is considered, at least by its own citizens, to be the most developed and religious country in the world, its citizens have been acculturated with a village rather than a global mentality. Little do they realize their votes to elect a new president, despite all the glitter and razzmatazz of their political conventions, is managed and decided by a shadow government. As Rothschild said, money can buy everything.

Ever since the robber barons learned obscenely that war is good for the economy, the management of money has been transferred to the devious care of the Federal Reserve. It became the great impetus for an increase of profit through war and carnage. This barbarous act initiated the huge inequality we find in our world today. The system was copper-fastened by what are called *fractional reserve* and *quantitative easing*.

This system of banking still prevails in our world today. In its most simplistic form, quantitative easing creates paper money out of thin air. It is a fiat and fake currency. It is easy to create fake money, but when debt which has been kicked into oblivion comes knocking on door, it becomes another story.

Banks give out credit with interest attached to it. They usually do not have enough reserves in their vaults to back up the credit handed out. The money they do hold from depositors is the fractional reserve. It is used as a backup measure. In essence, the common depositors' earnings are used by the banks to earn more money.

When the United States government needs money, it must borrow with interest from the Federal Reserve and pay back to the elites.

Even the least educated among us recognise that money and profit are the real cause of all the thievery and corruption in modern society. Anything can be purchased when the right sum of money becomes available to buy it. Rivers can be turned around to flow uphill instead of down when there is enough money to accomplish it.

Psychopaths start wars. The shadow government sells the machines of murder to countries which cannot afford them, with interest added to their borrowing. This in turn causes untold misery to the nations that purchase those machines.

This shadow government covertly causes internal insurgencies and stimulates disagreement through the tactics of divide and conquer. When war erupts, then bombs, bullets, guns, aircraft, and all other vessels of carnage are sold to both sides of the conflict, not to bring peace but more profit into the tills of the elites.

The ordinary men and women on the streets of the United States are not aware of the strategic plans which these evil oligarchs envision and enact in their name. The vast majority of American citizens consider their nation to be the most democratic and generous country on the face of the earth. The pledge of allegiance, which children in school repeat like a mantra, inculcates the idea that their nation is the most noble and exceptional on the face of the planet. Indeed the United States is a beautiful land. A multitude of its citizens are sensitively aware of its call to excellence. But the land that once accepted starving, impoverished people from all kinds of foreign lands is even now involved in the slaughter of their immigrant ancestors.

Not content with the immediate efficacy of bombs and bullets, spent uranium and Agent Orange have been showered down on innocent families who are interested only in feeding, clothing, and sheltering their children. What right does any nation have to genetically alter innocence with deformity? No matter the torture Hussein or Gaddafi may have visited on their people—that is far more tolerable than the mad rendition of freedom and democracy which the United States and Western Europe have visited upon them. Revolution must come from within, both physically and spiritually, if the onward push of evolution is to reach its natural conclusion.

The lie of the West and its control over mass media has not been introduced to save us from the terror without, but to curtain us from the elitist terrorism which crawls within. Wars of the past may have been justified somewhat because of the zeal for human rights and the emancipation of nations. The wars of the twenty-first century, waged by the West, have no such lofty ideals. They have been designed instead to swell the bank accounts of the psychopathic elites, so that ever more corruption and carnage will occur through money laundering and the sale of arms.

The elites' scheming tactics make their coffers ever larger. Because they engage in the end game, the sight of a cartful of money fills them with glee, whereas the sight of a cartful of young children and their mothers, hacked to bits by their murderous weapons, is passed over glibly, chalked up to and called by the undignified name of *collateral damage*.

The elites' armaments are no respecters of nations. Elites cross hurriedly over every border for the sake of money. More atrociously, they create false-flag enemies, turning the murderer into the victim and the victim into the murderer. In such a topsy-turvy culture, the devil becomes the saint and the saint the devil. Up becomes down and down up.

It is this bunch of elitists that drives nations into bankruptcy. Like a yo-yo, they play up and down, in and around with the interest gained from mortgage debtors. So severe are their terror tactics that many see no solution but to commit suicide. The most dreadful fact about this gulag enterprise is that the money they have grown rich on—to the point of five hundred trillion dollars—is money gained from the interest earned on a nonexistent currency. Fiat money is only paper!

The question is "Who turned these psychopaths into God?"

The answer is "We did"

"And how did we do it?"

"By sacrificing our moral principles for profit and consumer trinkets"

A larger question remains: "How can a nation survive when built on such deceit and lies?"

We in the West live in a world which has become more and more centralized around a religion that only concerns itself with the offerings of materialistic atheism. There is no justice in a world where only the economy of money matters. War crimes are committed without consequence. The warlords who commit the most atrocious crimes live in Europe and America. They do not live in Afghanistan, Iraq, or Syria. Fortified in opulent enclosures, their only concern is power and control.

Anyone can print money, but it is only worth the paper it is written on. The only money that is real in this whole deal of indebtedness is the interest that middle-class people pay back to these Zionist psychopaths.

A nation is only great insofar as it is moral and well ordered. Our modern world does indeed need a new world order, but one that is constructive and not destructive. The United States Constitution, probably the most just ever written, is slowly being devoured and rewritten by the Zionist illuminati, whose only concern is profit and expansionism. Their vision is atheistic. The God in their decision-making is the God of destruction. The old God of the Judeo-Christian religion is slowly being replaced by Shiva, the god of destruction, without the balance of Brahma, the Hindu god of construction. Through the new world order which Zionist illuminati envision, destruction of the old order must be enacted according to the blueprint of their structure. Psychopaths always use evil means to confirm their own perception of superiority and domination. If this confirmation is not attained democratically, then they will buy it.

Not content with control of the money supply, they are covertly planning a new world order in which the middle class will be wiped off the face of the earth, thereby creating but two classes: the elites and the slaves, who are the rest of us, passively serving them. This new world order will surely happen if humanity does not wake up and become consciously aware of our present reality. We need a new world order, but one with the primacy of God to substantiate it, not one that is diabolical.

From observable phenomenology, we can clearly see the interrelationship, interdependence, and interconnection of all living things on this planet. If we do not start to hug, kiss, and appreciate even the most inconspicuous forms of being in our sphere, our world will spiral ever forward into an Armageddon of ultimate destruction. For instance, when humanity's pollution frustrates the bee's pollination, starvation becomes the consequence. When the earthworm reneges on its appointed mission, then the soil, depleted of oxygen, will in turn refuse to send green sprouts as shouts of praise to the eternal heavens.

Atheism is the ultimate act of humanity's pride against God. It makes itself into the only god, which must be adored and worshipped. It arrogantly announces to this world that the elites are the only true form of sentient being to have emerged from the evolutionary process. Evolution has put them on the top rung of the ladder. The atheistic elites claim that from the beginning of time, they alone have been the full resolution of the purpose of evolution. The rest of us in the battle for survival of the fittest have been left behind in a less developed state. To their psychopathic minds, we are the leftovers, disinherited in the evolutionary struggle.

Since we are the ones who have not adapted, we must be erased. Atheistic elitism deems us to be vermin and useless eaters who are destroying the planet environmentally—hence Agenda 21. Life on this earth, with all of its complexity consciousness, has had but one purpose according to the illuminati, and that is to turn them into superior beings with all the authority of a monarchy. The rest of humanity has been robbed of self-worth and dignity.

The illuminati have turned Western Christianity on its head. As Christians, we have passively colluded with the elites in our own destruction. We no longer battle for our Christian entitlement to self-nobility and dignity.

The biggest enemy of Christianity is not our cultural religious differences from people in other parts of the world, but the abolition of the universal God from our midst. If this world is to survive, then the murder machinery of the atheistic elites must be converted to the more gentle approach of Christianity.

Evil cannot be fought with evil. The good is the only possible tool with which to conquer evil. The Christian West has acquiesced so much to the overpowering onslaught of atheistic propaganda that it no longer has the courage to challenge atheism. Political correctness in the interest of peace must always prevail, according to the atheistic political agenda. It was a huge crime to be anti-Semitic, worthy of the death penalty during the Bolshevik Revolution. But the same moral outrage cannot be afforded Christians, it seems, when Jewish comedians make disgusting jokes about Jesus.

Atheism has so ensnared the West that the whole body of the globe has become the carcass of its deceit. Everything about atheistic materialism is meant to exploit us, drain us, and destroy us. There is a shadow government manipulating the political process to such a degree that legislatures are bought and presidents selected rather than elected.

To bring the idea of God into any political deliberation is considered suicidal and not practical in the halls of human debate. However, the truth remains that God will not be mocked. There can be no morality or ethics without a spiritual consideration. To overconcern ourselves with economic and material solutions is not progress. It is retrogression. To disdain the fact that we are above all else spiritual in our orientation is to give credence to materialistic atheism.

When we become awakened to the scope of our inbred consciousness, even tragedy and the treadmill of dreary routine can become animated with purpose. Agony can be turned into ecstasy with the right attitude and an acceptance of our natural odyssey into God.

> Without God this world is a vaudeville of devils.
>
> —Dostoevsky

The signs are already shoving their ugly and belittling heads all around us and within us. They are plain to see, and yet the Christian West no longer has the courage to arrest the growth of this all-consuming diabolical diatribe and strangulation.

Atheism is the greatest form of terrorism ever perpetrated on the human mind. It is far more heinous and destructive than horrors of ISIS. Yet perversely the morally bankrupt, unawakened Christian West continues to deck the halls of the elites' castles with tidings of good news and "peace on earth".

The egotistical greed of psychopathic elitism is incrementally releasing its poison on this, our little blueberry earth, with stupefying malediction and progressive enslavement. It has so surreptitiously consumed our mindset that we no longer know right from wrong.

Science has already verified that the invisibility of consciousness is the unifying field of all matter. The cosmos is one. We are all one. Compassion unifies each one to the other. There is no separation in this world or the next.

Quantum physics has verified there is a hereafter. Body and soul are a continuum, one into the other. The body finds itself in time, and while it disappears materially, its spirit lives on eternally. Whether we like it or not, we are hardwired spiritually. This is the only paradigm worthy of humanity's perception and appreciation.

Atheistic materialism will not accept this paradigm because atheism denies the spiritual urge in this world, capitalizing completely on the ego. Organized religion will not accept it either because it separates the good of God from the bad of evil. God is made totally separate from the evil of the body. This approach is dualistic.

Quantum physics, however, verifies the clash of opposites. Good and evil are the one reality. Consciousness is unity. Obviously organized religion has made a huge mistake in its approach to God, but it at least recognized the transcendent future for humanity. Its mistake is in the how, not the why.

Atheistic materialism has done unspeakable damage not only to the how, but even more ferociously in its denial of the why.

Mass media, which is totally controlled by the illuminati, is now used in such a way that, as passive receptors, humanity has surrendered its consciousness to a synthetic, virtual world of depravity and violence. Psychopathic planning to lead humanity towards destruction often appears as a shill. The message of evil is often so cunning and deceptive that it seems like goodness on the surface. A people deprived of a righteous message through control of the media soon becomes a people who can no longer discriminate between good and evil. So intent are the moguls of mass media to corrupt the conscience of the modern world that what is good about the human story is replaced by what is bad. When ugliness comes in, it kills beauty. The mass media content which the elites broadcast is infected with viruses so crass that they vulgarize instead of civilize humanity.

Western society has become dumbed down to such a degree that, as pliable and amenable animals, we thrive on the sensational much more than the rational. Atheistic science, with its emphasis on objective, rational truth, has so twisted the mind of humanity that what is mere sensationalism and fantasy is now considered rational and acceptable and often terribly funny. Satanism and the occult have replaced the existence of a benign Force at work in this world. Profit has become grace in our liturgy of Devil worship.

A mass media which only reports the lies of its own bias turns its victim into a dangerous terrorist. Meanwhile the perpetrators of its murderous crime-soaked message live in luxury, totally free. Mindlessness, with its idiotic content and canned laughter, is now considered comedic. Intelligence is reduced to cleverness at best, and wit is the stuff of stooges.

How can every new program be considered the greatest and "awesome"? When art becomes deviant and devoid of any uplifting value, it loses the justification for its existence. When art is judged by the measurement of the external alone, then greatness is judged by immanence only. Classical beauty cannot enter consciousness if a person does not have the spirituality to recognize it.

The West has allowed the judgement of atheism to determine the possibility of creativity in all human endeavours. We have become so distracted by the economy of life which it proposes that we now live life only on the periphery. Atheism has so indoctrinated us that we now live with acceptable insanities.

When we are unendingly propagandized by messages which glorify murder and carnage, the human mind itself becomes a killing field. The human heart grows hard when compassion is never part of our value system. Through mind control, a person can become a killer who obeys the command of the programmer. He or she becomes fodder for the coming war, incapable of differentiating between the celluloid and the real.

Everything becomes upside down when consciousness is taken out of consideration. The Devil comes out to play when God goes away. People are fooled into thinking that barriers will protect them. Even though they have never actually met an approaching enemy, they fear that enemy terribly. Generate enough fear and humans will forfeit all their individual rights for the sake of security.

It was in such an atmosphere that the Department of Homeland Security (DHS) in the United States was initiated. Through this tactic, the United States turned itself into an open-air prison at the behest of the Zionist illuminati.

Evil can be greatly enhanced when fear is established. Fear is a ploy for control. Organized religion did this through its indoctrination of hell and damnation. DHS in the United States has done precisely the same thing. The fear of hell is nothing in comparison to the reality of an unseen enemy, now known the world over as an Arab terrorist.

Physical barriers are of no advantage when the mind has to battle with lies. Through a lack of consciousness, the ordinary American citizen has not yet realized the evil enterprise being hatched out in their own backyard. There is no homeland security to keep the terrorist out when already he is within!

The Ten Commandments for this new world order are already prescribed on the Atlanta Guide Stone. It seems incredible that the human mind can lower itself to such an insufferable psychosis of wanton savagery. The elites have chiselled their intent to get rid of five billion human persons. Henry Kissinger agrees with this.

Devoid of any consciousness, these men play a diabolical game. They have invested themselves with the power of decision about who among us shall live and who shall die.

The warlords of the West, with an all-seeing eye, look down from their impenetrable pyramid high in the sky. They declare crime to be good and compassion evil.

The illuminati's vision for the new world order has been meticulously planned. The five billion souls they wish to exterminate cannot be obliterated in one huge nuclear scoop. Such a vision must be planned incrementally and slowly. The noose must be squeezed a knot at a time, so that the choking rope on the periphery will not be noticed. Create an atmosphere of stress and fear, and human rights will soon disappear. Willingly, following a herd mentality for the sake of security, naive people soon give their freedom away to a false saviour in sheep's clothing.

The incremental planning has been done covertly. Mass media, which is rooted in materialistic atheism, concentrates our minds on the ego and denies any room for the human spirit to expand. Remove consciousness from the human project, and the only prospect is selfishness. Replace compassion with a zest for violence, and soon the human spirit, without a moral compass, will devalue the sacredness and beauty of all life.

The gratuitous violence beamed out by US mass media across the world develops the impression that murder and might are the most central solution to all human altercations. A gluttony for blood spews out across our screens to such an extent that we become convinced to kill another who opposes us. It is our moral duty. Death has taken such precedence over the sacredness and beauty of human life that we now seem to lust after it. Our most precious possession has been so cheapened that we presently accept it as amusement or entertainment. We fail to recognize the sinister decadence and deceit involved in such distraction.

The human psyche becomes degraded to such an extent that the viewer-receiver becomes as psychopathic as the controlling transmitter. When the value of righteous living has been stolen from us, we become as psychopathic as those who control us.

A vulgarization and cheapening of human life corrupts both transmitter and receiver. We have become obsessed with blood and murder. We glorify it—so long as it happens to others. We have become what the media has mind-controlled us to be: vulgarized citizens of a deadly conspiracy. We are like sick patients in a hospital ward, doing what we think will cure us. Little do we realize, the lethal concoction the doctor is preparing, with which to inject us.

Desacralization of the world in any form will eventually destroy all sentient life on our planet. Through the propaganda of the mass media control system, we become the unfeeling and dispassionate clients of the atheistic elites. Dumbed down, we become more manageable. Robbed of our feelings and intellectual competence, we become more amenable for the shadow government's final solution.

Zionist illuminati own and control Western media. Their aim is to indoctrinate the unsuspecting into thinking that crime is fun and vulgarity laughable. Valueless entertainment becomes the tool of manipulation. When all consciousness has been pumped out of the human spirit unaware, we reverse the evolutionary process and live like nonenlightened men and women.

Journalists, with few exceptions, surrender truth for lies, because without adherence to the illuminati agenda they cannot survive. Any program contrary to the elitist agenda will never be broadcast. Never once will Western media broadcast scenes of horrendous oppression and horrifying brutality perpetrated by Israeli militants on helpless civilians in Palestine. Its propaganda machine continues the same old, tired message about Hezbollah missiles. They so twist the truth that it is like an elephant complaining about a flea that has landed on it. Nothing justifies dropping white phosphorous on top of innocent women and children. It is a war crime! Both the United States and Israel are guilty of this.

The vast majority of Western civilization is scarcely aware of the nefarious project which is unfolding all around us. So deceptive is the operation of the illuminati that the new world order is already covertly preparing humanity's future history. Incrementally, these psychopathic lords—apart from lullabying us into zombie land—are even now poisoning our water with fluoride and our air with chemical trails. Our food is being genetically modified to look beautiful and uniform on the outside but lacks nutritional value on the inside. In an atheistic culture of conspicuous consumption, outward appearances are humanity's primary concern.

If living life in the twenty-first century were not so diabolical and obscene, then beauty and value would shine from the inside and not the reverse.

Advertisements in glamorous magazines turn the unquenchable thirst of the human spirit for something more into an immediately obtainable and available trinket of egoic distraction. A recent ad in a newspaper showed a picture of a beautiful antique table. The caption under it read, "If she does not like it, leave her." In other words, break up your commitment to your wife and children. Marriage is expendable. Moral values are of no importance in the acquisition of material goodies.

Glamour has replaced grace, and, like the commodified indulgences of the church, it can be bought. The mind is so exploited and manipulated that celebrities are presently more admired than heroes. So subtle is the elites' control of the media that the singer Madonna has been turned into an icon and made a substitute for the Mary, the Mother of God, who throughout the ages of Western civilization has always represented maternal love. No matter the mythological aspect of the story, Madonna the singer is not a selfless, universal symbol for motherly tenderness and love.

The pharmaceutical industry continues to earn billions through its corporations. Like all corporations in the West, it also refuses to recognize how life is interdependent, interrelated, and interconnected. Based as it is on the atheism of materialism, the medical field continues to work only on parts of the human physique, to the detriment of the whole. It separates body from soul, failing to acknowledge the spirit of a person, whose inner consciousness has a most profound connection to the part of the body that needs healing.

Educational institutions are funded by the illuminati. To the degree that a school supports the atheistic propaganda of the elites, to the same degree is it funded with generous grants.

Separation of church and state prevails in America, and this for good reason. No organized religion has the right to impose its doctrine on another. To exclude religious education for this reason is the morally correct thing to do.

For the same reason, however, the atheistic doctrine of the Zionist illuminati should also be excluded. This is not the case in the United States.

While never overtly indoctrinating atheism, the illuminati nevertheless buy the curriculum. Just as the illuminati control the pharmaceutical industry, so do they control the educational system. That system treats the child student as though that child is only a part, beheaded from the whole. As in the medical world, the educational world refuses to see the child holistically.

The theory of evolution must be taught in public schools, precisely as Darwin taught it. Man is but a body that ends with natural selection. But to end the human evolutionary journey on the level of the purely material is not integrative. Quantum physics teaches us this. Consciousness invades us and atomizes us into a dimension beyond its own possibility. Consciousness teaches us that we actualize our evolutionary journey into a more holistic integration. Quantum physics tells us consciousness is the unifying field beneath matter. If that is so, then the subject of consciousness must also be brought into the school curriculum.

Consciousness has no connection with politicized religion, but instead demands integration of matter with spirit. Without this holistic connection, education will ascend into a hell on earth. Pupils will become exactly what the illuminati want—dumbed-down robots who do their bidding. A school which does not uphold and teach the principles of consciousness will instead let evil men manipulate and control it for their own ends.

Atheism and organized religion cause dissension. Through mind control and indoctrination, both organized religion and atheism are toxic. Imbued with their own self-interest, they induce a sense of separation rather than integration. Atheistic science dismisses any actual consciousness, awareness, feeling, intuition, introspection, contemplation, value, or meaning. Objective, rational, materialistic science is not capable of teaching us anything about love, compassion, or wonder. It can tell us nothing about interior or subjective experience. On the other hand, organized religion is equally nefarious. It dismisses human intelligence with its myths and doctrines.

We have been given so much new information through quantum physics that a new paradigm of integration between matter and spirit is absolutely imperative. It is even now just a minute before midnight; we must wake up to the consciousness of our own dignity and worth. We must throw off the yoke of our slavery to both the religious and atheistic systems. It is time to reclaim the divinity entombed within us.

Consciousness does not separate mind from matter. Consciousness unifies all into one. The information has already been given to us. We are all grounded in the one great holiarchy. Consciousness does not discriminate. Consciousness makes our differences disappear.

We are the icons of each other. Divinity defines us.

CHAPTER EVOLUTION

Atheistic materialism considers natural selection as the end point and destination of the human journey. Fundamental theists consider the story of creation as told in Genesis to be revealed truth. More progressive Christian churches reject the literal interpretation of Genesis and embrace the Darwinian theory of evolution, but do not accept that it ends in natural selection. If the ascending story of humanity's process is true, the progressive theists ask, why cannot the human mind ascend into the invisibility of a higher consciousness?

Herein lies the great debate about belief and destiny.

The Enlightenment of the eighteenth century gave a whopping hammer blow to institutional religion. Once again, the findings of science contradicted the information about creation which Holy Scripture had given. Rather than confirming that man and woman, Adam and Eve, had been directly created by God, science proclaimed that conscious human life evolved slowly from lower forms—even from the one-celled amoeba in the sea.

This new understanding caused huge consternation in both the secular and religious world. It still unnerves people to this day. Christian fundamentalists insist that the Bible cannot err and every word in the Bible must be taken literally. Science disagrees.

The more enlightened Christian churches say the process does not really matter, so long as it is understood that God is the Creator of all life in the universe. Indeed, many Christian scholars admire the whole evolutionary process which Darwin uncovered. However, Christian scholars teach that evolution transcends the material and morphs into the spiritual.

Teilhard de Chardin, considered to be an astounding Christian palaeontologist, broke the process of evolution into five stages: He understood evolution to be future-oriented—always becoming more complex, from what he called the alpha to the omega.

1. cosmogenesis
2. biogenesis
3. noosgenesis
4. christogenesis
5. omega

According to de Chardin, the entire universe is in a process of becoming something more. This process yields to a growing refinement and complexity as it draws ever closer to omega. To evolve spiritually, one must become heretical by deprogramming the mind from the small, parochial concept we have of God.

Our understanding of God is formed by our small, inherited cultural patterns or through the mind control and propaganda of organized religion. Such restriction minimizes our intellectual capability. It insults us intellectually. A person does not become spiritual through apologetics, dogmas, or legally imposed canon law, but through the process of evolution, which always involves struggle. We detect this in the adaptation and survival of species. We humans thrive by love, not law. Like the forging salmon, we leap over jagged rocks and raging waterfalls in order to spawn.

Atheism, as taught in our schools, only tells part of the story. It stops with natural selection and aborts the spiritual dimension to the human story. Atheistic evolution accommodates exactly the profane dimension of its purpose. It deals with the ego only. It dogmatizes the yin through the abolition-death of the yang. It creates a woeful imbalance. Profit, consumption, and competition are its only value system. It totally omits the final transition of de Chardin's evolutionary genesis into omega.

Because the atheism proposed by the so-called Enlightenment was so destructive and all-encompassing, we have been left like cosmic orphans wandering in the dark. We have been left, as D. H. Lawrence said, in the glass bottles of our egos—squirrels running forever around in circles within our cages.

The great art of European Christianity has become nothing more than utilitarian. It reflects more amusement than wonder. The soul of the artist is seldom contemplated.

De Chardin viewed matter differently and considered it holy. Unlike Augustine, whose theology tainted human flesh with the whole matter of original sin, de Chardin understood matter as an interconnection and a continuum into the metaphysical and transcendent. De Chardin challenged the prevailing Augustinian philosophy, which was framed by the hierarchical church to serve its own purposes.

Organized religion is dualistic. It separates body from spirit. De Chardin's theology is unitive. Our present and our future are the one reality. Through our embrace of the sacred in the here and the now, we connect to the sacred in the hereafter. Matter and spirit are equally measured. We are already in eternity. We realize at best about five percent of our consciousness. The rest is left blowing in the wind. How scandalous! We remain too much in low frequency and fail to access the full light of our identity. Atheism wants us static but never dynamic. It is easier to use us for the profit motive in such a passive state.

The fact remains, despite the marauding intrusion of nihilism, that God is as near or as distant as we individuals choose. Every one of us is *Homo liturgicus*, a priest of nature. The higher self can be reached if we choose it. This obliges us to be careful in the way we direct the river flow of our lives.

We nurture the bloom of the wilderness and the wet when we dare to be spiritual. A bluebell rings so that a bee may seek its honey. Object and subject are always involved in all of our undertakings. Response is what joins them together.

When we lose this connection, our world deteriorates. Great literature, perhaps even more than any Bible, shouts this from its own mountaintop. Jesus did not speak Aramaic, Greek, or Hebrew. His language was poetry.

Without a rootedness in the turmoil and pain, the joy and happiness of this world, how can there be a growth into consciousness?

De Chardin knew this well. That is why the church silenced him.

This world deteriorates to the extent that it loses the consciousness of its poetry. Consciousness begins with cosmogenesis. The carbon needed for human life had its birth in the big bang. Stardust planned each one of us.

- *Biogenesis*: Biology is the sentient world of plants and animals. Consciousness resides here also but in a higher degree.
- *Noosgenesis*: *Noos* is the Greek word for mind. It is at this stage of genesis or becoming that the animal makes a quantum leap into the consciousness of being conscious. At this stage, consciousness becomes conscious of the self. The human person is evolution conscious of itself.

Dogs and cows are conscious, but they are not aware of themselves. Consciousness as an energy and an intelligence runs through everything. Because of this, the human person must respect animals and plants as sacred. Hindus see cows as holy entities. Celtic and Native American spirituality sees God in everything.

We as human beings now exist on the noos step of the evolutionary ladder.

Since atheistic materialism is the prevailing paradigm which controls our lives, we are led to believe we have no future. Evolution is declared to have ended with natural selection. From this point on, there is no process. There is no genesis. All that has happened in our evolutionary past came about by mere chance—so atheism teaches. There is no intelligence behind the genesis of our species.

Our progenitors changed and adapted in order to live. The claw and the tooth involved in the struggle to survive are still with us. "Competition instead of cooperation" is atheism's mantra.

The human species has made a quantum leap from chimpanzee to *Homo sapiens*. But sapience, according to atheism, has no spiritual dimension. It can only be used immanently. It is of no transcendent value.

Genetically we remain very close to the chimpanzee—so biology tells us.

There is no higher tier than the noosphere. Atheistic materialism teaches, "Nothing exists outside of matter." Consciousness amounts to electric impulses given off by the brain. The brain, when fully understood, will provide us with all the answers and become the exterminator of all things spiritual.

According to atheism, Consciousness gives no objective, empirical evidence. Therefore it must be rejected. This is as high as the human species can go. To believe in something greater is like drugging the mind to escape the torture of living.

Darwinism energizes atheistic materialism. The ego is all. Eat, drink, and be merry, because life is short, and tomorrow we die. Through facing our absurdity with courage and humour, we attain our only possible dignity. This is the central message in Samuel Beckett's iconic play, *Waiting for Godot*.

Every time I go out into the world it is suicide but
if I stay at home it is slow dissolution.
—Samuel Beckett.

No, I regret nothing, all I regret is having been born, dying
is such a long tiresome business, I always found.
—Samuel Beckett

All of old.
Nothing else ever!
Ever tried, ever failed!
No matter. Try again. Fail again
Fail better.
—Samuel Beckett

You're on earth. There's no cure for that!
—Samuel Beckett

Birth was the death of him.
—Samuel Beckett

In our present paradigm, to be an atheist is to be considered sophisticated.

The immense majority of intellectually eminent men
disbelieve in Christian religion, but they conceal the fact in
public because they are afraid of losing their incomes.
—Bertrand Russell

The danger of religious faith is that it allows otherwise normal
human beings to reap the fruits of madness and consider them
holy … We are even now killing ourselves over ancient literature.
—Sam Harris

The spectacle of what is called religion … has filled me with horror, and I have frequently condemned it … Almost always it seems to stand for blind belief and reaction, dogma and bigotry, superstition and exploitation and the preservation of vested interests.

—Nehru

Religion has actually convinced people that there is an invisible man living in the sky, who watches over everything you do, every minute of every day. And the invisible man had a special list of ten things, he does not want you to do. And if you do any of these ten things, he has a special place full of fire and smoke and burning and torture and anguish, where he will send you to live and suffer and burn and choke and scream and cry forever till the end of time. But he loves you.

—George Carlin

Carlin sounds clever, but his apologia is not intelligent. The God he castigates is the God of organized religion. It most certainly is not the spiritual God whom Jesus lived and died for.

The Judeo-Christian concept of God is very nuanced. Like all music, it is composed of arias and themes, of yin and yang, of the clash of opposites. When contraries are denied their complementaries, then they stay lifeless, devoid of interest. Like all great literature, the Bible is a story of rage and adoration, justice and injustice, anger and compassion. Carlin's dismissal tells only one side of the equation. It lacks balance and does not serve honest criticism. Unfortunately it is the dark and violent aspect of God, which atheists love to declare, that now consumes Western culture.

When audiences such as Carlin attracted hilariously applaud his seemingly enlightened remarks, they are clapping at their own ignorance. Ridicule is hardly worthy of serious scholarship. Carlin's objective was to debunk the notion of God's involvement in human affairs. He used comedy to promote his atheism.

If God is absent from the human predicament, as atheists claim, then why engage in his slaughter? Why make fun of others who believe the opposite? Cleverness has never solved any serious problem facing humanity. Only intelligent scholarship and careful analysis can accomplish this.

Any religion or political system which propagandizes fear is itself the fearmonger. It is itself the ambassador of terrorism.

In the interest of all that is sacred and hopeful about human life, it is imperative that the human race must arise from its slumber and topple the ruling psychopaths who plan to destroy us. Western civilization has been dumbed down to such a degree by senseless and violent entertainment that the human mind now accepts murder and mayhem as normal. This is called *parallel psychology*. We become what we have been co-opted to believe.

The elites covertly teach, through an inversion of mass media's creative possibility, that human life is cheap. Invariably, atheistic media preaches that if we want to be successful and survive, then conquest is necessary. We must compete and consume. Detachment only leads to anarchy. Bloodletting is exciting and cruelty necessary. Vulgarity of the most audacious kind is "cool" and considered very, very funny. Curse words like "fucking" are used to fill in the gaps when people can no longer complete a sequential sentence. The West has almost totally lost its capacity for eloquence.

Have all our great cathedrals and works of art been created just to be seen as museum pieces? Whatever happened to the inspiration of the times and the artists who created them?

The evolutionary process has been reversed in the West. European humanity has moved backwards in a process called *involution*. Our modern technological wonders are destroying the unseen spiritual wonders of our own bodies and our interconnection with the natural world.

Evolution by nature aspires towards something higher. Horrifically, though, the controlling power of the shadowy illuminati want humanity to stand still on the purely material level of the ego. The spirituality of Consciousness intends a glorious destiny for us. But our minds have been controlled to such a degree that we do not even recognize our slavery. The globalist elites who own 98 per cent of the world's wealth have covertly and incrementally pushed the spirituality of consciousness to the periphery. They have done this because without morality, murder and corruption better accomplish their agenda. A license to kill is not God's will!

We sense a growing vulgarity and a descent into crudeness growing more blatant every day. Euphemisms such as "collateral damage" are used by invading armies to smother the truth of the slaughter inflicted on innocent lives.

Distance makes murder committed by the invader invisible. It is very easy to kill for the sake of profit in someone else's backyard. At the same time, back home, citizens' minds have been propagandized to believe invasion is necessary and therefore justified. The only way to offset this devouring onslaught of nihilistic decadence is through the refinement which consciousness brings.

The spirituality of consciousness illumines the human mind and returns us to our original ground, which is both the nadir and the zenith of human existence. The only way to combat the insidious state of our contemporary preoccupation with consumptive materialism is to grow into an awareness of our divinity, in direct opposition to the atheistic agenda.

We are destined for glory—an Eden etched eternal. When we really appreciated the depth of consciousness lying potentially within us and make the effort to reflect it outward, then we know it is spirituality which will save us. We are best remembered by our good deeds. In its simplest form, the spirituality of consciousness is other-oriented, whereas atheism's primary preoccupation is ego-laden.

If this world is to move forward on the evolutionary ladder, then the next quantum leap for humanity has to be into the realm of Consciousness, which quantum physics already teaches is the unifying field of the cosmos.

The illuminati control and own the banks of the world, and thereby control most of the planet, turning the vast majority of Western humanity into a planet of debtors.

If the American people ever allow private banks
to control issue of their currency,
first by inflation, then by deflation,

the banks and the corporations
that will grow up around them
will deprive the people of all property
until their children wake up homeless
on the continent their fathers conquered
The issuing power should be taken from the banks
and restored to the people
to whom it properly belongs.

—Thomas Jefferson

The development of consciousness is the only force which is capable of combatting this system of slavery.

Through quantum physics, modern humanity has been propelled into a new and exciting arena of hope and faith possibilities. With the discovery of consciousness as the unifying field of all materiality, a death blow has been given to the atheistic materialism of the elites. Humanity's change to the paradigm of consciousness will save us.

To better understand consciousness, we must realize that matter does not exist as such. Life on this planet, when reduced atomically to its most fundamental structure, is not malleable at all. Our five senses register in our minds on a totally objective, material level. The spectrum of light which hits the human eye is infinitesimally small in comparison to the infinite availability of light in the universe. Anthropomorphically limited by our space-time, our minds constrain us to such a degree that we think what we see is all that is available.

In reality, space and time and our three-dimensional way of interpreting these are illusions. We are fundamentally a hologram. We are a part of the whole. The whole is inside of each one of us, just as a drop becomes the sea—though not the totality of it. The science of quantum physics teaches this. Consciousness envelops us all like drops in the one sea of reality. The whole is greater than the sum of its parts. The whole is the definition of the parts, while it remains apart. We are a part but not apart!

Science, especially since the so-called age of Enlightenment, has been particularly prejudiced against any proposition that could not be explained rationally and objectively. For this reason, any reality outside of reason and objective reality was, if not denied, at least held as suspect.

Quantum physics has changed this way of thinking. Because it has concluded that consciousness is the unifying principle which holds all matter together, it presents the possibility of a whole new answer to the mystery of the universe. For the first time in the evolution of our species, we have left the malleable and the material and gone into the amorphous. It has been through the tooling of science that we have been able to do this. Even though quantum physics does not tell us Consciousness is God (by whatever name), nevertheless it indicates that, through a metamorphosis, we can possibly express life outside of matter and natural selection. Quantum physics proves objectively that atheistic materialism has become an evil movement.

Alarmingly, this is the direction in which the illuminati of the new world order are taking us. Materialistic atheism disassembles life in the direction of evil. Ironically, the very promotors of matter as primary are the promoters of antimatter. They turn everything upside down, making man superior to the great nonlocal Intelligence who created the universe. Atheism as a discipline must necessarily be part of the human race's search for meaning, but when it is used to promote mere matter, it sets itself apart and becomes destructive. Integration of the parts is always necessary in our search for holism.

Instead of probing the possibility of a more glorious and life-enhancing future for the human person, the elites use matter as a strategy to swell their bank accounts. Their avowed pursuit is humanity's greatest curse. They want humanity to believe they are in search of "the God particle" through their atomic collider at Cern, Switzerland. In fact, they are attempting to blow matter and its natural companion, antimatter, apart. Such experiments are a violation of the natural law. With the least modicum of intelligence, the human race must put an end to them. Even love has to be limited by boundaries. So also evil.

Matter and antimatter are meant by nature to stay together. Like yin and yang, they complement each other creatively. If the two underlying progenitors for material life become separated, then a power of indeterminable destruction will be unleashed upon the earth. A scenario much more devastating than the biblical prophecies of Armageddon, which televangelists and fundamental Christians take so much glee in predicting, will convulse our world with terror. It is man and not God who will unleash the terror.

The atheistic elites are of such character that they pathologically think they are the masters of the earth. The idea of a prevailing, unitive conscience which glues the earth together is anathema to them. Without God, this bunch of psychopaths vests themselves with such control and power that the horror of murder and the terror which their wars bring to others are of no significance to them.

Our planet has almost totally been brought to its knees because the spirituality of consciousness has been eradicated from our choices. The elites have been in total control of our destiny. Transhumanism rather than transcendence is their next play toy. It is deemed to bring us great joy in our ongoing process into slavery. However, it will only expand the chasm between humanity and the natural law. Spirituality cannot be robotized, no matter our attempts to suppress it.

Russia is once again one of the most spiritual nations on earth, and its leader, despite the propaganda of the West, is a profound Christian.

Our machines, as cyborgs bereft of morality, will make all future decisions for us. In the world of the psychopathic illuminati, mathematical calculations will determine our future, instead of the accumulated wisdom we have gained from all the generations which have preceded us. Our feelings and emotions, which play such an important role in the way we live our lives, will be considered of no importance. The transhumanist agenda will rule humanity as a proxy for the whims of the elites.

Welcome, brave new world indeed!

The atom is 99 per cent empty space. So when we look out through our eyes, what we see is not really there at all. All that exists is the emptiness and invisibility of no-thingness, no-spaceness, no-placeness. This is what envelops us.

Our minds make us think that what we see is real. Our minds deceive us. We experience the world outside ourselves through our five senses. We think our mental experience is the fullest disclosure of the world of reality. The truth of the matter is completely different.

As Max Planck, the father of quantum physics, indicated, it is the mind that is the matrix of all matter. What we see is not reality. Our minds plays a trick on us, as it were. The deeper we go into reality, the more the world we think of in a material way dissolves into no thingness. There are no objects.

Despite the fact that atheistic materialism and the illuminati want humanity to remain on the evolutionary level of the animal, science is now teaching us that our future lies in the spirituality of consciousness. Mystics have always taught us this: "My me is God," said St Catherine.

Our future lies in the nonlocality of consciousness, which is, as quantum physics teaches, unitive. It is holographic.

We think we see the world substantially. The spectrum of light photons which reach our brains makes us think this. The reality which our minds make into a hologram is only an illusion. Consciousness is infinite awareness. The more we develop this awareness, the deeper our being finds its peace and resolution. The deeper we journey into infinite awareness, the more free we become from the slavery of the ego and the selfishness which greed and materialism cause.

Consciousness lies ever before us. Like a magnet, it forever draws humanity closer to its original ground and true centre. To become conscious is the initial blossoming of our personalities towards the good in life. It becomes the supreme accomplishment of the human race while here on earth. It is the nadir of our achievement. It is the point towards which evolution has been driving us since the big bang. Having achieved this plateau, we will never fear death, because consciousness is transmorphemic.

Having reached an awareness of consciousness while here on earth, and having awakened to the distortion which the low-level frequency of atheistic materialism brings with it, we begin our journey into the mystery of the unifying field of consciousness. Compassionate love for the planet and all that dwells in and on it erupts with an intense creative frequency. Life on earth is seen differently, with enthusiastic eyes.

We have outlined how nature intends evolution to process us into consciousness. But materialistic, atheistic science does not take the natural law seriously. Arrogantly, it flouts not only the balance needed in the ecological world, but divinizes itself to such a degree that, instead of promoting the affairs of humanity's heart, it continues to rob the human race of its humanity.

Rot and disease become rampant in a river which does not flow into its sea. Soon it becomes smothered with algae. The powerful and controlling elites refuse to allow the flow of consciousness to oxygenate humanity's deepest awareness. It is as if the controlling elites have hubristically assumed the power to divert the onward evolutionary process to obey their vision rather than following the law of nature. Atheistic materialism, through its denial of any ultimate meaning, thinks it can fiddle and muddle as much as it desires in the sphere of the body material.

Not content with the arrest of the evolutionary process, it propagates the myth that the tin and tinsel which technology brings is the final answer. Already the earth is moaning and groaning from the weight of too much machinery. Bombs and bullets have already caused horrific pain and terrifying screams from the murdered, innocent people of the earth. Madeline Albright, foreign secretary to George Bush, when queried about the unjustified killings in Iraq, declared, "The killing was worth it."

Technological innovation can be marvellous, but when it is created in defiance of the natural law, it cannot be accepted as innovative or life-enhancing. It is essentially destructive. The greatest tragedy facing our planet is that, instead of accepting the unifying field of consciousness, which quantum science demands, as the most fundamental component of reality, we choose to stay amused and drugged by insidious mind-altering propaganda. Mass media now controls us. The Ten Commandments of our new world order centre on the obscenity of genocide with no escape from slavery.

No matter the propaganda which the new world order splatters on our psyche, the fact remains we are doomed to be spiritual. Evolution from the big bang onwards had us in mind. We come from stardust, which by its very nature worked intelligently over a period of some eleven billion years before humans appeared. A process of incredible artistry has gone into our making. Surely humanity has not been made into such a nanotechnological wonder only to have its edifice smashed into smithereens which, like a broken egg, cannot be mended!

We are hard-wired for consciousness by the power of a great nonlocal Intelligence. The puny connections of our manmade technology, despite their achievement, are infantile and temporary in comparison to our connectedness with the infinite and the eternal.

Despite all the bravado and applause for our ingenious, creative, technological wonders, science never has nor ever can achieve a machine with a heart. Technology ensues from the head, and is as illusory as the atom is. It cannot feel. Though it may mechanically imitate, even to the point of outsmarting a human being, it will never be able to laugh, cry, dance, or sing. Most of all, it will never be tender enough to show compassion or identify with the struggles of another human being.

This world already has too much gadgetry. It is pushing us in the wrong direction. It materially gathers us but spiritually spatters us. It is time to stop our lemming run to the sea. Let's stop a while and contemplate whether technology is the real apple in our tart. Why can we not even try to experiment with our inbred energy of spirituality to change our planet for the good? Evil is destructive and incrementally grows ever more consumptive. Spirituality takes our world in the total opposite direction. Evil implodes but spirituality explodes. Atheism destroys but spirituality employs.

What an indictment—that while we slept and were lullabied into zombie land, atheistic materialism stole in through our doors and covertly coerced us to surrender our divine identity for a shattered pottage.

A society which is dumbed down to applaud and be wowed by the wonders of technology is out of touch with its own reality. We have much more in common with the veins that bring chlorophyll to leaves and the veins that bring blood to brains than we do with the wires connecting the machinery of our technology.

The difference between technology and the natural world is the same as that which exists between life and death. We have inverted our modern drive towards what is good, to such a degree that by our lifestyle we now choose death instead of life!

A civilization which is built on the accomplishments of the mind alone, despite hoards of money stashed away in holes of raped gold, will finally belatedly learn what scripture warns: "the moth eats, and iron rusts."

The atheistic materialism of the elites, within their manufactured illusion of involution, will one day learn that the natural law will not be mocked. There are moral limits which consciousness imposes. Humanity must recognize its parameters. To proclaim transhumanism and transgeneticism instead of transcendence as the future for humanity is a very dangerous thesis. When the natural law becomes hijacked, our technology becomes our atrocity.

We are coming into an age when everything will be smart except the human being. Even now our identities, assessed through our fingerprints, will enable us to access all the technology in our homes.

But again we must ask, "What good is a machine without a heart?" When the West begins to exercise its attention and energy on matters of the heart, then and only then will we build a new, relevant, and peaceful existence on earth.

Jesus proclaimed a different message than the one of atheistic materialism. He lived and spoke about the Godness that lives inside of each one of us. He asked that we dig deep in order to climb high. Even before quantum physics discovered it, Jesus preached that consciousness envelops the universe.

How ironic that George Carlin, a professed atheist, should have conjured up images of a cruel God to prove the absence of a divine Intelligence working in and through humanity. In fact it is atheism itself which is burning and choking the human heart from achieving its full potentiality. Even now, the elites, through greed and exploitation, are denying life to all sentient beings outside of themselves and incarcerating us in an actual living hell.

Atheistic materialism is taking the oxygen out of our air, the purity out of our waters, and the sustenance out of our food. What is necessary has been discarded and disregarded. Atheistic materialism makes us all into mannequins. When spirituality is removed, what is real becomes fooled. The Christian West thinks it is free, but we are living in a fool's paradise. There is nothing on the floor of this world that is so complete as the infiltration of atheism into every corner of our existence. It babbles like a baby, but it hacks like a chainsaw when the wooing is over. It is evil dressed like a coma.

Atheistic materialism is, at this moment, the cause of all the tormented cries from waterboarding, and the exhaustion experienced from sleep deprivation. Our so-called disciplined personnel render these torments on the already plundered and battered combatants in the Middle East.

When a man or a woman from the Christian West really understands what it means to be a follower of Jesus, then their spirituality, connected to the vital energy of another awakened spirit, will soon become a river of such pure, untainted water that others will be inspired to jump right into it. Purity and goodness are contagious. Spirituality, when enacted, becomes the only wind that can wipe away the atheistic stench of our decay and impoverishment.

Spirituality is central in our daily activities. It impacts on the decisions we make daily. Do I need so much stuff? Am I adding, even microscopically, to the torture of living, breathing things by my food intake? Do I ever see the connection between the cow and the cheese, butter, and ice cream I eat? Do I ever say, "Good day to you, Cow, and God bless you for all the good things you give me. I'll make sure to return the compliment to you. I'll put another forkful of hay in the barn this evening to feed you"? Do I ever talk to the beautiful plants in my garden, or wonder how all the fine-tuning in their symmetry could be stored up so perfectly in a tiny seed? How can a tiny watermelon seed produce a fruit two thousand times heavier than itself? Where did this know-how come from? Do I ever wonder what school or apothecary the flowers went to? Where did they learn such artistry of design and colour? What hand appointed them?

And as for the bees! Oh my God, there's intelligence for you! If humanity would work even half as well, we'd have a phenomenally well-ordered world. If only we could work together to pour golden, delicious, nutritious honey upon the face of our planet. There's no money exchanged in the bees' enterprise. Why can't we learn from them? We do not know the bees' language except for their dance around a new resource, but surely they would ridicule our way of economy.

Do we ever think spirituality is a precursor to prayer? Prayer is not possible without imagination and wonder. If we are not wonderers, then our prayers are vacuous. Wonder and curiosity are the precursors to genuine prayer. Wonder ignites delight, and that spiritual experience is itself a prayer. It elicits a response to the Intelligence beyond the mystery. Spirituality comes out of the everyday. It happens far more frequently in our kitchens than in our churches.

And all this is to say nothing of the mesmerizing miraculousness of our own bodies. Think of the potentiality for a perfectly formed life coming out of that egg which you have cracked open to scramble. Where is the fluff? Where are the eyes? Where is the beak among this yellowy, beaten stuff? When we begin to ask such questions, then we are beginning to be spiritual.

Atheistic materialism deadens everything. There is nothing that is life-giving within it. Never have we needed more a stimulus to give us life and replenish us, to replace the one that so deadens us. We are meant for more. Go to the shopping malls, where everything is bought and sold with only deadness present. There is no connection made between the orchard producer and the seller. There is only dead money. There is no reverence. There is no respect. There is just a sense of convenience and entitlement. Convenience and entitlement are ego-driven. They take the soul and the heart out of everything. This is precisely the point where atheistic materialism thrives and the self loses its spirit.

Spirituality is all about the ordinary. Spirituality is all about how we live every day in the midst of our community and in the smaller confines of our homes. Spirituality defines us as much as our sleeping and waking define us. Spirituality is much more about attitude than churchgoing.

Most of our attitude has been shamefully misled and directed by charlatans and thieves who do not give a damn about what is our deepest entitlement—namely our spirituality. So long as the money tills keep ringing, they accommodate while despising us. We fail to realize how we compromise our God alive within us on a daily and sometimes innocuous basis.

Atheistic materialism hurls at us its latest fanfare of gloriously coloured, alluring display, to attract us and, even more covertly, to distract us from the fact that we are more than our egos. Our response is to buy more and more stuff, which we stuff into our stuffed wardrobes. The deal is done! If we were more spiritually developed, we would act more intelligently.

The first question to answer is "Do I need it?" Can you live without it? Such scrutiny is the stuff of spirituality All along, until we begin to ask such questions of ourselves, we have not the vaguest idea that buying and selling involves our spirituality. We have become so twisted and turned upside down that our shopping malls and streets of taunting treasures have replaced our ability to seek the most precious diamond of all, our own spirituality.

When making our choices in the marketplace, have we ever tried to discover where our desired object was manufactured? Did we ever take time to think that the soles of our shoes may have come from the rubber trees in Africa, where the poor people who collect it are only paid seventy-five pence a day? We walk comfortably, whereas the poor who gathered the rubber walk around in bare feet. Connections are everywhere. Our spirituality is involved in all of our daily choices.

The atheism of the illuminati excel in false-flag making. When they are not blaming God for the evil of their own doings, they are blaming Islam for their own exploitation of the Middle East.

Corporations that outwardly pretend to be the saviours of humanity, through cut-throat competition, drive small farmers from the land. Huge conglomerates, more interested in quantity than quality, contaminate the food chain with chemicals that eventually poison us. Western civilization, like the fruit it produces, appears all shiny and perfect on the outside, but inwardly it is tasteless and nonnutritious. This is the state that we find ourselves in.

When consciousness is replaced with a hunger for profit, all the nourishing juice of the fruit becomes tasteless and often sour. The very trees thunder through their sun-drenched leaves and murmur, "This is murder." A tree may not speak the language of our culture, but in an inaudible, universal way, it begs for our undivided attention. Forests are our main oxygen providers and carbon consumers, far more precious than oil or gold. Yet we value our automobiles and tenderly take care of them much more than our sentient trees.

Jazzed up with grasping and greed, we consume much more than we need. We never seem to learn the insufficiency of all that is available. When we placate our yearning, the object of our desire soon loses its appeal. We become bored and never seem satisfied.

Atheistic materialism does not even answer the yearning of our ego, much less our spirit. The prevailing matrix of Western society has failed its people, both now and eternally. Is there a possible answer to our contemporary culture's unease with itself? People who choose transcendence over the immanence of matter declare uniformly in the affirmative. People who are aware recognize consciousness within and without. With this belief, they replace terror with courage and absurdity with purpose. They regard natural selection as another quantum leap to a higher dimension.

Teilhard de Chardin, whom I mentioned earlier, delineates two further spheres on the evolutionary ladder: the christosphere and the omega. People of faiths other than Christian should not reject the mention of Christ on the trajectory of the evolutionary ladder. Rather than judging him as the Son of the Christian God, see him in the evolutionary sense as a good man filled with God consciousness and a towering universal figure whose life on earth was ego-less, compassionate, and heroically generous.

The next tier on the evolutionary ladder completes the story of humanity's ascendency into the godhead. Chardin calls it omega. Quantum physics calls it consciousness. No matter the process, consciousness permeates all steps ascending from local into nonlocal or nonlocal descending into local, thereby sparking divinity in everything.

CHAPTER ATHEISM

It cannot be stressed enough that the paradigm of atheistic materialism, which found its source in the eighteenth-century Enlightenment, has wreaked havoc on earth. Through its debunking of God, we have been denied our capacity for praise, thanksgiving, respect, and reverence.

The governments of the West explain their game of war as that of freeing people in foreign lands from dictatorship. This is pure pretext. Love alone is the true conqueror. All the great poets and prophets have been preaching this wisdom hoarsely for thousands of years. Yet these macho men who rule the world never entertain this message. "It's not masculine nor scientific to believe," they say. "Only naive fools internalize such a message."

Propelled by greed and a lust for power, the elites pound spirituality into a pulp. God is screaming out at psychopaths, but their lust drowns out his voice.

Truly the West, with its use and sale of military armaments, brings disaster and destruction rather than peace to the earth. To follow the way of Christ is to disobey and be countercultural. Love is not tolerant of covert slavery. Elitism must vanish.

Atheism scorns organized religion as a virus and dismisses God as a consequence. It does not seem erroneous to atheists to dismiss a father for the sins of his children. A father can still live irrespective of the conduct of his offspring.

There must be love for love for love to begin!

Both atheism and organized religion must be thrown into the dustbin of history. They are imperialistic by nature.

The theory of evolution, as it is taught in public schools and generally accepted by the secular world, is true as far as it goes. But to a world more intellectually informed and advanced, atheism has been proven wrong through the discovery of consciousness as the unifying field of life. An invisible and spiritual dimension lies beyond the material. It invites evolution out of natural selection to grow with a genesis into a greater enhancement.

Atheism insists that there is no afterlife. It insists matter is all there is. We have had a past, but we have no future, according to atheism. This view is absolute. Because it is held with such conviction, it as fundamentalist as biblical literalism. Both atheism and biblical literalism are guilty of indoctrination. They both stay stuck in the immutability of their own self-serving convictions. They reduce the unknown ineffability of humanity's future to the limits of their own frame of reference.

To evolve into the future which Consciousness intends for humanity is to learn that our search on earth is itself the answer. Belief is made with doubt. The difference is what we do with it. Do we construct or destruct? Do we favour one side over the other and cause yin and yang to collide? With our spirituality, do we expect harmony and peace to dwell among us via the easy grace and disengaged prayer which organized religion offers? Or do we jump right into the fray and, through our personal suffering and self-giving, hammer out an answer which will carve a benign outcome into an evolved future?

If we spiritualize communally, we will mute the voice and the ways of a diabolical, egotistical system that is hell-bent on destroying the sacredness and dignity of each one of us.

The great irony of life is that a building which has taken years to build can now, with the push of a button, be blown away within seconds. Our potentiality to be destructive comes much more easily than our self-giving efforts to be constructive. When even one among us, through the conviction of an inner spirituality, courageously stands up, and in an alternative voice challenges the corruption of the political and religious powers who control us, then truly that person turns water into wine.

Atheists continuously cry out, "Give me the evidence! Give me the proof that God exists!" To give them a proof where only matter exists is impossible. That kind of proof is contrary to all logic. One cannot prove that the great, universal non-Local can exist in the local if the subject studying the object does not believe in consciousness. The veracity of an object depends on the subject who studies it. Truth is only possible when subject and object are connected to each other.

It is impossible, in the objective sense, to impose the visible (matter) on the invisible (spiritual) and end up with objective evidence which proves the existence of God. The problem with atheistic science is that it restricts itself to the exterior while dismissing the interior.

Atheism, consumed as it is with its own delusion of intellectual superiority, has already been called to task by quantum physics. It needs to become more enlightened. The science of quantum physics has dealt a death blow to atheistic materialism.

There are many other indicators—though not proofs in the objective sense—which point to God as the one great Intelligence who created and guides the cosmos. Among others, these include

- the moral code written into our very being
- the unquenchable longing for completion and satiation within each one of us
- the primordial acceptance of a deity by humanity throughout the ages
- the awe, the wonder, and the astonishment the natural world elicits through the majesty and beauty of the earth
- the incredible fine-tuning involved in the creation of the universe
- our own experience

We intuit far more than we know!

We misuse the intention of God when we torture metal into a gun or a bomb. In a world which no longer appreciates the interconnectedness and interrelationship of all things, war becomes inevitable. The body surrenders itself to evil when it is not connected to the spirit. A country which invades other countries and kills innocent civilians will be disclaimed by God. War is the ultimate act of irreverence.

To the extent that a government maims and murders innocent people, to that same extent does the nation rot from within, Evil is contagious, and no missile or nuclear weapon is capable of eradicating it. Evil can only be overcome by its opposite. Evil will gather like a snowball unless someone decides to stop its roll.

So ravenously and lethally has atheistic materialism been enthroned in the West that we no longer seem to have the will to stop it. As Teilhard de Chardin said, "The age of nations is past. The task before us now is to build the earth. ... It's adoration or annihilation." It is Christ or Nagasaki.

An enervating sense of helplessness and fear beyond our control consumes much of our contemporary thinking. Little do the powerless people of the West realize that the defence system which the Department of Homeland Security prescribes as necessary is more about its own people's incarceration than it is of terrorism spawned by a foreign nation. Fear is a master domesticator.

When home-grown fear is used as a yardstick to subjugate a people, we congregate and find comfort and support through one another. A people coerced by fear are made manageable and robbed of their individual rights. Big Brother then broods over them. If this world is ever to become free, love instead of fear will coax us into eternity.

The cosmos is one. No matter the plans of the elites, nature will have its way. Nature will have the final say

If the systematic indoctrination of militarism is not enough to contend with, our consciousness is further pulverized by the constant harangue of negativity in our latest news bulletin. Our morning papers reveal our helplessness when confronted by the relentless tide of drugs and armed robberies. Selfishness, greed, lust, anger, and hate are reported as rampant and very much alive in our vacuous lives. Chaos—instead of the utopia which atheistic materialism promised—now rules our lives.

Atheistic materialism has taken us into a dark tunnel which leads nowhere. The dark becomes our only reality—more and more of it, with no possibility of a light shaft allowed to enter this thundering tunnel of nothingness.

How can a human being exist without being conscious of being conscious? Surely this is the most lethal and horrendous torture of all on the face of the earth. In the evolutionary sense, to be conscious of being conscious puts humanity on a higher level than the rest of the biological kingdom. Since evolution by nature is future-oriented, why must humanity now stay stuck forever and ever in the sphere of natural selection?

Atheistic materialism retards humanity. It keeps us in a dark tunnel without hope or faith in the possibility of light at the end. Evolution urges humanity to climb higher. By nature, as the plant must turn its face to the sun for survival, so also humanity needs its own system of photosynthesis. We need God. Atheistic materialism denies humanity this process by denying us the possibility of growth into consciousness.

Not content to rob the body and therefore the ego of its vitality through a genetically altered, pathological bloodline, atheistic materialism has also tried to interfere in the appreciation of a realm which it is incapable of understanding. To deny the existence of God is the language of the unevolved. It like a donkey making pronouncements on a sphere of life where it has no authority, no scholarship, no poetry, and indeed no intelligence to understand it. Atheism is totally out of its element in respect to spirituality.

Atheism drives out all that is tender, good, and beautiful about life's experiences, designating them as mere linear electric impulses. Profit is the only content in life, according to our prevailing atheistic paradigm. We become decivilized as a consequence. By adopting atheism, we dismiss all the garnered wisdom of the ages. Socrates's warning has fallen on deaf ears in our Western world: "The unexamined life is not worth living."

My me is God.
—St. Catherine

What we search for is the one that sees.
—St Francis of Assisi

Through mass media, our minds become preoccupied with the nonsense of trivial occurrences, none of which are meant to inform or enlarge our perspective. The avowed aim of atheistic materialism is to indoctrinate humanity to such a degree that we become donkeys, ready to devour the fodder which is thrown at us.

Quite recently on an Irish television programme, *Would You Believe*, the host Gabriel Byrne asked Stephen Fry, the English actor, if he believed in God. He replied, "Bone cancer in children? How dare you? How dare you? You created a world in which there is so much misery and it is not our fault! It is not right! It is utterly, utterly evil! Why should I respect a mean-minded, capricious, stupid God who creates a world which is full of injustice and pain? I have no respect for him whatsoever! ... It is apparent that God is monstrous. God is a monster ... The moment you banish him, life becomes simpler, cleaner, purer, more worth living."

Stephen Fry's answer is rather typical of the atheistic point of view. His response to Gabriel Byrne was honest and sincere. When confronted by the awful reality of bone cancer in children, one must necessarily question how to reconcile the goodness of God in a world full of injustice and pain.

The question of human suffering cannot be responded to with the cliché answers which fundamentalist Christians resurrect from the Bible. Such answers are intellectually insulting and cause more pain than cure.

Mr Fry, of course, has repeated the whole cry of Job in respect to his question regarding suffering. Rather than staying on the purely acceptable plane of accusing God for his indifference to human suffering, might it not be more legitimate to say that chemical corporations such as Monsanto are the true monsters instead of God? Genetically modified and irradiated food tampers with the natural process. Cancer comes more from man's interference with nature than from the flawed design of God.

And, Mr Fry, is it possible that all the chemical poison spewed out from planes in chemtrails might not somehow be related to the cancer in little children? Chemtrails are part of the atheistic plan to get rid of us.

What about the poison of fluoride pumped into the toothpaste and water which children drink? Could cancer in little children not be related to such a poisonous intake? What about the mercury present in inoculations which children are compelled to take into their blood systems? Surely, Mr Fry, one cannot blame God for such heinous enterprises.

One of the most remarkable characterisations about the human species is the gift of free will. We can choose between good and evil. Cancer in a little child is an aberrant, evil thing. Is it not possible that the evil which cancer brings to an innocent child has more likely been caused by the malevolence of man than the cruelty of God? Man is a cocreator. We cannot blame divinity for the sins of humanity. Blaming God is far too easy when confronted with the problem of human suffering.

The question of human suffering has always haunted humanity. Writers such as Synge in his great classic one-act play *Riders to the Sea* deals with the subject. Often we can do no more than shake our fists at God when confronted by terrible tragedy. Perhaps to shake our fists at this insanity is our only prayer. The greatest form of prayer is most often the awful cry of the human heart. Such suffering is indeed an insult to the human mind. It just makes no sense.

When atheists ask questions, we must be prepared to sincerely listen. Atheism in many ways purifies theism. When the dynamism of atheism is laden with an urge to seek out truth rather than an outward dismissal of a Creator, then such search must be accepted as a genuine exercise in scholarship.

The truth is, as Tennyson said, "There is more faith in doubt than all the creeds of men." In another poem, he said, "Men may rise on stepping stones of their dead selves, to higher things."

To convert this poetry into prose, Tennyson dwells on what I would call the mystery of opposites. Creativity involves the clash of two opposing forces. There is a yin and a yang involved in all genesis. If there is only dark, we cannot know the reality of light. The two realities, when combined into a unity, allow each other to display themselves separately. A tree becomes more laden with fruit when it is first cut by a pruning knife. Suffering is joined to healing. Darkness is in the light and light is in the dark. They are the same reality. They are unitive. They do not separate. There is no duality in this world. One reality is the other. Evil and good are the one reality. God is One as the cosmos is one. To be one demands the paradox of opposites. For God to exist, evil must also exist. Without evil, there is no good. Without good, there is no evil. As Tolstoy wrote, "Without graves there can be no resurrections."

Courage and cowardice are one reality. Suffering and joy are one reality. A woman cannot have a baby without pain. Faith and doubt are the same reality. Quantum physics has shown that everything in this world is interrelated and interconnected. The cosmos is one, and we are all enveloped by the one consciousness.

Rather than the awful stopgap answers which organized religion gives in response to the legitimate question which Stephen Fry raised—rather than thinking in an anthropological way—the only answer possible is that the question of human suffering is integrated with natural law. This is the way it is. This law is immutable. We can believe or we can shake our fists at the idea of a creator. Yet this inbred law of nature remains immutable. As the character Maura said in *Riders to the Sea*, "No man at all can be living forever and we must be satisfied."

Death is life and life is death. The natural law teaches this. Atheistic materialism does not want to admit this because atheism only concerns itself with the ego and the temporary. It leaves no room for transcendence.

On top of all this, Stephen Fry should be further challenged on his claim that God is stupid, capricious, and a monster. As Sean O'Casey once said, "You cant blame God for the stupidity of priests." The same argument should apply to Stephen Fry. We cannot change the law of contradiction, which is integral to the law of nature. We cannot claim, as Mr Fry does, that this proves the nonexistence of God.

Could not the monstrous inversion of the natural law—an inversion concocted by corporations such as Monsanto—be the cause of setting aberrant cells to multiply and destroy the human body? Should people who believe in an intelligence greater than our own not have the legitimate right to question the atheistic purpose of fluoride in water, chemical trails in the air, and mercury in the injections we pump into children? Is it possible than an agent other than God is responsible for most of the illegitimate suffering caused outside the natural law?

Is God to blame for the obscene flow of the world's wealth into the coffers of the elites who control the Federal Reserve in America? Is the awful inequality and poverty in today's world caused by God or the illuminati?

At this point I would like to suggest to Mr Fry that surely he cannot blame God for all the slaughter of innocence in our world. Surely he should better employ his concern with the little innocent children of the Middle

East, whose lives are daily compromised, and even more appallingly the children of future generations, whose homeland has been saturated with spent uranium. Where is Fry's rage when it comes to his country's selling cluster bombs to Saudi Arabia, which daily destroy innocent lives in Yemen?

Evolution comes through a tangential drive involving violence to the life form which preceded it. The claw plays a necessary role in adaptation and survival of the fittest. Though we may not like it, the natural law requires it. Since neo-Darwinism is atheistic, surely it must agree that the old order gives way to the new through pain and suffering. Pain plays an integral part in the contest. God cannot be dismissed for not excluding suffering as a necessary component in creativity.

The bone cancer of little children cannot be answered anthropologically, in the sense that the natural law cannot change the reality that suffering is required for a healthy recovery. One cannot exist without the other. Holism is our only way to approach all our problems.

If there were only suffering, then health would never appear. As a matter of fact, it is pain which tells us we are not well. Pain is an integral part of the healing process. It is required for well-being. Suffering plays its part in nature. It is the tool of creativity. Like it or not, this law is immutable. The greatest wisdom is to accept it.

Suffering in this world cannot be used to abolish the idea of God. Nihilism, on the other hand, is its own answer. If there is nothing, then what is the point in searching for anything? Atheism strips humanity of its highest aspirations and accomplishments.

In respect to security and safety, it would be far better if the Department of Homeland Security could spend its energy on consciousness. Insecurity is our greatest wisdom. We must let go. Nature teaches this. We become refined and advanced as a society to the extent that we realize our intrinsic spirituality. This is wisdom at its best. Quantum physics teaches this.

Rather than the earth becoming a cleaner, purer, and more liveable place without God, might it not be argued that our planet is becoming more destructive and unliveable precisely because atheism has dismissed the possibility of divinity?

Atheistic, objective science always cries out for evidence. The proof is already available. God can be noticed as much by his absence as by his presence. We see the consequence of God's absence in the West today through our decadence.

The problem with atheistic materialism is that of its fundamental prejudice. If God is not, as atheists claim, then all life ends in oblivion. It becomes a vaudeville of devils. Death becomes the final arbiter and expert. This negative trajectory turns human life on earth into a tragedy and an afterlife into an impossibility. Whether theist or atheist, we all end up the same way if atheism is true. All atheism can prove by its own teaching is that it spoke the truth while it was living, but since atheists will be dead post factum, there will be no need for convincing.

Furthermore, if life has no purpose or meaning and there is no Creator who initiated it, why do atheists create such a fuss in their efforts to stamp out theism from the face of the earth? If there is no God, then let it be so. Why must atheists fight against a bunch of unenlightened theists? Would it not be far better, in the interest of harmony in the world, to ignore theists? There can be no argument if there is no God. Could it be that atheistic materialism is not nearly as interested in the God question as it is in making more money? If this is not the case, then why is materialistic atheism riddled with such passion, when there is nothing to be passionate about?

Could atheists' passion for argument possibly stem from an inner conflict with their own consciousness? The moral law is written into the very psyche of every person born in time. There is no escape from it. It is written there by nature. It may live in the subconscious and never be brought into the conscious, but it is there in dormancy within humanity.

We all know in the deepest recesses of our being that murder is wrong and love is right. This stamp from the natural law indicates a spark of consciousness within each one of us. If we are not at ease with our own divinity, then by hell we will try to get rid of it. Not content with the natural law, we try to fight it as though it is restrictive of human freedom.

In actuality, the total reverse of this frame of reference presents a much more freeing type of experience. The more we reach into our own consciousness, the more we feel free and integrated. There is no other way to overcome the tragic philosophy of the atheist. Good is more revelatory than evil. The natural world tells us this. The magnificent fine-tuning of the universe gives us a clue about a magnificent Intelligence at work in the planet's order. Such incredible and seemingly effortless works behind the world's mechanism go unnoticed. When good goes unnoticed, God goes with it.

Life has been turned inside out to such a degree that the innocent are regarded as bandits and the evil ones are considered the intelligent truth-seekers and planners. Psychopaths of the earth live free in their opulent, guarded estates with private jets at their back doors and billion-dollar yachts moored in private harbours. Disconnected from the killing fields, their bank accounts swell with untold profit from their collateral enterprises. Their own children, steeped in luxury, gurgle their first words while children in that other world far away have all the life squeezed out of them. Their last audible cry is "Mama, Mama, where are you? I can't see you. My eyes are gone out of my head. Mama, Mama, where are you?"

The true enemy is not over there or far away at all. It is within each one of us, growing under the false flag of patriotism. In fact the true patriot is the one who calls his country to account.

In a time of conflict, terrorism is not easy to identify. Most often terrorists are viewed as a bunch of fanatics who are hell-bent on murder. If the truth be known, terrorism is more a reaction than an action. Injustice always predates and predicts it.

It must be said that terrorism of any sort is never the right response. It only begets itself.

So who is the real terrorist in the Middle East? Has the Arab world ever invaded the West? Was the Middle East not in relative peace before the West moved in to destabilize it through the old British imperial ploy of divide and conquer, thus weakening its leaders' grip on stability?

Any nation with colonial intentions of exploitation and plunder violates the cosmic law of Consciousness. Such a nation will morally become accountable for its sin. It will be compelled, in the name of universal justice, to seek forgiveness and make retribution. Should it fail to do so, it will topple from within rather than from without. Its own obscenity, corruption, and lies will be the millstone whose weight will drown it.

Atheistic materialism is the cancer which is killing Western society. It teaches children how to be greedy, and that kindness or compassion are not necessary. It encourages "meism" and indoctrinates selfishness. At its core, it is antifamily.

Terrified of social revolution, the elites of the West, totally consumed with their need to control, plan incrementally the destruction of the earth's population. Through an atheistic control of the media, a utopia which immediately appeals to the ego is presented, while at the same time it destroys the soul of humanity. If future generations are to live without incarceration, then the prevailing paradigm must cease to exist. It has brought us to the brink.

Things fall apart
the center cannot hold
mere anarchy is loosed upon the world
the blood-dimmed tide is loosed
and everywhere the ceremony of innocence is drowned
the best lack all conviction
while the worst are full of passionate intensity
—William Butler Yeats

Quantum physics teaches that our future is consciousness. We move from particle physics into an immeasurable dimension far more mysterious than our three-dimensional perception. We move into the unknowable and the ineffable.

Rather than deterring us, this ineffable state of unknowability should stimulate our curiosity and sense of adventure. When the imagination becomes excited, there is always passion. We know what passion is like when we fall in love. So also can our enquiry and search for meaning become a very passionate experience. Consciousness is a passionate life experience.

Consciousness lives inside us and outside us—so quantum physics teaches. Consciousness does not discriminate. We all belong to it, and it belongs to us all. It is there for the seeking.

If schools, instead of their atheistic agenda, would change their curriculum to embrace consciousness in an applied and interpenetrating way, then the citizens of the future would be beautifully endowed to face life with enduring values and principles. Public education would surely serve the body politic and the health of a nation through the ethics and morality which consciousness brings with it.

Consciousness is nonsectarian. It rises above the petty peeves and differences which organized religion brings with it. It teaches limits and introduces boundaries for civilized living.

Atheistic materialism culturally indoctrinates young minds. It brainwashes them into thinking disrespect is acceptable. Lacking in no egotistical needs, future generations automatically think they are entitled to everything. This system of atheistic materialism robs future generations of their true identity, self-respect, and dignity.

Public education, substantially supported by the endowments of the elites, prepares its students for a job but not for life. Such a system perverts the law of quantum physics by excluding the whole to the detriment of the parts. An educational system which excludes the spirituality of ethical and moral concerns cannot but end up producing robotized automatons who willingly submit to the slavery and mind control of the illuminati production line.

Through these endowments which the illuminati offer, classical education becomes Pavlovian. Students are turned into amenable cogs in the whirring wheels of their assemblies. To the degree the atheistic agenda controls the education of a nation, to that same degree are students kept in a low vibrational state. To the extent we are kept in this low frequency of available light, to that same extent are we robbed of our growth into transcendency.

Atheistic education, without moral values, desperately wants society not to awaken to its divine possibilities. With a dumbed-down populace, control of the masses is more manageable. Atheistic education encourages and promotes the evil capacity we all experience within us. In an instant we are capable of degrading ourselves through an evil act. It is only our capacity to act against this evil force with love and goodness that turns our physicality towards transcendency.

Atheistic education, devoid of moral values, prepares students for a world of hedonism and debauchery. Egotistical expectations are hammered into the high-rise world of entitlement. One's personal life is all that matters. Competition instead of cooperation lies behind the mind-set of atheistic education.

The ingrained message indelibly marked on the vulnerable minds of immature students is that they must fight for survival of the fittest. Gouge more salary out of the corporation one works for. Live according to the rules and control system in which you have been programmed to believe. For the sake of survival, students from an early age are programmed to accept that their free will and individuality depend on the corporate world. The corporation, rather than the civilized world, has become our new moral compass. Decay and depravity are the north on it.

Dependency devalues and steals away our liberty. This precisely is the aim of the atheistic agenda. Control increases to the degree that liberty vanishes.

Education without values, as useful as it is, seems
rather to make a man a more clever devil.

—C. S. Lewis

When conscience is excluded from a school curriculum, compassion goes out the window. The secondary become a substitute for the primary. How can young minds possibly be educated in the direction of decency and civility when the system that endows and directs them is itself corrupt and diabolical?

The shadow behind the governance of education is valueless in content. Billions of pounds have been endowed to schools which further and support the atheistic agenda. The purpose of this expenditure is mind control. It is to direct the emotional state of young minds. When young children are vulnerable and impressionable, they are perfectly suited for the indoctrination of atheism. The Jesuits in a far more Christian atmosphere used the same approach to indoctrinate the young in the opposite direction. Atheism is absolutely determined to use such mind control in all of its social undertakings. Spiritual values are its main target.

At all costs they must be undermined. Young minds are like sponges. The more deceit is pumped into them, the more impressionable they become.

Consciousness respects the whole person, body and spirit. It is holistic. It is not exclusive. Unlike the fundamentalist atheistic approach, it is not closed but open to the possibility of an unending, eternal love experience.

Consciousness has but one commandment. It is easier to learn than the Ten Commandments of old. The commandment of Consciousness is compassion. With it we can put an end to war, live nonviolently, and recognize the all-encompassing Consciousness in each other. Compassion turns separation into oneness. Quantum physics teaches that the cosmos is one.

Ceaseless, useless entertainment continuously bombards the human masses, to such a degree that no room has been left for an examination of conscience. Atheistic materialism has turned the human person into an automaton, out of tune with the earth and its natural process. To the degree we are removed from the soil of earth, to that same degree do we become dysfunctional. What we throw out by the back door comes in to haunt us through the front door.

In a world so deceitfully dumbed down, there is little room for consciousness. If society is to be cured of the disease of atheistic materialism, then the balance of morality and a healthy spirituality must be intertwined with the needs of the body. Money and profit are too paltry a god for enlightened human beings to follow. Atheistic materialism has already caused untold harm through its indoctrination. It divides and creates the illusion of separation. It despises the other as a competitor, when in fact the quantum particle goes into the unity of consciousness, making of life an experience of cooperation instead of competition.

If we love ourselves and the planet we inhabit, then the power of consciousness lives in us. We cannot live or love without it.

Atheistic materialism might have hubristically triumphed in its present domineering context. Ultimately, though, it has no future because it violates the natural law of consciousness. In so doing, atheistic science has dismissed the invisible for the visible and the subtle for the concrete. In essence, this system takes all the music out of life for the sake of the literal.

Quantum physics connects the subject to the object and makes the whole greater than the parts in an interrelated and interdependent way.

This has dealt a serious blow to atheistic materialism. Just as atheism hammered religion in the Enlightenment, so now quantum physics has begun to ring the death knell of the atheist. A new praxis is beginning to emerge whereby science and spirituality are becoming bedfellows.

Through quantum study, a new biology is beginning to shed light on the inner working of human genes. Atheistic materialists have always insisted that our genes determine not only our human characteristics but also our morality. In other words, while still in formation, our genes were predicting our future.

Bruce Lipton, in his study of the biology of belief, has made an astounding breakthrough in his pronouncement that it is the environment rather than our genes that determines our future. He calls this study *epigenetics*. This is another huge hammer blow to the negative determinism of scientists such as Dawkins and Hawkins. It is nurture, or what happens outside the cell, rather than what is within the cell that determines our future.

Quantum science has turned its face away from the conventional atheistic view that has prevailed in the West for the past three hundred years—the dominant view which has led our world into the vale of tears we find ourselves in.

If quantum science has pulled the veil back to give us a more enlightened view, the world of astrophysics has also enlarged our understanding of the universe and our place in it.

CHAPTER SPIRITUALITY

Since quantum physics has brought human enquiry from chronological time into the eternal and replaced thingness with no thing ness, humanity's search for meaning and purpose cannot be found in the realm of matter alone. Quantum physics has brought us to an axial turn in our search for meaning. With the understanding that this new science provides, we know insubstantiality underpins all existence. The particle morphs into consciousness. We leave the land of the atom and enter into the land of the spiritual. Consciousness embraces everything. It is the before and the behind, the below and the top, the alpha and the omega, the nadir and the zenith of everything. It is the beginning, the cause and effect of all that is. There is nothing outside of it and that which is inhabited by it. Like a drop in an ocean, there is no possible way of getting out of its entanglement. Its law is immutable. There is only oneness!

This cosmic oneness of consciousness, ever respectful of humanity's evolution into the sphere of the mind, now endows free will to the humanoid. The human person becomes the most divinized of all the specimens on the floor of the earth. Humankind has been set apart from the rest of the animal kingdom because of intelligence and the addendum of free will which accompanies it. For the first time in the evolutionary process, the human specimen has been endowed with the ability to choose and become a cocreator.

Having arrived at this axial turn, consciousness provides humanity with the ability to manoeuvre in any direction. It provides as many possibilities as our species is capable of imagining. For the first time in the history of evolution, humanity can choose good or evil. We can put ourselves above the natural law of consciousness by separating ourselves from its oneness, thereby severing the connection between body and spirit. Or we can steep ourselves in the all-embracing oneness of consciousness. To do the former is to attend to the ego alone. To do the latter is to grow spiritually, fully cognisant that immanence is congenitally tied into transcendence. The "now" of time intrinsically bears the potential to morph into the eternal.

Through spirituality, heaven surrounds us even here on earth, laden with wonder, appreciation, and thanksgiving for all our blessings. The great God of Consciousness is so respectful of our free will that we are invited more than compelled to become a vessel of righteousness. Consciousness, ever expansive and infinitely limitless, surrounds us and envelops us. We are within it and outside of it. It encompasses the universe. Consciousness defines us. We are eternal consciousness limited by a human experience.

We have been conditioned by an overriding atheistic agenda, which, in the interest of enslaving us, uses mind control to subtly manipulate us into conformity. This contradicts the infinite possibilities we possess through consciousness. Our identity as spiritual beings has been squeezed out of us. We have been disconnected from our infinite consciousness. The sense of our own spiritual dignity and worth has been replaced by a placebo which atheism promises will answer all our human needs and psychological pains. Western society has been so deceived by the trickery of the atheistic agenda that it is now perceived as the great solution to all our problems.

We need a huge surge in wakefulness if contemporary Western society is to shake off our destructive lethargy. Only the reclamation of our inherent spirituality can save us from disaster.

We are never predetermined by our genes, as atheistic scientists like Hawkins and Dawkins so passionately claim. If that were so, then the most treasured endowment of our species—the gift of free will—would lie tattered. Atheism would indeed then have a valid argument in its denial of God's existence. Bruce Lipton, in what he names epigenetics, has proven that it is our environment and not our genes that determine us. This being the case, both the consciousness which quantum science proves and the new biology of epigenetics have given a huge hammer blow to atheism.

Atheistic materialism is diabolical in its drive to smother the human urge to seek out a higher resolution for its hard-wired yearning.

The murder, the mayhem, the crime, the corruption, the disrespect, the lies, the gloom, the darkness, the pessimism, the all-encompassing slavery to shopping malls, the emphasis on celebrity, the murder of the innocent, the madness of war, the stealing, the double-speaking, the pornography, the sale of arms for huge profit—all of this is blamed on the invaded instead of the invader. That is how atheism works. It converts the mind into thinking up is down.

The utter insanity of the Israeli occupation of Palestine is because lies have been turned into truth. The same is true of the war crimes of the rich nations, which go unreported. Bankers who have committed genocidal atrocities in their safe offices are still allowed to live freely in the luxuriant palaces.

The atheistic agenda has failed humanity miserably. We have the ability to put an end to it by becoming more conscious of consciousness. Atheistic materialism loves spiritual laziness. It says, "Luxuriate in the ego. Lie on your couch and be entertained by the ceaseless, useless, vacuous programs we broadcast to you daily. And yes, oh yes, lest I forget, please learn how to kill, because one day soon we will need you as fodder for our next war!"

Atheistic materialism becomes intoxicated by the power we surrender to it. Like all that it exploits and sells, we have become a product. Our value is determined by our purchasing power. Glamour becomes our ultimate achievement. The more expensive our attire, the more we become the envy of others. The more we cover ourselves with the smell of cosmetics, the more we think we are exceptional. Cosmetic alchemists, in a frenzied passion for their own product, speak of it as an intelligent agent, capable of obliterating all the cracks on an aging face. Atheistic materialism turns things into human beings and human beings into things. If we notice and really listen, it is Italian shoes and French handbags which do all the talking in the ads we are watching. Only the spirituality of consciousness, both individual and social, can put an end to this madness.

New possibilities always emerge from their opposite. The only way to combat the evil of materialistic atheism is our refusal to be enslaved by it.

When we recall our recent history, it is people like Gandhi, Martin Luther King Jr, and Mother Theresa who have left an indelible impression on our psyche. It is truly remarkable that these three people are so much appreciated to this day. The contribution they made to the world emanated from their spirituality. They dug deep into their consciousness and brought out compassion instead of hatred to ease the pain of our hurting world. Such is the power of spiritual consciousness.

Each time we destroy innocence, each time we steal from one another, each time we hate, we kill a universe, because consciousness tells us the cosmos is one. We are all in one another. As Hinduism proclaims, "Thou art that."

In its essence, spirituality is about coming home to our own centre, which is truly divine. Much as atheism wants to take away this precious rootedness, we must oppose it in any way possible by becoming countercultural.

Paradoxically, we feel best about ourselves when we give ourselves away, either through presents or presence. Spirituality is about detachment. Less becomes more through spirituality, just as lessening the seed creates more plant. To become conscious of the tiny seed is to wonder how this bit of matter contains the opulence and the sequence of the flower. The more we pay attention, the more we wonder.

All sentient beings are crying out for attention and compassion. The plant looks to the sun for its nurture and the clouds for its water. Animals look to us for shelter and food. But when it comes to atheism, humanity has no one to look to for sustenance. Economy does not address the needs of the spirit. Spirituality enables us to become caring, wise, and compassionate people, who through their own witness influence this world for the good.

Since we have now moved into the noosphere, which in no way ends with natural selection, as atheistic science claims, we look to consciousness to bring us into the realm of spirituality. How we live out our spirituality is determined by each one of us. It is not the genes within us that determine our future; it is the way we handle our consciousness which determines our spirituality.

Spirituality is an act more than a prayer. Going to church on a Sunday morning out of duty does not mean we are thereby spiritual. Spirituality is about going back to the source. It is a decision to enter more deeply into the arena of higher being.

We were created to be spiritual. We are hard-wired for God. There is no escape from the haunting of the divine spark existing within each of us. This unquenchable longing, whether conscious or unconscious, is part of our evolutionary allotment. We can't get out of it, whether we like it or not.

It is a proof that we are not complete yet. We are not satisfied. We cry out for something more. We are never at ease with life as it is. Unfortunately, atheistic materialism has hijacked this longing and tortured it into something nature never intended. It twisted the river flow of our lives and pointed it in the opposite direction.

One hundred years ago, Freud recognized this unquenchable longing: "Humans are driven by irrational forces ... which must be always controlled ... Because of this control humans will always be discontent ... they must be invited towards a naive faith which is a necessary illusion."

A few years later, Edward Bernays, Freud's nephew in the United States, pushed his uncle's teaching that humans are driven by irrational forces. Bernays, as the founder of modern propaganda, capitalized on Freud's thinking by turning desire into the main purpose for human existence. He manipulated humanity's collective unconsciousness into a desire for material things, thus fully ushering in the hurricane of atheistic materialism. From then on, consciousness became a secondary preoccupation.

This in turn ushered in perhaps the greatest neurosis ever to beset the psychology of Western civilization. It is the underlying cause for our modern stress, disharmony, and anxiety.

A conscious and intelligent manipulation
of habits and opinions of democratic societies
can be engendered by an invisible government.

—Edward Bernays

Buddhism, to the contrary, teaches that desire is the cause of human suffering. By twisting the primary desire of the heart to reach for its higher self, Bernays twisted humanity's purpose towards the material instead of the spiritual.

This manipulation of the human urge for transcendence has been one of the greatest mistakes in human history. It lies at the very heart of man's separation from his spirit. Through this manipulation, atheism succeeded in separating humanity from its source. When we move from our centre, we lose our self-respect. Edward Bernays, through this ploy, substituted for creative inspiration a lust for mediocrity and kitsch.

When great art appears in our contemporary world, as indeed it does, it displays its integrity through spiritual questioning rather than atheistic conviction. Becket's *Waiting for Godot* is a classic example. The atheistic view of Beckett is more of a challenge than a statement, and is therefore a work of art and refinement. It proposes more than it discloses.

It can be claimed that atheism produces more kitsch than enlightenment. Competition and product are our greatest achievements, according to atheism. Shopping malls have replaced our cathedrals. Reverence has become repulsive in a duped world bereft of consciousness. Lemming-like, we rush unconsciously towards an edge which offers only death. Computer chips, when used to control instead of enhance the human journey, give ammunition to further accomplish our death warrant.

When humanity becomes removed from what is natural and ordinary, so-called progress is considered extraordinary. The fact remains that catastrophe always becomes inflationary if some intermediary or arbitrator does not try to stop it.

Atheistic materialism is snowballing us. In our lust for progress, we will arrive at a stage when machines kill us. Robots will decide who among us shall live and who shall die. This is the agenda behind the atheistic elitist agenda. Never does the human heart more need to be reassured spiritually: "Come to me, all you who suffer and are overburdened, and I will refresh you."

How can there be progress on earth when only the mind and never the needs of the human heart are being met on our journey? Progress on the purely egotistical level leads to disaster.

Should we still be unaware that even now the snowball of atheism is gathering momentum and rolling life close to the edge, far more immanent is the use of artificial intelligence. This atheistic control mechanism is called *singularity*. The human race through the atheism of natural selection has now arrived on the rung of a tangential ladder, rather than a radial one which pulls us ever forward into consciousness. We become fascinated and enthralled with the promise of artificial intelligence. Atheistic materialism does not believe in the radial energy which invites us to develop spiritually. Sadly we enshrine and canonize our technological wonders, but desecrate humanity's capacity for spirituality.

Artificial intelligence, generically called transhumanism, will end free thought. We most often gain technologically at the cost of our place in the infinite spiral of consciousness. The triumph of the ego over the spirit is almost a fait accompli. To the extent that our technology addresses and satisfies us externally, to the same extent is the human prospect impoverished spirituality.

Materialistic atheism has become so aggressive and grasping, at the expense of all that is interior and primary, that it will not be satisfied until it totally destroys the human soul. All of our technology thus far has been external, an outward extension of the human body. But ever more our machines are becoming invasive, intruding on the internal. The singularity of artificial intelligence is an affront to humanity's capacity to make moral decisions. Unless we decide to end this madness, cyborgs instead of the human mind will make all future decisions for us.

What this world needs most desperately is not the singularity of technology, but the singularity of Christ's message: "Do unto others as you would have them do unto you."

William Butler Yeats said that the greatest journey the human person will ever take is the one into one's own soul. Atheistic materialism proclaims the opposite message. Without the mystical, enlarged vision which transcends the limited availability of visible sight, this world becomes more intolerable.

Despite the impoverished state of consciousness we now live in, perhaps—please God—there is enough sense among us to stop the ticking clock of our destructive technology. We already have more than enough.

The only cure for our planet's sickness is the development of our eternal and infinite consciousness. The less we conform to the mind control of atheistic materialism, the more we grow into the mystical understanding of our no-thing-ness. Our greatest achievement is our insight. Our greatest delight comes from the intake of our eternal consciousness. Instead of atheistic materialism branding us, we can fight it through our own unique spirituality.

In the sphere of consciousness beyond time and place, we will exist in the nowhere of everywhere. Then even the smallest punctuation in the script of life will add to the vocabulary of our literature. The birds will sing songs to us, and rivers will pour music over waterfalls in our honour. Through cosmic consciousness, remembrance of things past will become obsolete. Days and years shall be torn into tatters. Human speech will be useless. Anticipation and expectation will no longer be tinkered with. All will be instantly spontaneous and satisfactory. Our satiation shall put an end to all our longing and desire. Experience will displace explanation. The eternal will still our muted cries of the temporary. All that is good will be now, forever. The need for security will evaporate. Our fulfilment will become official. Our joy shall be complete, without the possibility of a crack in its glass. Deprivation shall be circumvented. Laughter will topple all tears. Peace and serenity shall be the only infection. This is heaven! This is our inheritance. We are all parts of the one interconnected, eternal, and infinite consciousness.

This is what the great nonlocal Intelligence has planned for us. Our future is interwoven with the winds which blow through the heavens. Our future is our insubstantiality. To reach the fullest experience of this ecstatic experience, it is necessary that we cultivate our sense of insubstantiality through our temporary substantiality. The now of eternity, alive in our material lives, cannot be wasted on trivia. Maturity depends on the cultivation of enlarging principles in the minds of our childhoods. Our excellence depends upon our efforts. Now is our most precious moment. We must begin to behave morally in the now if we are to develop our consciousness.

Atheistic materialism promises us Olympian gold medals but discourages us from making the effort necessary to attain them. The claims of atheism are asinine. We attain only to the degree that we cooperate and exercise our consciousness. To the degree that we stay unaware and spiritually illiterate, to that same degree will we fail to experience the full breath of consciousness in our hereafter.

In the lunatic landscape of contemporary Western society, the human spirit is being demolished. Where are all the courageous voices shouting caveats against this slaughter? Once more, our silence is our only eloquence. The unquenchable longing for something greater has been extinguished. Consciousness has been boxed into paper parcels.

Since atheistic propaganda is in such stark contradiction with the wisdom of the ages, why do intelligent human beings not ponder more and ask life's most intelligent question: "Without a who? Why a why?"

An emotional connection to product was established by Edward Bernays. Passive consumers changed from a needs-based society to a desire-based society. Western civilization through this ploy forfeited its unquenchable thirst for God for the sake of such stuff as an insignificant bottle of Coke, which proclaims, "This is it!"

As the media is, so will the mindset of the nation be. Marshall McLuhan implied as much with his famous dictum, "The medium is the message." Atheistic materialism, through the ownership and use of mass media propaganda, has calcified life's meaning and purpose with such rust that we no longer recognize truth.

Jesus possessed the most authentic, singular voice in all of human history. But the only guidance in our new future will be the singularity of transhumanism. Wisdom and guidance concocted by the brain of a machine will drown out the singular message of Jesus Christ. Machines, more than the affairs of the human heart, now guide us. According to atheism, the gadgetry of machinery is our only destiny and purpose. Humanity, on its evolutionary journey, has arrived at the full stop of natural selection. According to atheism, the only future for our species is mechanical.

Evil triumphs over good in such an atmosphere. The signs of our collapse, expressed multifariously through our decadence, become more shocking and heinous every day. An atheistic, mechanical life without a heart is as despicable as the depravity it produces and teaches.

Our planet will collapse from within unless we bring our spirituality back into the marketplace. The holy name of God has been obliterated from the constitution of the European Union. The hydron collider in Cern, Switzerland, is a glaring attempt to wipe God off the slate of humanity. It is generally understood that the illuminati worship the Devil instead of God. Shiva, the Hindu god of destruction, in statue, adorns the front entrance to the hydron collider. Of all symbols in the history of our mythology, surely the choice of Shiva is the most sombre indication of the atheistic agenda.

The elites who sponsor the experiment of the hydron collider consider themselves the zenith of the evolutionary push. They consider themselves the enlightened and informed ones. Natural selection has chosen them. The rest of us, as low-caste underlings, are merely slaves to serve them. It's a paradox that this group of obscenely wealthy elites can so easily choose the Devil and evil over an avatar who gave his life for the good of the world.

Since the planet is already overpopulated, around five billion souls will be exterminated, if the elites' plan becomes a reality.

Because atheism precludes the God of consciousness, absolute evil can prevail without any moral responsibility. This vision is best encapsulated on the tablet of the Atlanta Guide Stone. The plan is to destroy most of humanity before all the nonrenewable sources of the earth are consumed. According to the shadow government, most human beings are useless, inefficient eaters. They must be eliminated.

To be yourself in a world that is constantly trying to make you into something inferior is a human being's greatest accomplishment. To be yourself is to spiritualize your personhood. In our deepest core, we are spiritual. On earth, we live as spiritual beings in material clothing, not the other way around. The natural law tells us this. We think the falling leaves from the autumn tree have little relevance. But their hymn of beauty tells a far deeper story. It is only the awake who can hear and see the fullness of the natural world's telling.

We have so much energy within us that we can invite a new messenger to take hold of our being at any moment. We have the power within us to be our own spiritual prophets of Consciousness. There is a life task awaiting each one of us, which must be awakened by ourselves alone.

The spirituality of consciousness is the one denominator that we all share. It embraces our ability to embrace our common humanity. It transcends all cultural differences. It makes us one as the cosmos is one. This is what Hinduism calls *cosmotheandric*.

The term *cosmotheandric* should not be confused with the one world religion, which the atheistic new world order envisions as a means of control, as Constantine did with the first Christians. It is the exact opposite! It calls for a revolution in the spirituality of consciousness. This is not the same as remaining faithful to the dogmas of organized religion, nor does it have the covert purpose to make us all one, religion and all, under the same central management of power and control. Rather is it the founding principle on which we base our commonality under the same spiritual flag of consciousness.

A spiritual approach to life changes everything.

Some great nonlocal Intelligence has radially and tangentially pulled us from a sphere of intelligence (noosphere) into omega, which is the God of consciousness. The illuminati resent this evolutionary arrangement. It distracts from our egoic selfishness.

Contrary to the indoctrination of atheistic materialism, through spirituality, we surrender the needs of the selfish ego for the sake of the common good. This demands sacrifice. When sacrifice is understood properly, it means love. Compassionate love, such as Jesus taught, is the dynamic involved in spirituality. Spirituality is not about going to church on a Sunday morning. It is more about what we carry with us into the church.

An old Irish monk once told one of his compatriots, "If you are going to Rome to seek Christ, better that you stay at home, because you won't find him over there."

Spirituality is relational. It involves the subconscious as the floor for the conscious. It turns even the smallest surprise from the natural world into a gift of wonder. To be spiritual is to realize that in everyday life, it is the little happenings that feed our conception of God—dim and dusty at first, but then, through an alarming wakefulness, we find the tranquillity to anchor our emptiness.

As Graham Green points out,

> "Pools become oceans ... and God is in everything.
> "I believe that a blade of grass is no less than the journey
> of the stars ...

the egg of the wren is a chef d'OUVRE for a five star
restaurant …
the narrowest hinge in my hand puts to shame all
machinery
and a mouse is a miracle enough
to stagger sextillions of infidels"

With God ever before us as the attracting magnet of our being, the raindrops on the windowpanes of the world will be turned into diamonds, and the soil of earth will become our new garden of Eden.

Atheistic materialism might respond more objectively to organized religion if the church itself were more spiritual. Missionaries still do all the hard work and live selfless lives, often spending themselves in slum poverty while their overlords live in palaces. Surely there exists a vast chasm between that cave in Bethlehem and the Vatican. Gold and opulent gemstones were never worn by Jesus of Nazareth.

None of the major religions in the West have moved an inch in the direction of cosmic consciousness. They still retain a tribal mentality.

With or without ecumenism, the religions of the world must selflessly come together in the defence of a God who is surely being daily crucified by the onslaught of atheistic materialism. Exposed and threatened by the same common enemy, the churches' particular tribal differences will have to dissipate for sake of a more spirit-centred and integrated universe.

When we live with the spirituality which consciousness brings, we begin to realize that ordinary life is not an endurance test but a dancing child alive within us, always full of wonder and curiosity. Spirituality, when understood properly, sets us free to become what we are meant by nature to become.

Ruminants munch peacefully. Carnivores wait patiently. Trees bend their branches in a storm. They do not uproot and move to another lawn. All creation lives with its natural flow of cosmic energy. There is but one exception to the natural law, and that is man. It is the gift of free will which makes us different from every other reality on earth. We can choose between evil and good.

Would you care to say which side of the great divide our guiding paradigm of atheistic materialism is leading us toward? When the nuclear bomb falls, we cannot blame cows for the radiated milk they bless us with!

Spirituality brings out the divine child within us. It will not come out to play unless we seed the meadows and fields that produce the crops which sustain us. Spirituality will never arrive miraculously. As with all things living, the dark is the first harrowing necessary for the seed to reach light. Spirituality has its own way. It provides no harvest instantly. We have work to do to make it come alive. It will not happen if we continue to sit on our fat backsides. Spirituality is not escapism. It gives us the courage to meet the catastrophic moment of our lives. We have to dare to be spiritual.

As Aeschylus wrote,

> He who learns must suffer.
> Pain that cannot forget falls
> drop by drop upon the heart
> And in our own despair, against our will,
> comes wisdom
> by the awful grace of God."

Egotistical atheism bent on nihilism abhors at all costs the awful truth of human suffering. Invented and sustained by psychopaths, human suffering is irrelevant to psychopaths. So long as it is at the cost of others, they thrive on it. They gather their riches through it. The more war, the more gain. The more pain, the more disdain.

Contrary to the huge dung heap of indoctrination which atheistic materialism has dumped on the human mind, little sprouts of spirituality come shoving through the smothering. It is often the smile and the courtesy of the one who serves that leaves the greatest impression on our minds. It is the spirit of the human person which most impresses us. What atheistic materialism offers will in the end be eaten by moths or corroded by rust. But the smile, the trust, the hug, the kiss, and the acceptance of a stranger leaves the greatest impression and will live on after the material package is forgotten and gone.

By the gurus of atheistic materialism, we are considered with as much esteem as the packages they sell. We represent no more to them than the allure of their packaging. Atheism packs its boxes with bundles of desire.

To combat this strategy of manipulation, we must return to the spirituality which the God of consciousness intends for us.

Surely, there exists somewhere the justification for our unquenchable longing. It is to our shame, both individually and socially, that we curse the light instead of the dark. It is time we individually light penny candles again. It is time we returned home to the beehive, laden with the honey that is our spirit.

Life itself teaches that God will not be mocked. Ultimately, if we live out the obligations which are unalterably tied to the privilege of free will, God will set all our crooked ways straight. To accomplish this, as John F. Kennedy said, "God's work must become our own." We are all obligated to cooperate with the Creator's will for the universe.

God never created our planet to be exploited and despoiled in order to sate the greed of atheistic, elitist psychopaths. It is absolutely imperative to put an end to the ferociousness with which the illuminati and their corporations are attacking the fragile biomass of our common earth. It is time we applied Agenda 21 to them instead of them applying it to us. It is time for all the poor on our planet joined in one spiritual union to apply austerity to those egomaniacs who have imposed so much austerity on the struggling people of the earth. We can accomplish this if we engender our cause with spiritual energy.

One person can change this world for the better. One singular man did it as he was dying a death by asphyxiation on the wood of a tree. "Father, forgive"—are those not the most haunting two words ever to cross the lips of a human being? They contain the most essential element in all of the earth's diplomacy. They enable us to see the other as the same as me They transform us into one another. They make us brothers and sisters. They turn us into the one family.

Why does the West continue to negotiate without an embrace of this message? It can work if we will it. Bombs and bullets can never conquer it. Why are we so unwilling to entertain it? Why are grown men too tough to say it? Why is bodily might always right and physical weakness always wrong? Are these two words too feminine to be considered by macho men? What turns a man into a hero? Is it what is within him, or is it his outward appearance?

No matter what the outcome, spirituality is always the determining factor. Why then are NATO, the US, and the UN too terrified to mention the teaching of this most impressive Singularity who gave such a message of peace and hope to this bedraggled planet? He was a nonviolent passivist. All who follow his way must be the same.

We change our world by changing ourselves. We begin the process by waking up to the fact that we are slowly being despiritualized and desensitized to what is essential.

Once we have named the enemy, then we can fortify ourselves against further infiltration. We can start our spiritual conquest by turning off our mass media, which only pumps out propaganda. We can teach our children to again appreciate the delicacy and wonder which the world of nature provides abundantly. We can convince ourselves that the games of plunder and murder which young minds absorb from mass media lead to a deadening of sensitivity to the wonder of life. Boys as much as girls must be disengaged from the horror of killing. All war games in a Christian home should be burned.

If only the governments of this mad world would try to inculcate a message of hope and love and make it come alive in their debates, then surely stability and security would ensue. The time has come when each individual must end the mind-control game and refuse to purchase any product which is not needed. We must end inbred obsolescence.

The time has come for us to recognize the sacred interconnection and relationship we have with the earth.

Edmund Burke, the Irish parliamentarian, argued, "For evil to triumph all that is necessary is that good men do nothing."

The darkness drops again; but now I know
twenty centuries of stony sleep
We're vexed to a nightmare by a rocking cradle,
and what rough beast, its hour come round at last,
slouches towards Bethlehem to be born?

—William Butler Yeats

The holy name of God has been banished from the European Union's constitution. Allegiance to the very concept of divinity is never contemplated nor indeed implied in its modern halls of justice and legislation. The God of all consciousness has been denied. Divinity is never called upon for assistance in Western humanity's arbitrations and decision-making.

The account of European history must again be rendered in such a way that its marvellous creativity and refinement are narrated as arising ultimately from God and not atheism. Instead of being appreciated as a living testament of Consciousness, our magnificent cathedrals and monasteries have become hollow and empty places. Scandalously, they are best appreciated as heirlooms, or reinvented as museums, where uninspired zombies trod and gape rather than passion-filled believers singing psalms of praise. If modern humanity's sense of the real could be elevated to the realm of pure consciousness, then these sacred places would fill up again with the cries of the human heart and songs of supplication. Terribly, the wild caws of the crows are the only psalms now heard amid the tear-laden stones of Ireland's beautiful medieval monasteries. There can be no spirituality without awe and wonder. The crows' caws are not enough. Man's songs of wonder and praise must accompany them.

We have arrived at that axial point where we must reinvent ourselves again and move our direction towards our source and end. Atheism has had its day.

The primordial flaw underpinning contemporary Christianity, in respect to its God, is its own history. Atheists rightly claim that the church's approach towards the transcendency of consciousness has been horrendously biased and cruel. Atheism is brutal but honest in its condemnation of the Christian religion. Most of its arguments are valid and help to refine Christian followers to use their God-given gift of intelligence. Atheism refines organized religion when used constructively. Atheism purifies as it plunders religion.

It is plain to see that we as a species have made a quantum leap from being conscious to having consciousness of being conscious. Of all the animals on earth, we have been the most blessed with the gift of intelligence. If evolution has any validity, then of course we have been created to use our intelligence.

Atheism would agree with the argument so far. It is at this precise juncture, though, that atheism and theism part ways in their vision. Theism purports to have a future orientation. Atheism states that progress is only possible on the material level. It suggests spirituality is only a figment of the brain, which will be better understood when neurons are better understood.

The human being has arrived. And that is the end of the story, according to atheism. There is nothing more to report. There is no future. Life on earth is randomness and came into being by pure chance. Life is self-regulatory, according to atheism, and needs no mind other than the human one to mechanize it.

Theism takes the opposite view and sees humanity as a work in progress. *Homo sapiens* is future-oriented. The best is yet to be. Theism proclaims that humanity is meant to transcend—to go beyond the baggage of the flesh and morph into spirit.

Organized religion embraces this approach, but once again, humanity's spiritual journey reaches another conundrum. Christian fundamentalists embrace the Bible literally, and refuse outright the theory of evolution. They insist that the Bible is the exact Word of God and must be adhered to in every detail to reach heaven.

The Catholic church, challenged as it was by Copernicus and Galileo, no longer insists that the Genesis story is scientifically correct. Pressured by atheistic science, the powerful Catholic church came down from its hubristic pulpit and admitted that science was indeed correct in its assertion that earth is a planet rotating around the sun.

The Catholic church, seldom recognized for its humility, was pushed into such an admission. Atheistic science, however, not content with its triumph, kept attacking what it considered the superstition of the church. To offset the incredulity of atheism, the church created a moat of defence and declared itself infallible in respect to its pronouncements of faith and doctrine. Consequently, a huge rift between science and religion erupted.

Atheists such as Dawkins, in his book *The God Delusion*, have hurled all kinds of arguments for the abolition of religion, considering it a cancer in society. Much of his criticism is legitimate. The pity is that, like his fellow countryman Stephen Fry, Dawkins dismisses the existence of God because of the sins of the church.

Like atheism, organized religion has played a role in stultifying the onward process of evolution. Instead of living spiritually, it also, like atheism, became a blunt instrument in its blockage of humanity's river-flow into consciousness.

Not only did the Vatican refuse to live the lifestyle of Jesus of Nazareth, but this placebo church turned his house into a den of thieves. Constantly, as it grew richer and richer from the peasant money it garnered, it imposed ever-increasing tedious and controlling laws which hindered the poor from legitimate experiences of life's joys and pleasures. Consumed with its own hubristic power, it became a dictatorship, dishing out dogmas and laws that obscured the essence of the Nazarene's teachings. Like a bunch of lawyers, they converted the simplicity of the Jesus message into an immeasurable expanse of legalistic jargon, using words the likes of which Christ himself never used or contemplated. The dogmas these hubristic men promulgated are often totally incompatible with the natural law.

God has blessed us with intelligence, and divinity demands that we use it. Intellectually, it is inconceivable that a virgin can give birth to a baby, or that any human body can ascend with a full complement of atoms into an insubstantial realm. These types of dogma are an insult to the greatest of all our endowments—namely, our intelligence.

Today, I heard a man say that he was an atheist because he could not believe in an afterlife. I asked him why. He responded, "Over these millions of centuries, billions and billions of people have died, and the church says they either go to heaven or hell. I refuse to believe that."

"Why?" I asked again.

"Because there is no place big enough to hold all those bodies," he replied.

This is the illogical state of thinking into which religion has brought us. More shockingly still, there has been little attempt to educate the laity into spiritual competence. The same old, tired drills in rosary recitation still prevail in our religious education classes.

So much for an informed theology. The church still tolerates this spiritually destructive ignorance, content to let a sleeping dog lie. Theological unenlightenment prevails horrendously, because a secular understanding of our planet sounds much more intelligent than the spiritual one. Organized religion is growing ever more irrelevant. The church continues with its own solution because an ignorant faithful are more acceptable to its control system. "Don't wake them up because they might bite us" seems to be their mantra. "Let them be superstitious; otherwise they will ask too many awkward questions to which we have no answers. Let them stay with their sixth-grade mentality."

The atheistic elites want organized religion to remain precisely the same in its teachings, because, in keeping with its own agenda, dumbed-down people are easier to control and dominate. While we remain in a state of ignorance, we are vulnerable subjects for exploitation and slavery. In this sense, organized religion has become a bedfellow in the accomplishment of the atheistic illuminati agenda.

A people deprived of their own indelible truth become easy to control and manage. Robbed of a sense of eternal self-worth, we lose esteem for the machinery of our own bodies. We hand them over to a bunch of slave masters whose sinister plan is to use them as ploughs and combine harvesters. This adds more gold to their bloated silage containers on Wall Street. Unaware, it is we who contribute to our own slavery.

To be conscious is to awaken to the fact that what is internal to every person is eternal. It cannot be obliterated by a momentary planned agenda. The elites, through their atheism, deny this because the idea of self-worth is the arch-enemy in their war for control and profit.

Consciousness and spirituality are synonymous. Spirituality concerns itself with a sense of the eternal self's worth and dignity. When we awaken to this, we will not allow any system—be it the atheism of elites or the hierarchy of organized religion—to control us.

We are at an axial turn in the process of our evolution. In times past, organized religion controlled us. It caused more mayhem and exclusion than resolution to the human prospect. Presently the gurus behind the future direction of our planet are the illuminati. They attempt to influence, direct, and supply every human enterprise with copious amounts of money obtained obscenely through their system of indebtedness and interest. In the end, they incarcerate us both materially and spiritually.

It is time for the human race to awaken to the obscenity of the inequality which prevails, not only in the wealthy countries of the earth, but more especially in the poor countries. The obscene culture of the few can and must be obliterated from the face of our planet if humanity is to have a future.

The spirituality of being conscious bears the possibility of promise. The obscenity which surrounds the privileges of the illuminati can only be altered by our individual consciences. We must join as a family, living as one on this same small blue planet hanging in space. The privileged few do not have the right to steal from the many their rightful inheritance.

Ignorance and a dumbing down of society are promoted by the illuminati as seduction and sedation on mass media. They cause illiteracy and mediocrity of moral fibre. Amusement and entertainment have corrupted and invaded the territory of the human mind to such an extent that we cannot any longer distinguish between genuine comedy and pornography.

The elites, who gorge themselves with riches stolen from the poor of the world, are atheistic because atheism, which is amoral, suits them. The immorality of the elites' atheism is totally suited to waging war, always far away from the nation which initiates it. The riches accrued through the sale of armaments swell their already obscene bank accounts with untold billions in plundered money.

Any approach which furthers the cause of blunting a developed conscience is cleverly used to distract and oppose humanity's ingrained need for spirituality. Organized religion becomes an easy target for atheism. If, on the other hand, the church remained true to its mission, it would have concentrated more on spiritual literacy than politics. Even now, when it has been chastened by so much scandal, its arrogant preoccupation with and concentration on dogma and canon law discloses how unreal and removed it is from the ordinary concerns of its followers

It would seem the Roman Curia ignores applied theology and the gospel of interpenetration. The official prayers of Catholicism are more credal than personal. They are inductive much more than deductive. They dissipate more than associate.

Humanity needs to learn that we live between two great darknesses, but that does not spell deadness. We already know in a metaphorical way that this does not put an end to the mystery of living. Gestation happens through an astounding connection of couple consciousness in silence and darkness. What is even more astonishing is that all this happens so effortlessly and in anonymity. Surely when we consider the birth of a baby, we must be awed by the marvel of its body's perfect machinery and also by its determination to reach out and connect with a loving attender.

It is not enough that organized religion be apoplectic about abortion without having first evangelized its followers concerning the sacredness of matter as a continuum into the interior, spiritual realm of consciousness.

Obviously the population of eight billion people already on our planet cannot go on exploding indefinitely. But that does not give us the right to discriminate about who should live and who must die. Love for all the newborn children of our world cannot be compromised nor negotiated. Once life is, then to end it is a serious crime, unless the foetus is doomed to die anyhow. The mother's life always takes precedence in such circumstances.

The very name "religion" introduces the unifying principle of connection. This is scarcely the case, however, in a church so separated from the natural world, whose laws and distinctions are etched out in sterile, comfortable offices, far removed from the muck and tatter of a broken world. If organized religion is ever to speak authentically and legitimately, then its priests and bishops will have to replace their pens and computers with spades and shovels. Pens need paper and computers need software. Software and hardware must work as one. A *sensus fidelium* must become the bishop's law instead of the other way around. God is more often found in the kitchens and sculleries of the humble than in the mansion rooms of the elites. Matter and spirit must act as one, or else there will be Armageddon.

As we have seen, one of the great gurus behind atheistic materialism is Edward Bernays. He turned humanity's unquenchable longing for something higher into a narcissistic desire for consumer goods. What is literal is much more appealing in our world than what is lateral. It appeals to the ego instantly. Bernays knew this. The elites have managed to turn the unquenchable longing of our souls for something more into something less.

This has been the most deceitful con job ever perpetrated on the human mind. We now sell dog food and cat food with greater flair and conviction than religion does its own wares. All the dimly lit corridors of our ancient monasteries, where monks scuttled by candlelight to sing "O

Holy Night", have been censored and replaced with "Rudolph the Red-Nosed Reindeer". The mystery which the monastic candles engendered, displaying more shadow than light, has now been all blown out. Nothing remains to remind us of our transcendency. Our shopping malls and neon lights have blown all such mystical experiences out of mind and out of sight.

Religion stays stuck with its linear approach in a world which is consumed by the glamour and colour of mass media. If religion were to take on the mantle of spirituality and project its meaning through art and compassion, then instead of vulgarity and coarseness, humanity would awaken through the media to a message of the nobility, the beauty, and the blessings of ordinary life. When the heart is touched, the head follows. A new world order based on the principle of spirituality is possible if we choose to make it happen.

If evolution is to find its conclusion, then it must be allowed to arrive back where it started from—namely God. Instead of transgenetics or transhumanism, our future is transcendence. There cannot be any other resolution to our human journey.

Both the atheistic illuminati and organized religion have caused untold damage to an onward evolutionary process into the invisible. Atheism dismisses the possibility of an afterlife. Organized religion, while admitting it, only tolerates its own interpretation of it.

The church's usual response to questions it cannot answer is "It's a mystery" or "God can do anything supernaturally". Always the cop-out or the stopgap measure when its authority is challenged!

To be human is to be uncertain. There is so much we do not know and have yet to learn. Theology develops. It is not static. All the answers are not in yet, nor is God finished with our human story. Far better to leave the discovery of God an open book than to close divinity in the seedy pages of an ancient manuscript. Far better to say God is dynamic and always hides around the next corner.

Contrary to Richard Dawkins, atheism has brought far more pain, suffering, and death into this world than religion ever did. Communism wiped fifty million Russians from the face of the earth.

Organized religion is equally guilty of mind control as the atheism of the illuminati. Indeed, both hierarchical systems are agents of slavery: one of the mind and one of the body. If a new world order is ever to arise, then it must find its authenticity through spirituality. Neither organized religion nor the atheism of the illuminati shows any compassion to a world which is becoming ever more lonely, stressed, and desperate. The system of both agendas favours the few at the expense of the many.

Both systems deem themselves as the only viable authority on earth. All laws and governance are legislated to promote the security and self-interest of the elites, with a few crumbs from the table of their providence falling to feed the poor and hungry masses. Both organized religion and the elites have twisted our upside-down world to such a degree that soon trees will exhale carbon instead of oxygen and the cow will eat the lion instead of the other way around. Something has gone incredibly wrong within our present matrix. If we do not design a new paradigm for the planet, then surely the Armageddon which Christian fundamentalists so gleefully predict will eat up humanity. Ironically, religious fundamentalism is as spiritually destructive as atheistic materialism.

The vast majority of civilization cannot make a distinction between religion and spirituality. Spirituality is not religion. Spirituality is about transcendence. Religion is about politics. When politics enters, spirituality usually goes out the window. One can go to Mass every day of the week and say a thousand rosaries, but such exercises are mere hypocrisy if they do not morph from egotistical reverence into a full complement of responsibility. There cannot be worship of God without a commitment to leave our safe sanctuaries, go forth into the arena of our everyday world, and incarnate the divinity dwelling within us. We must first become drops in the water with which we sprinkle our asperges.

Christians should not go to Mass on a Sunday out of submission to a church command. Prayer is a cry of the heart, and unless there is forgiveness and compassionate consciousness in the heart, love is absent in our prayers. We should only go to church with the right disposition of heart.

Unfortunately, prayer in organized religion is basically theatrical and credal. Prayers are uttered mostly to substantiate doctrine, and seldom as an inspiration or motivation to play one's little part in compassionate creativity.

The terrible tragedy about religious worship in contemporary society is that believers confuse religion with spirituality. When worship becomes the rant of rushed credal prayer, then surely it is an insult rather than a reverent acknowledgement of the God of creation.

We might as well stay at home and watch TV, which so covertly and insidiously robs us of our spirituality. Worship has to be passionate. It should be celebratory and festive. Reverence and thanksgiving are the hallmarks of happiness, gratefulness, and forgiveness. When this passion is missing, then worship is empty and worthless.

Liturgy is as much lateral as it is linear. It has to interpenetrate the experience of the contemporary. Theism has much to learn from the expertise of atheism in this respect.

Never has society been so taxed, so drugged, so wasted, so intellectually mistreated by the distracting and confusing immorality broadcast by mass media. We are terrorized to death by an enemy we have never encountered. Is this just another war game played out for our viewing in order to keep us addicted to verbiage? Fear engendered is just another system of control. Manufacture a false act of terrorism, and through lies and propaganda, the masses will subjugate themselves to the lies of their government just to be protected.

This procedure is but a repeat of what organized religion has done to Western civilization. The fear of hell and damnation often lurks heavily even in this, our more enlightened world. The tactics of the church in our terror-tortured world have now been usurped by the state. We are confused and conflicted, without a moral compass. Where do we look for guidance? The promises of both organized religion and atheistic materialism have failed us.

We need a new world order.

The question is what kind of order will it be? What kind of a world will we bequeath to our children—an elitist, atheistic materialism, or a cosmotheandric spirituality?

In the West, to mention the holy name of God is almost considered vulgar and unclean, People have become so intimidated that, like anti-Semitism, it is considered politically incorrect. In the whole tragic, egoistic celebration that Christmas has become, profit and economy have expelled the honoured guest from the birthday table. We celebrate a crib with no baby in it.

Slowly, imperceptibly, covertly, and incrementally, our Christian heritage has been stolen away from us. To the church's credit, faith in a supreme being was kept alive through the teaching of religion right up to the Enlightenment. The faithful remained subservient believers through the indoctrination of a fearful God, but it was God nonetheless. We had not till then totally thrown the baby out with the bathwater.

Through all the turmoil, the church clung to the idea of dualism. God was the Greek Aristotelian version: up in the sky, apart from matter. Instead of integrating immanence with transcendence, the here and the now with the hereafter, the church considered this world a veil of tears separating matter from the hereafter. As we have indicated, quantum science now teaches the exact opposite. Matter and nonmatter are a continuum. Quantum science integrates. It does not separate as the church does.

Good and evil are the one reality. We cannot have one without the other. Time and eternity are on one continuum. Heaven starts where the foot falls. In this sense, religion and atheism are the very antithesis of integration. They each are built on the opposite extreme. They never come to the middle They both introduce imbalance.

Spirituality, on the other hand, can be totally reconciled with quantum physics. This is accomplished through the morphing of the observable atom into the realm of invisibility.

Materialistic atheism is in total opposition to the spiritual journey of the atom into consciousness. It denies what is deepest about our higher being. It cries out for attachment to matter as our only reason for living.

Spirituality cries out for a detachment from the ego and growth into selflessness. Spirituality calls us into a unifying field of consciousness where the "I" is the "thou". I am in fact my brother and sister. We are all one in the great One of consciousness. When we realize this, all wars will cease.

Matter is the means and consciousness the end. Spirituality invites humanity towards true self-esteem, recognizing that spark of divinity which we are in each other. Atheistic materialism invites selfishness, whereas spirituality invites compassion.

The banks of this world thrive on debt. They are the crowning achievement of the masterminds behind materialistic atheism. The more money paid out, the more money raked in because of the interest paid on the loan. Banks bulge through the human sweat of enslavement. On the scale of humanity, the balance always avalanches in favour of the banker but never the depositor. Such is the injustice of atheistic materialism. Only God can possibly change this system.

Central banks,—all interconnected, interrelated, and integrated— have done a far better job in the paradigm of atheistic materialism than organized religion has in promoting true spirituality. With such a glut of money, the top lords of the universe are its money lenders. With money, it is now possible to rob human beings of their self-respect and dignity. The psychopathic elites have built another golden calf to worship in a Middle Eastern desert. What is highest and noblest about the human person is incrementally eroded by the evil paradigm of atheistic materialism.

We may argue that it has always been so. Unfortunately, if humanity continues to approach life without the balance of spirituality, now as never before we are on the brink of the greatest catastrophe our planet has realized in human history. We say this, not because of the usual jargon which fundamentalist Christians drag out of the book of Revelation, and not only because of the misuse of nuclear energy, but also because atheistic scientists arrogantly continue to seek the flip side of consciousness. Compassion has never once entered the equation in their search for truth. Truth cannot be found with such an imbalance because it totally violates the natural law.

A truly spiritual vision teaches this. It is the primary law and final dogma maintained throughout the ages through the wisdom of humanity. Yet the arrogance of atheistic science is such that in boycotting humanity's accumulated wisdom, we challenge the power of divinity and unleash Armageddon upon our planet.

The Cern experiment, not content with the answer which quantum science indicates concerning consciousness as our unifying principle, is arrogantly hell-bent on pushing enquiry even further. The mass media message, as ever engaged in mind control, conveniently summarises this enquiry as a search for "the God particle". But how could such an experiment be objectively undertaken when already the subjects who study it are consumed with a hatred for a spiritual solution which might possibly answer our human dilemma?

Their search is not for the God particle, since God has already been killed off by their atheism. Rather, it is a search for a particle which will better serve their agenda. It is in effect an experiment to legitimize their evil agenda for the world. Its avowed purpose is to release the negative, dark side of matter from its inbred attachment to the positive, thereby releasing a devastating force, the likes of which our world has never known and is incapable of controlling.

If the atheistic agenda which controls our media were truly honest, then the captions on our information transmitters would read, "Cern searches for the Devil particle"

Every force in life, as we have seen, is not dualistic but unitive. Consciousness is unitive, which is positive and directed towards the good and the beautiful in the human experience. But it necessarily has a dark side, which, if unleashed, will be a purely diabolical source of torture on our earth.

This is not some fairy tale concocted by some fundamentalist preacher, but a true report of the facts of what is happening at the hydron collider in Cern, Switzerland. The statue which greets one upon entering this experimental lab is of Shiva, the Hindu god of destruction. Should the dark force of matter ever be released, then what in heaven's name is to become of the earth? Will atheists such as Stephen Fry still blame God and call him a monster?

The only certain fact about human life is that the visible, material body morphs into consciousness. The invisible spirit lives on in a realm unimaginable. Restricted by the five senses, we only receive a glimpse of our possible future. All we know with the certainty of science is that the full embrace of consciousness awaits us. But it is not just quantum science which gives us a spiritual perspective; we receive millions of clues every day, in the midst of the ordinary. As Oscar Wilde said, "Mystery is in the seen; not the unseen."

We find our spirituality by vesting ourselves with new eyes and a different way of seeing. We walk on holy ground. Not a bird sings nor a tree uplift its branches but in response to God's presence. As Celtic spirituality instructs, there is only a thin space between heaven and earth. People in the West of Ireland still say, "Heaven is but an inch and a half above the head of a man." Patrick Kavanagh, a spiritual Celt to the bone, said, "God is a pearl necklace hung around the neck of poverty.

God's Spirit moves through everything. God is as near to each one of us as we are to ourselves. God is very available. You do not have to make an appointment to meet divinity, nor is divinity a respecter of schedules. You do not have to pay money for God's counsel in the psychiatric office of your inner being. Euros and dollars are of man's making. If we allow them to control us, they become a neurosis. Cheat, lie, steal, and swindle though we may, the truth remains. "There's no pockets in a shroud," as the Irish say.

We are vessels of infinite awareness. The greatest catastrophe is to allow divinity to die within us. We reach the full embrace of divinity to the extent that we become conscious. God is the inner flame, while we are the sparks emanating from the centre.

CHAPTER THE EXISTENCE OF GOD

Science promotes the idea that one day we will be physically forever young. But who would want that? Already the challenge of living our ordinary daily lives can be quite burdensome. The poor of this earth are in such dire straits that their existence draws tears out of stones. If there is no life after death, a person might as well commit suicide.

Often we see that it is the suffering people of the world who smile most and remain hopeful. Even if it is for the wrong reason, who gives arrogant atheists the right to take this away from them? Hope is always a right for the living. It is of no concern to the dead, and atheists are, by their own admission, already the dead.

Suffering retards arrogance and promotes a reaching out to others. It engenders compassion. It is hammered out on the anvil of one's own personality. We cannot become spiritual without the tooling of suffering.

Atheism has such a stranglehold on modern psychology that any suggestion of a higher life is totally forbidden. Subjects such as suicide and death are discussed on the purely physical level without ever mentioning a spiritual dimension. It is as if psychologists today are embarrassed by the idea of God ever entering the equation.

If there are any subjects in life worthy of a spiritual dimension, then surely the bereaved need to be reminded about the possibility of an afterlife. The unifying field of consciousness teaches this. But why have we arrived at this diabolical stage when, in the West, we dare not even mention the holy name of God in our various professions?

We seem to be terrified of this, especially in the arena of economics and politics. Corruption erupts because God has not interpenetrated our lives. God is missing in the West, but we Christians do not miss him. We have a lot to learn from Islam.

This world has surely gone mad when we support the armies who spill their bombs on those who are too poor to manufacture them. We even rob the murdered corpses of any respect and refer to them merely as "collateral damage".

Atheists dismiss the idea of a good God because of human suffering. Not only do they not accept the yin and the yang in the natural world, but they consciously upset the balance, favouring evil over good. They discriminate and alter the natural flow of life to such an extent that our rivers, instead of replenishing us with pure water, have now become putrid swamps from all the poison dumped into them. Atheists blame God for the malformation of the world, when in fact it is they who are the agents of evil.

The accumulated wisdom of the world teaches that suffering instructs. We seek to cure our physical ills because the signal sent by our bodily suffering is a message to alarm us. Without physical suffering, our bodies would die from rot. Suffering is an emissary from a higher realm. It pounds us all into the same level. It teaches us compassion. We knowingly walk in another person's shoes because of suffering. Suffering connects us to the flow of contradictions. We can rise to a higher plateau because of it.

Suffering gives meaning and purpose when we connect it with our primal scream. It is not for nothing that we often say of the death of a loved one, "I can't believe he's dead." There is an echo of transcendency in many of our colloquial expressions: "Where do you think you're going?" "Where have you come from?" "Who the hell do you think you are?"

Suffering is the prerequisite for healing. God cannot be denied because of it. Materialistic atheism pretends to be the antigen for our ills. Its evil philosophy has taken most of the accrued wisdom from Western society. Stupefied by its prevailing, rampant rot, we deride and dismiss matters that really matter and spend our lives in pursuit of trivia—inconsequential nothings. This is what materialistic atheism has done to our human enterprise.

The Christian world has succumbed and handed over to a bunch of global, fascist, Orwellian thieves its mandate to bring peace and serenity to our world.

The only constitution the elites follow is the one which they have written. But as truly as there is a divine hand at work in this world in accordance with the natural law, good will triumph over evil—even if that means the Creator of the universe gets rid of us as a species. The wisdom of endurance or any other noble achievement can ever be born out of greed and exploitation of others.

Atheism demeans us. Evolution, if anything, is about refinement. To have arrived at the level of natural selection where humanity is now conscious of itself is to ponder the question, "Now where do we go?" Surely over the four billion years of our evolutionary journey, humanity could not possibly have struggled to express itself in such a vulgar, selfish, crass, exploitative, murdering, greedy, grasping, egotistical, and evil way?

Even if there is no God, it does not seem logical or tolerable that the convulsion of the universe's purpose was to spawn the human species for such a Frankenstein scenario. We are meant for more.

Nothing constructive is possible without its opposite. Evil will always yield evil unless we use it and will it to attain its opposite. Joy cannot be experienced if there has not been the previous experience of pain by which to measure it. The great nonlocal Intelligence does not—because it cannot—suspend the sequential flow of the natural law. To do so would mean that the preordained way of life is somehow flawed.

So-called miracles reflect the power that is already within us. They reflect a deeply held trust in the power of spirit over matter. Prayer, like the butterfly effect, can literally change the world. That is why it is so important that we come together and pray communally. We still know very little about the power of the neurons in our brains.

Perhaps the full blossoming of synchronicity—which birds have already mastered—and mental telepathy—which we all experience—will be ours for the keeping one day. As Jesus said, "If you have faith you can move mountains." There are energies within us that we have not so far discovered, and they will all be explained as natural occurrences one day. The most fantastic thing about life is that still-unknown miraculous potencies lie hidden within our bodies. They have been all planned from the beginning. They have lain dormant since the big bang, but in some future time we will discover them. When they appear, they will have come—sensational as they may seem—out of natural process and not some supernatural intervention. God does not interfere with the evolutionary push. All miracles are natural. That is why prayer can move mountains. If enough of us come together in faith, we can disarm the armies of the world.

The illuminati who prescribe bloody onslaughts and war machinery for the sake of profit are atheistic materialists because their agenda is best supported by greed and exploitation. Most of the human race hopes for more. Belief in a better future is the primordial philosophy which at all times appears in the history of the world's tribal past. Victor Frankl wrote, "He who has a why to life can bear with almost any how." With atheistic materialism, our only why is the belly of our ego. Thus ends humanity's search for nobility.

Spirituality tells the story of logo-therapy. Hope springs eternally. The roots of belief are so deep inside the soul of humanity that they cannot be eradicated. The communist revolution in the Soviet Union tried to stamp out Christianity, but at this present moment, Russia under the leadership of Putin can rightly be considered the most mystic Christian country in the world.

Fyodor Dostoevsky, one of Mother Russia's most mystical writers, suffered horrendously in one of the Siberian gulags set up by the communists. It was in such a setting that he rediscovered his faith in Christ. In such an awful place of deprivation and pain, he at times experienced tremendous serenity: "There is nothing more beautiful, profound and manly than the image of Christ."

Dostoevsky's spirituality, gained through suffering, became the very foundation for his masterful writing. Through his experience, he became, as it were, a suffering servant who enabled humanity to reach for something higher. Only spirituality can give us the courage to face our own death and the death of others.

Dostoevsky was an adamant critic of Western civilization. He called Europe a beautiful cemetery. All his writings centred on the soul of man. Spirituality is the heart of the matter. All the main experiences of life concern the spirit and not essentially the body. Take spirit out of the equation, and we are dead before we live. Dostoevsky's writings are in total opposition to the demeaning purpose for which atheistic materialism prepares us.

Within each one of us lies the devil and the saint. We have a choice to make; we have free will. We are not determined genetically.

Our spirituality is such that we are called tangentially to move horizontally in a compassionate way. When we have accomplished this, we move vertically into the full completion of our consciousness. Evolution intends this for us. But when a society is indoctrinated to move in the opposite direction, it becomes corrupt and acts in an antispiritual way. This is why Dostoevsky called the West "a beautiful cemetery".

Since a sense of morality is stamped on our psyche by nature, we automatically know the difference between good and evil. Natural law always veers in the direction of the good. Though suffering is involved in the process, it leads to the noblest outcome. We carve out our spirituality at the precise intersection between the horizontal and the vertical. Our free will determines our future. Through our decisions, the energy of holiness or the energy of evil enters our world. Compassionate consciousness avalanches when we choose the good. Evil rushes in when we choose the bad. At the precise intersection between the horizontal and the vertical, viciousness or greatness enters the world.

So far, we have made the case that materialistic science is harmful to the earth—not only because it destroys the planet for its own exploitative purposes, but also because it obliterates hope and belief from the human prospect. It has turned our world into a flabby, empty, and vapid place. Can we make a case that the God of compassionate consciousness has the power to turn all this around? Can we prove that this supreme Intelligence exists at all?

Atheistic scientists, who study only what is local, demand evidence for the existence of God. From their point of view, God must be turned into an object before their study of a deity can be reasonably verified. If this cannot be done, then there is no proof that God exists. There is no evidence. Metaphorically, this is akin to saying that because just a drop of water exists, the waters of all the seas on earth do not exist. A drop can never prove an ocean. The great nonlocal Intelligence, ever working in and through the local, can never be discovered in terms of the local alone. The local does not give a definitive answer, but it does provide a clue. The atheistic approach imposes on the visible and local proof of the nonvisible and nonlocal. This can never be given. All we live on are but clues—and there are many of them.

The science of quantum physics points out that the whole is greater than the sum of its parts. The whole stands out from its parts. Quantum science has also discovered that the final particle of matter moves into consciousness, which lies in the realm of invisibility and no-thing-ness. Since this is true according to the objective study of the atom, how can no-thing be studied in a some-thing way? Quantum physics takes science into the higher realm of no-thing-ness and invisibleness. Quantum physics has taken us into the realm of the mystical.

Scientific, atheistic materialists do not have the credentials necessary to enter the room of this speciality. From their own premise, they have hubristically thrown the key away. They can rant all they want about how religion has done so much damage to the earth, but they have absolutely no right to make a judgement about the no-thing-ness and invisibleness of the Creator. Consciousness, by their own admission, does not lie in their remit, since from the start they have abandoned it.

For those who are awake to consciousness there are millions of clues exploding around us in our everyday world which disclose divinity to us. Despite the fact that we are exposed to ugliness and terrible evil in contemporary society, still millions of miracles explode around us every day in the midst of the ordinary.

Terribly, both organized religion and atheistic materialism have replaced awe and wonder with the tedium of ritual and the false indoctrination of consumer consumption. Atheistic materialism has attempted to dumb us down flabbily and vapidly. It has reinvented and twisted the story of our humanity to such a degree that it insists we evolved by mere chance, with no purpose except to fulfil the desire of our egos.

The steady-state theory of atheistic materialism abolishes the idea of a divine Creator, since without a beginning there is no need for a starter. Atheistic science believes that the earth has always been in existence.

Through the study of astrophysics, atheistic science has been proven wrong. The Hubble telescope in outer space has replaced the steady-state theory with the theory of the big bang. Our universe was born about fifteen billion years ago. Cosmic waves of that beginning have been observed by Hubble in outer space Another discovery of staggering proportions is that matter continues to expand throughout the universe. This is called entropy.

If that first spark in the universe's time had ignited creation even by a difference of two seconds, gravity would have pulled matter in on top of itself and disappear into a black hole. As a consequence, we would not be here to tell the story. If, on the other hand, gravity at the time of the original spark of creation had been greater, matter would only be vaporous and the galaxies, stars, and planets could not exist. Stephen Hawkins wrote that had the spark been smaller "by even one part in a hundred thousand million million the universe would have collapsed."

Through Hubble, we have also learned that our sun, huge as it seems to us, is but one of trillions in our own galaxy of the Milky Way. There are over one hundred billion such galaxies. Even more awe-inspiring is the story of our own little planetary home. We dangle in outer space with such accuracy that some kind of supreme intelligence must be behind the precision. For us to be here in our Goldilocks position, conditions also had to be precise. In order to survive, sentient life needs such chemicals as hydrogen, oxygen, nitrogen, sodium, carbon, and phosphates. If hydrogen and oxygen were missing, water would not be possible, and without water, there could not be crops to feed us. Nor indeed could we be. The marvel of the big bang is that all the chemicals needed for the human species to appear and survive on earth were there from the beginning. Zinc for our digestive system, calcium for our bones and iron for our haemoglobin were all present in the big bang. The macrocosm was connected to the microcosm. Our bodies are made of stardust.

If we were to become conscious of who we really are, we would surely spend more time in reverential prayer and contemplation. Each cell in our bodies contains in its nucleus our nervous, digestive, respiratory, excretory, circulatory, skin, reproductive, skeletal, and muscular systems. Each cell is an intelligent being. It can survive on its own. It has within it all the functions needed for life. It is by far more complex than any big city with all of its organisations to deliver food, take out garbage, and so on. Truly we are deified atoms and units of consciousness.

The automated factory of the cell carries out as many unique functions as all the manufacturing activities on earth. It is capable of replicating its entire structure within a matter of a few hours, and yet this remarkable piece of machinery that possesses the capacity to construct every living thing is several million times smaller than the smallest piece of functional machinery ever constructed by man.

Shamefully, we are more awestruck by our own creativity than by the construction of every cell which effortlessly builds our bodies. We admire man-made machinery but seldom take time to meditate on the marvellous craftsmanship in the intricacy and fragility our newborn babies.

Our brain is the greatest construction of all realities. It processes about one hundred million bits of information every second. But we remain unconscious of this invisible, silent, flawless intelligence working effortlessly inside us.

Atheistic science hubristically demands evidence, but reason evolves into intuition. Intuition is a higher way of knowing. Even atheistic scientists know this. It is impossible to use the parameters of the tangible to measure what is invisible and irreversible. This knowing which exceeds rationality must become the guide for human wisdom. It is anti-intuitive to release darkness or antimatter upon this world. Atheistic science will rue the day it releases it.

Intuition leads to a space outside of time and place. It indicates that, without the logic of mathematical, rational proof, we can recognize a space more heavenly than earth.

The wisdom and intelligence always so exquisitely labouring behind the mechanism of Mother Earth, though not totally understood, still indicates that good is more revelatory than evil. If the ear is out of tune, how can it ever understand the music of Beethoven?

One cell has the capacity to connect with fifty trillion other cells to form one body. Since consciousness is unitive, so also do all human beings on earth have the potential within them to become one family upon the earth. The cosmos is one, and in it, through consciousness, we are meant to be one in each other. Consciousness is the unifying field which glues all life together as parts to a whole. To act contrary to this universal law of nature is a sin.

War and killing violate this law of nature. If *Homo sapiens* evolves into the higher sphere towards which the natural law is attracting us, then peace and serenity will reign—not only in this world, but in the one hereafter.

The great Intelligence behind the evolutionary process has created us, with all our complexity, for this purpose. Consciousness has made us for eternal love. This is our destiny. When the materiality of the cell is coerced to flow against its own purpose in nature—as in transhumanism, Cern, and transgenetic experimentation—then antimatter will be released upon the face of the earth. An apocalypse, the likes of which Christian fundamentalists could never envisage, will devour humanity. Caught up in their preoccupation with Armageddon, hell will physically consume them too, even though they think they are the chosen few.

Through the indoctrination of atheistic materialism, we have been so diverted from consciousness that we no longer realize the darkness we live in. Our vision has been stunted. We no longer see the face of divinity within the cellular construction of our own bodies, nor in the beauty of the flowers who scatter their perfume on us free of charge. The greatest gifts of all are given to us freely. But we seldom say thank you to the sunlight or the rain. We continue our lives consumed with concerns that keep us from kneeling.

Complex unities do not come about by mere chance. They speak of Intelligence. The sin of atheism squeezes all mystery and awe out of everything. It separates us from our beginning and casts a disparaging look on humanity's project and prospect.

The fine-tuning of the universe is awe-inspiring and reflects the majesty of an ineffable Creator. *The God Delusion* was promoted atheistically to destroy the idea of divinity. It reflects more realistically the small-mindedness of its author than the authenticity of God. The likelihood of life coming from chance and randomness sounds like intellectual madness. It is estimated at one chance in a trillion multiplied by twelve trillion. Christopher Hawkins, the theoretical physicist who doubted God's existence, said that life could not exist if things were different by one degree.

The genius behind the universe, according to Albert Einstein, "has to be an intelligence of such superiority, that compared with it, all the synthetic thinking and acting of human beings is an utterly insignificant reflection."

As though this is not enough to prove the existence of a Creator, the new science of biology has begun to point to a Creator whose intelligence is evident behind the human body.

The biology of the human body presents us with amazing facts. Most of us are not at all conscious of the invisible, effortless, intelligent functioning behind the various parts of our own bodies. We readily become impressed with extraordinary events, but the greatest miracles of all happen every day in the midst of the ordinary. Our consciousness has been so misdirected that, even when surrounded by the holy and the sacred, we live on the unconscious level. Preoccupied with delight in what is purely material, we substitute what is secondary for what must be primary. There is a shrine within each one of us, but, conditioned to be materially Pavlovian, we scarcely ever visit it. We reserve our greatest praise and appreciation for the machines of man, but scarcely ever give the same reverence and respect to the ingenious machinery of our own bodies.

Each day our bones manufacture one billion red blood cells. Our ears can discriminate between three million tones. The human eye translates photons of light into an image with a speed that no computer is capable of analysing. Our fingertips have thirteen hundred nerve endings. We hear a ten-billionth of sound under the noise of a jet plane. The human brain, weighing only three pounds, is capable of analysing more information than all the computers of the world put together.

The consciousness of God the Creator is working silently and effortlessly inside of each one of us every day, restructuring the bones of our bodies to accommodate our needs and making endorphins in our brains—endorphins which are twice as potent as any drug manufactured to bring mental stability into our lives. All this is given to us for free.

There is an invisible spirit at work inside each one of us, organizing the chemicals in our bodies. As our bodies develop, our senses grow and our nerves, muscles, and glands expand. All these creative happenings occur within our own bodies, but we scarcely notice them. Intuitively, though deep down, we know they have been orchestrated by a benevolent Intelligence.

Wrapped around the forty-six chromosomes in each cell of our bodies is a string which, if unravelled, would be 196 million miles long. The complexity of DNA, as the brain behind each cell in the human body, is truly amazing. Francis Crick, the codiscoverer of DNA, believed, like Richard Dawkins, that natural selection was the last stop on the evolutionary train. But when confronted by the marvels of the DNA, he said life on earth could not be explained materially: "An honest man, armed with all the intelligence available, could only state, that in some sense, the origin of life, appears at the moment to almost be a miracle, so many are the conditions needed to get it going."

With the unravelling of the DNA running through every one of the fifty trillion cells in the human body, Crick and Watson discovered that there was but a tiny register of difference between humanity and other primates. This discovery shocked atheistic scientists to the core, since they believed that genetically we were leaps and bounds ahead of our lower primate cousins. They had always proposed that our genes determine us and not a creator God.

To add another nail to the coffin of atheistic materialism, biology, which was so adamant about an atheistic explanation for life, has begun to move in the direction of design. Bruce Lipton points out in his book *The Biology of Belief* that it is our environment rather than our genes which determines us. We are not the victims of our genes.

Since the environment of the twenty-first century is culturally atheistic, it becomes immediately clear that we are not genetically disposed to be evil. It is materialist atheism which is determining us. The corruption, stress, horror, murder, and mayhem which we experience in our world today is all the result of the atheistic agenda with which the Zionist elites control us.

Truly, heaven starts where the foot falls. Hell does also. It is up to each one of us to untie the knot which binds and enslaves us. Our own spirituality is the only warranty. We are in eternity already. Indifference carries over into the hereafter. We are our own definers!

Our planet is a holy place, created magnificently. With a different perspective, we see that earth is a small blue berry hanging in outer space, almost insignificant in terms of the universe. And yet of all the places in our solar system, it is a Goldilocks paradise, placed carefully in the exact right position for our species to sustainably survive. Locked in by gravitation, our streams and our rivers flow into a sea moved inexorably by a moon. Do we ever wonder about the power of the ocean as it plays its daily game of golf? What precision and what a swing—it scores a birdie every time.

We fly on a spaceship at the rate of 187,000 miles per hour, and yet we are not cognisant of the movement. We do not feel the rush of air all around us. All seems stationary and solid. Without any human radar to guide our spaceship, we land as though we hadn't even begun. What a smooth run!

We have become too complacent with the ordinary and the seeming. Material atheism has dulled our imagination much too much. Consciousness, however, turns the ordinary into the extraordinary. The trees, the tall green trees of the forest, build spires of reverence into the heavens, offering their hospitality to the little creatures who seek seclusion and the serenity of their own eternity among its branches. With a balance in their intake and exhalation, they clean and they build quite equally. There is an effortless process always at work within the forest. Day and night, they pump out oxygen perfectly scaled in the correct equation. If oxygen were emitted at 20 per cent, all breathing animals on earth would asphyxiate. At 22 per cent, sentient life on earth would incinerate.

Consciousness runs through everything.

There is enough energy in a single leaf to electrify a city the size of New York for a day. We take delight in the moss-dappled greenery at the foot of a tree, the likes of which no spinner on earth could weave. A deer darts, splitting the sun apart. A blackbird sings a melody as profound as any symphony. And every breath on earth is a hosanna. God's voice is inaudible, but the language of divinity is unmissable. You will hear it in the patter of the rain on a tin roof, or in the hurried rush of a mountain stream over rocks. If you listen intensely, a stream will speak to you. It will tell you that life is infinite departure. The coloured leaves on the autumn trees say goodbye as they morph into their own sort of eternity. Everything that lives is transient. The only constant is metamorphosis.

Say hello to the natural world always, because you are a part of it and it is a part of you. Hold hands with each other and sometimes hug and kiss a bit. Never become an abstraction to presence, because that will release negative energy. There is already too much of it. God does not like it.

There is more serenity to be found in the midst of the natural world than in all the distractions and amusements of man. Go more to the seashore and listen to the swell and retreat of the waves. Nothing is possible without its opposite. Every swell and retreat of the wave echoes the pulsation of your own heartbeat. We are all in the one nothingness.

When we awake to consciousness, an enveloping compassion will take hold of us. We will recover the sense of our own self-worth and kindle respect for the other that is within us. We will never again feel alone nor like cosmic orphans wandering in the dark. We will return to our invisible nothingness, which is our source and completion. We are but a happening between two great secrets.

Atheism has its source in the null and the void of body and soul. It is even intolerant of agnosticism. Where opposites are not allowed to clash, there can be no creativity. Spirituality is built on inspiration and hope, but atheism is built on its own conclusion. It is intolerant of its opposite—even though, as it so often proclaims, the mind is tooled by curiosity. Atheism is not open to the subtlety of wonder nor consequent reverence.

Why are we so timid to leave the material and jump into a new possibility? Nature teaches us to let go of our security and make a leap into the unknown. Why are we so afraid to surrender when the natural world, through all the paintings in her book, suggests surrender?

When you listen to something as simple as the sound of water, you are like a rich man entering heaven.

—Seamus Heaney

"God is in the bits and pieces of everyday, a kiss here and a laugh again and sometimes tears, a pearl necklace round the neck of poverty"
And the beautiful beautiful beautiful GOD
shows his face in a cut- away Bog.

—Patrick Kavanagh

Dostoevsky offers no solution for humanity except spirituality. Born with the same capacity for evil or good and blessed with free will, we each have a choice to become a part of civil society or be swamped with corruptibility. We can, if we so choose, move into the oneness of consciousness by becoming more aware. If we open ourselves to the possibility of our highest instincts, then we will find serenity. Such awareness will help us overcome the jagged rocks of suffering in the surrender of our river-run to our sea.

It is only through such a surrender that even the fear of death can disappear. Though terror be all around us, with our focus on the eternal, we can make a quantum leap into that realm where serenity will complete us. Through the discipline which spirituality imposes, we will find our collectiveness as parts flowing into the one whole.

Dostoevsky—in total contradiction to Karl Marx, who disdainfully dismissed rural life—praised the beauty of the earth and its sacramental nature. "One has to grow on the soil where the trees and the corn are growing." Dostoevsky recognized the natural world and our fellowship with all creatures as the source from which all our inspiration emanates.

Brothers, do not fear man's sins. Love man in his sin too, for such love
resembles God's love, the highest possible form of love on earth.
Love God's creation, love every atom of it
separably and love it also as a whole.
Love every green leaf, every ray of God's light.
Love the animals and the plants and love every inanimate object.
If you come to love all things, you will perceive God's
mystery inherent in all things; once you have perceive
it, you will understand better every day.
And finally you will love the whole world with a total universal love.

—Dostoevsky

CHAPTER CONSCIOUSNESS

I t seems incredible that every cell of my body replicates me. Each cell of my body can live alone. The totality of me is in each cell just as each cell is my totality. Living humanity lies in a nest of consciousness joining us together in the unity of the great Oneness. Mesmerizing as this sounds, not only am I in the universe, but the universe is in me.

Consciousness means to be in the one great circle of the universe. To live fully in this world is to manifest what is unmanifest about us. We are made for noble purposes. When we internalize this, we become integrated and happy. Even mortal death is transmuted when we live consciously. The more we become conscious of our own interiority, the more we recognize our oneness with the beauty of the earth. To live consciously is to hear the true melody in every integrated aspect of earth. Chaos is always resolved by harmony when we live consciously.

We need to bring our own presence to beauty before we can appreciate it. Our presence cannot be present when we live unconsciously. Our presence is the greatest present we can possibly give ourselves. We spend 95 per cent of our time absent from our presence. We do not know how to be still and kiss and hug ourselves. Instead of morphing from the unconscious into the conscious, we spend most of our precious time on earth in shopping malls.

We are out of tune. We sell the nobility of our souls for trinkets that will not, because they cannot, ever satisfy us. We give our at-one-ment with consciousness away for a tube of lipstick or maybe a car. In the end it does not matter anyway. Lonely stays the heart that does not dig deep into consciousness. Smell, taste, touch, hearing, and sight are in reality invisible. It is only by inviting them up to the plane of consciousness that we can appreciate them. When they lie on the plane of our unconscious, they lose their reference.

When the unconscious prevails, presence disappears and the conscious heart is absent. The unconscious becomes dominant without consciousness and manipulates the mind to attend to stuff instead of God.

A deep unconsciousness has a gravitational pull into corruption, such as we see in the West today. A government whose main preoccupation is the economy and the profit gained from selling military arms becomes corrupt, which in turn produces greater moral problems on the home front.

Beauty and truth are only present to the extent that we are conscious. God cannot come alive unless we are present to consciousness. It is not possible to be present to truth when we live a lie. The beauty of this world escapes us when we live unconsciously.

When we allow ourselves to be controlled by atheistic materialism, we pander to a false identity. A consumer culture loves spiritually dead and illiterate citizens, because it is easier to manage the hordes and sell to them that way. Its best clients are the ones who live unconsciously, satisfying only the desires of their egos. If truth were ever allowed to surface, we would see that what is profitable to the shopping malls drains away our moral fibre.

Edward Bernays, member par excellence of the elites, has changed the frequency of universal light into something obtainable through the spectrum of visible light. He has hijacked humanity from its higher vision. Bernays was the man who capitalized on our unquenchable longing. He used it to promote the selling of desirable material objects as an answer to our search for God It was a clever move because it enriched the elites and catered to the human ego's needs without any spiritual responsibility.

The devastating results of turning the body into something supreme is exploding around us daily. Corruption arises without moral guidance. Elitist atheists, through their total control of mass media, have distracted the Western mind with such an incredible amount of lust and violence that their dumbed-down clients accept it as normal. "Life is cheap" is the mantra of the elites. The main aim of the illuminati is to dethrone our mystical capability. Contemporary entertainment is merely a shill which the elites use to distract us. Shocking as it may sound, the passion which sports generate has been propagandized to such a degree that men cry more over a loss in a sporting match than they do at the sight of their newborn babies. Competition more than cooperation invites passion in our big brother world.

If a spiritual paradigm is allowed to emerge, what we consider but a chapter will become the benign conclusion to our book.

Psychological manipulation turned humanity's search for something transcendent into an immanent object, which brought cessation to our eternal longing. The more beautiful and fashionable the object, the more humanity craves it. The more the craving, the more the dismantling of our satisfaction. God has been turned into an object to be bought in a shopping mall.

To live consciously, we must shift away from all the indoctrination pumped into our unconscious behaviour patterns. Most humans live out their lives unconsciously, with the same values by which the environment has shaped them. If the environment has been negative, then the person will grow up as a victim, thinking more negatively than positively. If a child grows up in a home where there is no affirmation or compassion, then that child will evolve in an emotionally deprived way. Henceforth the child will search for some substitute to replace the loss of conscious love.

The compassion which consciousness offers is a universal entitlement. To the extent we are denied it, to the same extent we remain deprived. Material objects are seldom bought out of necessity, but as an exercise to satisfy the deprivation of the affirmation our spirit yearns for. Atheistic materialism serves as a substitute for the searching and the longing of the human spirit. It is the very antithesis of a fulfilling existence.

When we live consciously, we live sustainably. We meet our human needs while at the same time respecting the heart and lungs of the earth.

Our contemporary paradigm of atheistic materialism becomes more and more energized through the fakery of its offerings. It destroys our consciousness of being conscious and sends us metaphorically in the direction of hell rather than heaven. It tells us we will stay forever young or totally satisfied if only we will buy its latest offering. It is because we live mostly on the unconscious level that we drink in the indoctrination of atheistic materialism.

On the other hand, if we live on the conscious level, we know we need the love and the compassion of universal consciousness to sustain and complete us. If we do not begin to live on the conscious level, then not only the self but the whole earth will incrementally collapse. It is dangerous to live atheistically. It is the abandonment of all that is deepest, both inside and outside of us. We becomes more spiritual to the extent that we live consciously.

In order to live on the conscious level, we must, as Jesus said, "to thine own self be true". To be conscious is to face our inner and outer truth. To be conscious is to know the interdependence, interconnection, and interrelationship of all living things. To be conscious is to know all that lives is caught up in the oneness of consciousness. This is what spirituality is all about. To be conscious is to know the world we live in is a sacred environment where even the smallest happening is a theophany. A million disclosures can exist underneath a rock, there for our discovery. Worms are the ploughers of the soil, without which no food would grow to sustain us. Without the honeybee, humanity would die in as little as four years. The big bang continues to spark in the midst of the ordinary, but because we live unconsciously, we have lost our connection with the natural world.

Atheistic materialism disjoints us, insisting only on egotistical superfluity, while our spirit yearns for the literacy of unity. To live consciously is to learn to appreciate the interconnection of all living things. To integrate spirit with matter is the primary call facing the human race. To accomplish this, we need to shift from unconsciousness into becoming conscious. It is through being conscious that we learn not only our own individual, truth, beauty, and dignity, but also the same splendour rampant in the totality of humanity.

We cannot give what we do not have. Consciousness brings with it association. Its very existence is built on unity. Like concentric circles, it draws us back to the centre with the same energy in that first spark of creativity. We are all one essentially. We have already noticed the magnificent creativity so gloriously alive in each cell of the human body. The next step in our trail of glory is to drive our evolutionary genesis into the oneness of consciousness.

Rather than humanity's drive towards a higher consciousness, atheistic materialism insists we disassociate from a future of transcendental meaning and purpose. Cells get sick in the environment of atheism. Just look at what is happening to Western civilization. We have learned too readily to sabotage life, thereby giving oxygen to atheistic materialism.

The more we allow ourselves to be victimized through atheistic materialism, the more powerfully will fear and insecurity incarcerate us. False flags create terror and make us more amenable to control and subjugation. A society frightened out of its wits by the fear of terrorism usually looks in the wrong direction to discover its source. Propaganda and mind control have their source far closer to home than we could ever imagine. Only spirituality will tell us the truth. It is the sins of our own nations which should be feared most. In a world turned upside down and inside out, the saint is the real sinner and the sinner the real saint.

To live consciously is to choose love over fear. Love is a state of being. When we choose love, we radiate love. By choosing the higher frequency of love, we live positively. We negate all the evil stuff involved in the formation of our unconscious. Through the power of love, we can change the dominating power with which atheistic materialism controls us.

To be conscious is to know the very core of who we really are. What we seek is what we are—quantum physics teaches us this. If we accept the tenets of atheistic materialism, then we are allowing atheism to do our thinking for us. Atheism is a destroyer. Consciousness is a restorer.

We are infinite awareness. Consciousness assures us we are made in the image of God.

I raised you up and have given you a place in the heavens.

—Isaiah

What a piece of work is man!
How noble in reasonably
How infinite in faculties
In form and moving how expert and admirable
In action how like an angel

In apprehension, how like a God
The beauty of the world
the paragon of animals.

—Shakespeare

Atheism is not happy with this plan. In a culture of nanotechnology, man spits the Creator in the face, robbing humanity of its glorious destiny. In a world where only matter matters, human beings become transmuted into cyborgs.

We look out upon the exterior world, and we are absolutely convinced that what we see is three-dimensional reality. In reality, it is our thinking that is creating this vision. The human mind, and through it the human eye, only reflects a very small part of the energy existing outside itself. What we see is but a small interpretation on the backs of our brains, which registers as external reality. That reality is not in the brain. It exists apart from its interpretation. So the material world is really an illusion.

Quantum physics teaches that consciousness is the groundswell of everything. It is what is within us and outside us. Akin to the human cell, consciousness eternally replicates itself, gathering all life into the unity of living. It is not possible to live apart from the embrace of consciousness.

We are finitude enveloped in the infinite. We are a part of ineffable infinity. When we become aware of the fact that divinity defines us, a passion arises within us to conduct ourselves in the direction of the good. We live outwardly because of the consciousness within us. We learn to live compassionately because of the love inside of us. God, in creating us, has made us with a first love, and our mission now is to create a paradise here among us. We are called to be ambassadors of love. That is what consciousness consists of. We throw a rose to a rose.

The atheism which the Zionist illuminati propose demeans our divinity. By denying humanity its dignity and positive self-image, the Zionist illuminati aim to keep themselves in luxury while we as their slaves eat the crumbs from their tables. Through the indoctrination of mass media, Western civilization, instead of standing erect and acting intelligently, lies low on lullaby couches, filling its belly with bromides and its mind with lies.

We are deified atoms and droplets in an infinite ocean of consciousness. So long as we know this, no power on earth can control us. When we learn that we are made for love and stay on the level of consciousness, no fear on earth will overcome us.

The energy of consciousness lies deep within us. The deeper we dig, the more radial energy enables and inhabits us. The more we live life on the conscious level, the more radial dwelling will be the energy of the world.

Atheism invites out of us the lowest possible vibrational energy. Its aim is to totally abolish critical thinking. It is terrified of social unrest.

When a revolution of social consciousness arises, humanity shakes off the shackles of fear that were created to control them. Energized by consciousness, the spiritual new world order becomes one of love instead of fear.

There is a source and a powerful presence within us at all times. It is our higher consciousness. When we consciously choose to tap into it, we become passionate about all that is primary and of moral significance in this world. When we choose to be conscious, we enter a source field that is filled with the energy of the entire universe. The deeper we seek the source, the deeper we discover vibrational energy.

Consciousness essentially relates to connectivity. It is more about being than doing. For those who live morally, there is a source, a power, and a presence working through them. By living conscience-ly, we enter the all-embracing field of consciousness. We are vessels of infinite awareness.

The nihilistic approach which atheism preaches in declaring the death of God can never be successful. Atheism fails to recognize that the death of God on the outside can never lead to the death of God on the inside. The invisible realm is eternal. Even though atheistic materialism dismisses God, the fact remains that the invisibility of the spiritual lies in a higher realm. It will continue, no matter what dogma atheistic science propagates against it. We are doomed to be spiritual. We are hard-wired for consciousness. If we really knew who walks along with us, inside and outside of us, we would never fear again!

Our mental energies become depleted through atheistic materialism and consequently emit negative vibrations. We become the realization of our unconscious. On the other hand, if we live on the conscious level of our deified dignity and self-worth, we live love because we are love. With this attitude, we can overcome even the fear of death itself.

Where consciousness lives, there is no dust. What is deepest about us becomes enlarged, no longer hampered by the body. Free at last, the spirit is consumed with the consciousness of love.

We heal ourselves to the extent that we give our conscious energy to the unifying field of consciousness. Unfortunately, 95 per cent of our ordinary lives are spent unconsciously. We live most of our lives preoccupied with the trivia with which atheistic materialism has indoctrinated us. Not only has atheistic materialism robbed us of the wonder of our precise and miraculous place in the universe, but even more dangerously, it has robbed us of the realization that we are all in one another. The cosmos is one. Atheism turns us into geocentrists and egocentrists.

Our contemporary concerns are generally about money and the temporal. We give most of our energy to the fear of insecurity. Atheistic materialism desires our desires never to be sated. Its profits grow to the extent that the suffering which desire causes mounts up inside each one of us. We give most of our energy to this concentric circle which holds us in subjugation. Desire is future-orientated, aroused by the insufficiencies of the past. In the very centre between past and future lies the now of our focus.

It is the time to make a critical decision. This is the moment which never existed in the before or the after of our lives. It is the epiphanic moment in our existence. What we do with it determines our eternity. It is the moment we decide to live consciously or stay bunked down, passively living unconsciously.

It is precisely because we live on the unconscious level that we condition our fear and insecurity. Anxiety, depression, and stress come from the fear which our environment produces. It is we ourselves, both individually and collectively, who allow the karma of the subconscious to swamp our lives. Then, like the soft receptivity of a sponge, we absorb the indoctrination which the slave master uses to control us. We will die with our music still in us.

This planet has been brought to its knees. It has grown tired and weary from all the negative, aggressive energy poured upon it, both collectively

165

and individually. Through the habitual savagery of atheistic materialism, the divinity of humanity and its connection to all living things has been tortured. All that matters to the bloated overlords is that their own inflated egoic needs be satisfied.

Consciousness, which is the unifying field of the earth, never intended that 2 per cent of the world's population should have dominion over the remaining 98 per cent. Such an arrangement cries out to heaven for justice.

Humanity needs an axial turn into consciousness. We need to connect matter with spirit. There can be no future for humanity without God in it.

When we begin to live as the natural law of consciousness demands then we will be more concerned with hugs and kisses than the economy. When we decide to put back into our portrait the great nonlocal Intelligence who is the totality of all consciousness, then human suffering and death will be better understood. Through consciousness, when death confronts us, we are enabled to stand tall and face it like Cuchulainn, one of the great heroes in Irish mythology. The wholeness of consciousness overcomes all our fears and worries. Death engenders birth when we enter the world of consciousness.

Jesus of Nazareth has probably been the dominant figure in the history of Western civilization for the past two thousand years. The very date of our calendar was first installed in memory of his birth among us. Many both pray and curse in his name. His existence lives in our unconscious. We often blurt out his name in consternation, but more often in petition and aspiration.

The gospels of the Evangelists portray Jesus as a man of compassion, courage, humility, and impeccable moral character. More books have been written about this central heroic man than anyone else in Western civilization. His aphorism, "Do unto others as you would have them do unto you," has been the bedrock for all laws based on justice and equality. In his time, he lived in a totally countercultural way. He treated women with dignity and not as a bunch of brood mares, as the Semitic minds of patriarchal men did in his time. His Sermon on the Mount created a new paradigm in morals and ethics.

Inspired by his message of compassion and love, all kinds of humanitarian institutions such as schools, hospitals, and clinics have been instituted. H. G. Wells said that Jesus left the greatest legacy in human history. That being the case, why is it only now in our vulgar culture that the magnificence of this holy man's witness can be so easily blasphemed? Despite the terrible defilement and usurpation of a church which hijacked his message, why are Talmudic Jews and atheists allowed to attack Christ and never be condemned? Is this not like Christians smearing all Jews with the tenets of Zionism? Why, in the so-called Christian West, do Christians feel so pressured to omit the name of Christ in Christmas? Even if the story of his birth is purely mythological, why on earth must the name of Christ be excised by an "X" at Christmastime? What is so wrong about remembering the poetic teachings of the Beatitudes? Why must believing Christians be accused of insensitivity in the recall of this magnificent man's memory?

The West achieved its greatest expression through the edifice of Christ's teachings. Christians, like everyone else, love the poetry and civilizing teachings of their founder. This man Jesus, who was such a magnificent universalist, never preached hatred, but precisely its opposite. Why then should believing Christians feel so guilt-ridden and burdened with the baggage of insensitivity in the celebration of this luminous figure who brought good tidings to all men of goodwill? Why does the memory of such goodness threaten the atheistic materialists especially, while hypocritically they gather millions in profit from the desecration of his holy name at Christmastime?

If Jesus is part of the cultural identity of Western civilization, then despite the misrepresentation and true dispensation of the love and compassion he taught and delivered, why should Christianity bow to any other religious or political system?

The foundational value of his teachings is the greatest of all messages— not because of a church, but because of Christ, who is its core. The message of Jesus is cosmotheandric. He has unapologetically taught this message to a world which needs a new social construct. The terrible tragedy of Christianity is that it has not taken his message seriously. It has instead allowed the creeping virus of materialistic atheism to chew us up.

Convinced of our own dignity and self-worth, we can bring healing to others by our own witness. We can do it by loving. We each can become our own scripture.

Christianity is caught. It cannot be taught. It is up to each one of us to release ourselves from the hospital ward we have placed ourselves in. It is time for the Christian world to wake up and reclaim its heritage.

Jesus singularly told the world in an iconic way that love conquers all.

I mentioned in an earlier chapter that on the evolutionary ladder, Teilhard de Chardin placed Christ on the rung of a higher achievement. De Chardin called this step christogenesis. This is now called the era of the cosmic Christ, in terms of theological parlance. Placing Jesus on a higher evolutionary plane than the rest of struggling humanity may be considered discriminatory by the vast majority of people who do not profess Christianity. But if we look at Christ in a spiritual rather than a religious way, we cannot but stand in awe at his heroic goodness and courage. Even though he had never heard of quantum physics or the message of consciousness as the unifying field of humanity, he lived it like no one else before him and very few since. Even Nietzsche, as a nihilist, was very impressed with the life of Jesus the Nazarene. He deemed Christ as the only person in this life who had lived in a Christian way. Dostoevsky warned that if Jesus Christ had never lived, then the human race would have had to create him. Jesus the man has achieved the ideal which humanity is called to be.

G. K. Chesterton wrote, "The only thing wrong with Christianity is that it has never been tried."

When Gandhi was asked what he thought of Christianity, he answered, "It is a good idea."

It would seem that Edmund Burke, the Irish parliamentarian, was right when he said, "For evil to survive, all that is necessary is for good men to do nothing."

Christianity has become somnambulant. We are the good men who are doing nothing. Atheistic materialism has made us into stooges. We have been sleeping while atheism has been making hay. We have allowed the atheistic agenda to take our rights away. Those who were supposed to watch the gate fell asleep and became accomplices to the assassin.

Rejection is never enough. Reconstruction is necessary. Even though the old guard may not realize it yet, a stone a fortress can be toppled without even one stone being disassembled. Rot comes from within and inevitably will happen unless there is sufficient enlightenment to change it. Lust, desire, and power are its worst enemy.

If we, the laity, will wake up from our passive, indifferent way, this earth of ours will become a different place. Atheism will scurry to the periphery instead of covertly controlling us. The teachings of Jesus plead that we come home to our own centre and Godness.

We have been brought forth out of an eternal love, and we return with that same embrace. To live consciously is to be aware of our beginning and our return. This is our main task on earth. We have been created for and with a deep spirituality. Jesus knew this as the primary reason for human existence. He asked that we get our priorities in order. "Look to the birds of the air ... they gather nothing into barns ... Look to the lilies of the field ... not even Solomon in all his glory was arrayed like one of these ... Will not God the father provide for you in the same way?"

"Naive and utterly insane," the atheistic materialist says!

We are inexorably taught that "the wisdom of insecurity" is pure nonsense. Trust is impossible.

People of flesh and blood cannot reasonably live this way. We are meant to upgrade the human condition into an ever-expanding infinity of convenience and progress.

Jesus warns that this attitude will ruin not only our environment but our own place in it. "The moth eats and the rust devours." Jesus teaches there is no way of escaping from this, the command of the natural law. To keep constantly in touch with the teachings of nature is to learn the wisdom of the ages. Walk the path less frequented. Go the other way. Invest your eyes with a new way of seeing. Surrender and accept. As Maura, a character in the play *Riders to the Sea*, says, "No man at all on this earth can be living forever and we must be satisfied."

To vehemently oppose the wisdom of the natural law with empty promises, as atheistic materialism does, is an insidious insult to human intuition. To deny the existence of some great, beneficent Intelligence always threading the cobweb of life and holding it together is to break the interconnecting threads and hubristically take delight in the plunder.

Despite our human prejudices—caused mostly by culture and religion,—the fact remains that on the human level, Jesus the Nazarene is surely a man for all seasons. If Jesus were physically present with us on this earth today, he would interpenetrate humanity's psyche with the same message. We are meant to live as one, under the attention of the one Consciousness. Consciousness embraces each one as a part of the whole. There is no separation of the human body and its continuum of spirituality into the afterworld.

Jesus told us that the kingdom of heaven is within us. We have the free will to accept it or reject it. The decision is our own. We can live precisely on our paltry, threadbare couches with our minds desacralized, or we can choose consciously to trust the intuition that we are made for more.

Atheistic materialism is so terrified of death that it faces it by denying it. Why is humanity so ready to believe in the darkness before death and so terrified to accept the darkness after death? Consciousness is a continuum. It is a birth-death experience. Death is the train which brings us to a new station. It cannot be measured through special location. It is the only nonnegotiable reality in this world.

Consciousness continues forever. It is the bedrock of an ongoing river-flow. To be human is to know that in its respect, we do not know very much. All we can do is surrender to it. We should not fret nor worry about it, because a Presence is already within us which turns immanence into transcendence. But for the awakening of our consciousness, we are home already.

> The dead are not under the earth
> They are in the tree that rustle
> They are in the forest that groans
> They are in the water that runs
>
> —Francis Nnaggenda

Jesus, as one of us, lived what he preached. He lived out his God consciousness magnificently. No one among us has lived forgiveness as he did. Even in his last moments of torture, he cried from the wood of a tree, "Father, forgive them." How can this world ever forget this new message of love, which was so counter to the law of his culture: *lex talionis*, an eye for an eye and a tooth for a tooth.

This law of forgiveness was iconic then, as it is even to this day. If the whole human race were to follow this law of the Nazarene, the bombs and the bullets of the world would be turned into butterballs. Humanity would be beautifully served if the mighty powers of the West incorporated a meditation on the essential meaning of love and forgiveness, instead of staging their Bible breakfasts while hypocritically engaging in violence. Such hypocrisy is a pure mockery to the love and forgiveness which the consciousness of unity demands. It is time for a new paradigm.

The central mission of Jesus was to show us the way to reach our own Godness. He spent his life trying to lead the culture of his time towards a loftier horizon. The full complement of vibrational consciousness arose within him. He was determined to join heaven and earth together. Consciousness was a living, physical experience for him. "That they all Father, shall be one, as you are in me and I in you."

As in contemporary society, evil ran rampantly through the political and religious institutions of Jesus's day. At the age of 30, with a passion for a growth in consciousness, he trod his dusty land, living and teaching that there is a higher way to reach the fullness of life than the egoic one. He recognized the material impoverishment which the Roman Empire imposed on the Jews, and he raged against it. But he preached nonviolence as a way to accomplish justice. He never wielded a gun or a bomb, and yet two thousand years later the world still remembers him.

Martin Luther King Jr accomplished great things for his race because of the teachings of Jesus. "Do unto others as you would have them do unto you" is the most unifying message of justice this world has ever heard. This must become the central message which the governments and religions of this world attempt to inculcate. In comparison to this, the rest is gibberish.

This message of love and forgiveness impressed the heart of Western civilization for almost two thousand years. His story, of course, has been intercoursed by a church with its own agenda. While the details of the message cause dissension and disagreement, the core of his message still stands clear to haunt and challenge humanity.

Jesus spoke like no prophet before him. He blessed the ordinary events of the everyday. He made God as proximate and available as the pumping vigour of the human heart. He told us clearly that God rambles in everyone and everything. His parables and aphorisms applied to the routine of daily experiences. He spoke paradoxically. Opposites, when turned around, yielded new meaning, such as "find by giving away" and "receive by losing". No one, as far as the peasantry of his culture were concerned, had ever spoken like this before.

"Let him who has never sinned, cast the first stone."

"Love your neighbor as yourself."

"Do unto others as you would have them do unto you."

"Love one another as I have loved you."

"Which of you, having an ass or a cow fall into a well on a holy day will not try to retrieve it? … The Sabbath was made for man … not man for the Sabbath."

Jesus turned many of the tenets of his culture inside out and upside down. He was a truly a countercultural, courageous man. He broke the Sabbath law on his mission of love and forgiveness. He excoriated the religious leaders of his day. He chased moneylenders from the Temple. He gave comfort to sinners and confronted the self-righteous. He stayed far away from the illuminati of his day and recognized the atrocities they committed against the impoverished and the innocent.

His Sermon on the Mount remains one of the most devastatingly beautiful and hopeful testaments to the power of love in this world. He told impressive stories which ended with an unexpected message. They were totally countercultural, such as the parables of the Good Samaritan and the Prodigal Son.

In recounting the incident of the Samaritan woman at the well, Jesus acted in an anticultural way. Not only did he give women their due dignity, but equally important, he gave respect to Samaritans, who were the most despised tribe in the Semitic world.

In a world where atheistic materialism reigns, the story of Jesus the Nazarene, who by all accounts was a compassionate and gentle man, has become sneeringly intolerable. Isn't the central truth of his universal and nonjudgemental message as appealing and relevant to a hurting world as it always was? Why has this iconic man's message been so disastrously rejected in modern society? Why is he, of all good men, no longer considered our greatest Western hero? Why has Santa been allowed to become his impostor? Does there not seem to be some hidden agenda to erase his name from our cultural history? If he were ever again to be deemed the most iconic man in our history, then the tills of the West would jingle-bell less and be replaced by an exchange of compassion.

To offset the lie of atheism, it is now imperative that the Christian world wake up and resurrect the Christ message all over again. His second coming has to be now or never.

The reality is, Jesus is A MYTH
Christianity along with other theistic systems is the fraud of the ages
—Peter Joseph

Atheism, in its attempt to bash Christianity to death, has used debatable scholarship and illogical argument, mistaking the particular for the universal. Even if many of the details in the story of Christ's birth and death are myths, his central message must be taken seriously as the great hymn of a new earth.

Atheistic materialism uses mass media in such a way that, apart from its political propaganda, it more insidiously encourages us to gorge ourselves on the distraction and amusement it fantastically dishes out to us. Then, when we have been initiated into a longing for the horror and violence, atheistic materialism is ready to sow its seed of total control and disempowerment. Like a praying mantis, it will devour us. We will end up in the gulags they are essentially preparing for us.

Witness for instance the Ten Commandments of the new world order hacked into the Atlanta Guide Stone. How could any nation whose very constitution has been so sensitively crafted through the inspiration of Christianity allow the agents of atheism to so arrogantly and confidently proclaim such a vision?

An agenda of diabolical, incremental proportions is even now unfolding in our midst. But the Christian West has yet to awaken to its malevolence. We are dehumanized of our individual dignity. The elites see us merely as cogs in their machinery of slavery. The sprawling crawl of atheism is everywhere. It is in the silence of organized religion! When has the voice of the US church been heard to condemn its government for the slaughter of innocence in the Middle East? Silence becomes the tongue of acquiescence when consciousness is absent. Religion is as corrupt in its silence as atheism is in its propaganda.

We have arrived at a juncture in the Christian West where the Golden Rule has become expendable. Pay enough money to an atheistic lawyer and be judged an innocent man for the murder you have committed. Give a big endowment to a school and it will inculcate the atheistic agenda of the elites. Money can put the final payment on any educational system. Like organized religion, there is nothing the atheism of the elites despises more than critical thinking.

Who controls money
controls the world.
—Henry Kissinger

The supranational sovereignty of an intellectual Elite and World Bankers is surely preferable to the national auto-determination practised in past centuries.
—David Rockefeller

We are confronted by an appalling and devious enemy. The heritage of Western Christianity is about to be thrown on the dump hill of life by the creeping virus of atheism. The Christian West is allowing its past to be obliterated with scarcely a protest. When it's gone, it will be missed, because with it goes our worth and human dignity.

Atheism can and should be a tool in refining the insufferable nonsense of Christian fundamentalism, But when it becomes the outrageous force that it is today, invading and threatening every corner of Christianity, then surely the pendulum of its arrogance must be pulled back to a more reasonable middle.

Atheism makes a mockery out of organized religion, and rightly so, for its barbarism and extreme fundamentalism. The time has come for the Christian West to call atheism to task for the collapse of modern society and its devious plan to control and dominate it.

As life unfolds, materialistic atheism is now in a position, as the church was in the Middle Ages, to totally control human intelligence. Since man was less technologically developed in the Middle Ages, the potential for total disaster is now much greater. Without a moral compass, the dominant atheistic force will bring the human race to the edge. Only the balance which spirituality brings can save us.

A church which still concentrates on its own agenda and the security of its tenets will become more and more irrelevant. A totally new social construct is necessary to combat the rampant atheism which now controls the world. Families instead of churches will necessarily have to become new centres of spirituality, which will be lived rather than learned from our penny catechisms.

In the new world order of our Christian future, science will be appreciated for the magnificent contribution it has made to our understanding of the universe. We will learn to appreciate the Goldilocks position with which God has blessed us. With all that consciousness entails, our new church must be cosmotheandric. Our spirituality rather than religious education classes will erupt with astonishment at the marvel of creation. We will no longer separate science from religion but see both disciplines as an interconnecting whole. We will forfeit what were once considered the mysteries of the rosary and replace them with the mystery of divinity's unknowability, engendering the right questions rather than knowing preordained answers.

We will learn to stand in awe and wonder at the incomprehensible complexity of our own bodies. Our football and *Star Wars* will be much less exciting than the offense and defence games our white and red blood cells play with each other. We will never take life for granted but approach it reverently, enthusiastically acknowledging the divinity dwelling within it. We shall learn again our relationship with nature and all sentient beings.

We will know that butter comes from a clash between milk and cream. Life is comprised of a clash between opposites. Struggle is endemic in creativity.

Our future church shall involve itself with environmental issues and be much more concerned with the preservation of the species than burdening human sexuality with a fundamentalist orthodoxy. Linear liturgies which contain a theology inapplicable to the experience of contemporary men and women will necessarily be abandoned. Readings from the great literature of the world will become interspersed with scripture. The central message of Jesus will be lived rather than shoved to the periphery. There will be no need of an intermediary. The inner light will be the only legitimate governor. It will be the source of righteous behaviour. Science, relieved of its atheistic baggage, will guide rather than divert humanity towards its holistic future.

It is through this reconciliation alone that peace shall reign in our threshold world.

We will know in our new paradigm that explanation is never enough. Information necessarily leads to experience, and experience is metaphysical.

Pleasurable matter is an oxymoron. The moment we allow pleasure to register, we have allowed spirituality to enter in. Our notion of spirituality is much too small. It is much more than a chattering of prayer in a church on a Sunday. It needs attention as much as we need it. It is our own intention which creates it. Spirituality comes when we kiss it and put our arms around it. It can happen anywhere, instantly, if we attend and intend it. We create our spirituality by our careful nurturing of it. The peeling of a potato can be a prayer if we do it with care.

We live spiritually when we live sustainably. Spirituality is involved when we join our agricultural sustainability with our city living. Our eating with thanksgiving interpenetrates our living and joins heaven with earth in a unifying consciousness. We carve out our spirituality in the precise space and place of our own locality. We pray by our will to make a connection with what is deepest about us. Divinity dangles in the upside and the downside, the inside and the outside of our everyday. The only thing missing is our "hello".

We can objectify beauty through our attitude towards it. Our attitude makes the choice between evil or good. It is our conscience which tells the outcome of our choice. There is no escape from this. Desire dooms us into a spiritual choice.

It is our misuse of our spirituality which causes all of our terror and warfare.

Atheism restricts itself to the realm of the rational only. It cannot appreciate myth, which is an intuitive and higher way of knowing. It robs us of our ability to find a resolution for our unquenchable yearning. There remains an insufficiency in all things available.

The cultural approach of the West is rational and masculine. The philosophy upon which organized Christian theology is based is Aristotelian, logical, rational, masculine, and dualistic. The Eastern approach to consciousness is far more inclusive. It unites rather than divides. A yin cannot exist without a yang. The stress of opposites is always maintained. A creative process cannot exist without the intuition of the female joined to the rationality of the male. The Eastern approach to the one great Consciousness is unitive. It sees immanence as a swelling into transcendence. It does not separate body from spirit.

Jesus lived his life precisely in this manner. He applied the feminine side of nature in that he recognized the divine child living inside himself. That is why he coloured his message with reference to all the little unfolding mysteries surrounding his everyday routine: "Look at the birds of the air they gather nothing into barns … Look at the lilies of the field, not even Solomon in all his glory was arrayed as one of these." Jesus was a tender and caring man, attributes we usually assign to the feminine side of our characters.

He was gentle and nurturing—but such attributes do not fully describe his personality. He was totally integrated. When the moment arose to show his masculine convictions, he did not hesitate to courageously call the religious leaders of his day wolves in sheep's clothing, masters of deceit, hypocrites, and whitened sepulchres. It took the refinement of his own masculinity to demonstrate such manly courage.

He showed his masculinity when he angrily whipped the moneylenders out of the Temple. He had no interest in gathering money. "Render to Caesar the things that are Caesar and to God the things that are God's." Wall Street hates him. His life was lived in total contradiction of the way the Zionist illuminati or the patriarchal church lives today. Jesus lived the Eastern way.

He had huge respect for the environment he lived in, basing many of his teachings on his observation of the natural world. He spoke not only about the pruning of a tree in spring as a necessary prerequisite for a bountiful harvest, but also of the pruning of a human person from an overattachment to his ego.

Jesus the Nazarene is certainly one of the most masculine men who ever existed, simply because he integrated into one the masculine and feminine sides of his nature. As a male, he lived a life which was totally countercultural to his society. More astonishingly, he still stands as the most countercultural voice to the masculine control and dominance of the West.

Jesus knew that he would not, could not ever kill anyone. Yet it is the Christian West which has done most of the killing in our contemporary world. The exquisitely blessed and beautiful land of North America, from its very inception, was carved out through the shameful slaughter of sixty million native people whose very spirit was joined to the natural world in a sustaining and sacred way. The mass media, in retelling this story, has turned the beautiful, integrated lives of these gentle people into a propaganda which best suits the assassin's agenda. Stories of the Wild West are grossly propagandized and exaggerated to tell a tale of the white man's courage. Native Americans find it inconceivable that anyone can proclaim ownership of the land. Everything belongs to the Great Spirit and cannot be owned. It is only on temporary loan, according to Native American wisdom. Ownership is a purely rational, Western idea.

If North America and its allies could live in accordance with the spirituality and wisdom of its own native people, then for sure this world would endure more sustainably and securely.

The suppression of the feminine to the dominance of the masculine is the main cause for the hell that is erupting in the West. The masculine approach is purely rational. By its very nature, it causes disruption in the natural flow of things. There can be no creativity in this world if the feminine is not connected to the masculine. Nothing is reasonable if rationality is not joined to intuition. When immanence is severed from transcendence, humanity has no reason for living. Suicide becomes our most reasonable option.

The Zionist illuminati are purely masculine. They are psychopaths. They have no feeling or compassion. They have severed their hearts from their heads. Reason has castrated them. It has cut the hearts out of them. They are empty shells who take glory in hell. They are cut off from what is deepest inside of them. They are not enlightened, although they call themselves illumined. Their illumination comes from the dark side of matter. That is why they possess genocidal intentions. The Atlanta Guide Stone is their bible.

A world that is purely masculine becomes a terrorized place in which to live. The masculine West, with its schizophrenic personality, is the true terrorist. It is the West which manufactures most of the war machines in the world. It is the West which either directly or indirectly commits most of the murder in this world. It is the West which produces most of the unmanly men on earth. Their guns symbolize the power in their penises.

A world which continues to separate the feminine from the masculine disregards the findings of quantum physics. The masculinity of war games in the West disassociates humanity from its unifying field of consciousness. If we continue to live with the present paradigm, hell will break out on earth.

Hell is far worse than the materiality of fire. Hell is a spiritual experience of passionate love never requited. Hell is to stay eternally separated from the pure consciousness residing within us. Hell is an eternal heartache. Hell is to never realize the joy of unity. Hell is a house divided from itself. Hell is an internal regret for the energy we have wasted pursuing trivia. Hell is the experience of a cosmic orphan crying out in the dark for a parent's love.

Hell is a regret and a longing, in which the lifestyle of the past has precluded the possibility of ever coming home again. Hell is the result of not attending in time to the recognition of our higher being. Hell is like sowing a seed in good ground but never having the compassion to water it. Hell is to be forever thirsty.

Hell is an Olympian course with no finishing place. Hell is the river run of our lives with no sea in which to satisfy the demands of the ego. Hell is to remain forever restless.

The damnation of hell does not happen in an afterlife, nor does it depend on God's judgement. We ourselves are our own judge and jury. It happens here. We damn or redeem ourselves by the way we live in immanence. The possibility of heaven or hell lies purely in our decision-making.

We have been created to be cocreators. If our awareness of consciousness prevails, then we will have scattered the seed necessary for a paradise hereafter. We determine our hereafter to the extent we cultivate or neglect our consciousness while here on earth. Our here and now is very important. Growth or retardation comes from our performance. The more we develop our consciousness, the more we become spiritual. Spirituality compounds like a snowball tumbling down a hill. The more we gather, the more we swell and increase. The greater the increase in our spirituality while physically living, the closer we come to the centre of all consciousness. The closer we draw near the great nonlocal Intelligence, the greater our ecstasy.

Time, space, and place, though temporary and chronological, can ultimately only be measured by infinity. Mathematical measurement and rational evidence lose their potency to finally explain when it comes to matters mystical. As we live, so we reap the fruits of our spirituality. We draw near our heaven or our hell to the extent we grow or retard our spirituality.

The more we live by our ego, the more we determine our distance from the conscious centre of the universe. The more we determine our distance from consciousness, the closer we come to the experience hell. The more we determine our closeness to the centre of consciousness, the deeper we experience heaven. Because of free will, we ourselves determine our depth of consciousness. Nature teaches this. Not one of us exists apart from this determination.

Unlike the determinism of nihilism that scientific atheism teaches, it is humanity itself which, through the gift of free will, makes the determination. Our moral choice between good and evil, made while here on earth, determines our closeness or distance from our Creator. We are meant by the great nonlocal Intelligence to be cocreators.

A conspiracy of fear was proclaimed through the hell which the church created during the Middle Ages. The only hell possible and the only fear feasible are the ones we create within our own being. If we choose to live morally, then obviously fear does not even enter the picture. If we live selfishly and refuse to live compassionately, we create a division between our being and a higher consciousness. To separate from the unity of consciousness is to choose hell. If fear and hell exist, they do so because we have caused them internally.

The only way to overcome fear is to realize that essentially we are divine, endowed with a noble dignity. No external power in this world, neither state nor church, can take that away from us. If we live morally in accordance with the unifying field of consciousness, no external control system on earth can destroy us.

Control of the body is possible through the covert actions of evil men and nations. But with God inside of us, we will remain always free. The human body may be whipped and tortured by diabolical men, whose macho acts may give them the assurance of their masculinity, but it is the human being they torture who is truly the integrated one. Power and a sense of superiority may win a temporary victory, but a hubristic conclusion corrupts far more than it heals.

True victory is a thing of the interior. It is never exterior. Until the war-waging, profit-gouging countries of the West realize this, there will never be peace on earth.

It's time for a new paradigm centred on the unifying field of consciousness to begin. Max Planck, the father of quantum physics considered consciousness fundamental: "I regard matter as derivative from consciousness. We cannot get beyond consciousness. Everything we talk about. Everything that we regard as existing, postulates consciousness."

The stream of knowledge is heading towards a non-mechanical reality.
The Universe begins to look more like a Great
Thought than like a great machine.

—James Jeans

"The most beautiful and profound emotion we can experience is the sensation of the mystical.

It is at the root of all true science.

That deeply emotional conviction of the presence of a superior reasoning power, which is revealed in the incomprehensible universe is consciousness'."

Consciousness is an interior experience. If it is missing, as it is in atheism, then the music of Mozart or a sense of the good, the true, and the beautiful can never be fully appreciated. Art is mythical. It is intuitive more than it is rational.

Atheism destroys the possibility of transcendence. It robs humanity of its ability to be imaginative and creative. Ultimately atheism creates agony but never ecstasy. It is incapable of harmonizing the disjointed notes of life.

On the other hand, spirituality integrates the duality of opposites to create unity. It expands the frontiers of the emotions and elevates them to a higher perspective. The lessons learned through bafflement and bewilderment become a creative part in the development of a great symphony. The spirituality of consciousness is not closed but open to change. It attempts to capture what is indescribable and indefinable. Great art has its roots in spiritual consciousness. Unlike atheism, it proclaims rather than disdains the glory of living.

Atheistic materialism demands concrete, logical, rational evidence. It dismisses belief in God because believers cannot objectively prove his existence. But just because we cannot prove the love of a mother for her child does not mean her love does not exist. As Thornton Wilder points out in his play *Our Town*, it is only the poets and the saints who appreciate life. And then, maybe, only some. A psychopath can never appreciate compassion.

If science does not put its heart as well as its head into its investigation, then this world will never become integrated. Atheism is built on the dark side of matter. Enlightenment cannot come if the light and the spiritual side of matter are not allowed to enter in.

Atheists declare religion to be just a deliberate illusion, invented by power seeking priests ... I do not need to explain that after its victory, not only are the most precious treasures of our culture would vanish, but even more any prospect of a better future.

—Max Planck

Irrespective of the historical truth of the Jesus story, it remains the greatest story ever told, simply because it integrates matter with spirit. When it is interpreted and applied correctly, this world will be truly directed by the Consciousness which Jesus himself related to, in the interiority of his own being. His compassionate message of love in a new way will push away our atheistic ways and lead us to the omega point.

Jesus gave us the ultimate criteria for how to live. He preached consistently to boycott any system of power that was not based on love and mutual service. "Turn your swords into plowshares." He preached a radical freedom from every law but the law of love.

One of the most mystical icons ever carved by the hands of man stands in the ruined monastery of Monasterboice in Ireland. It is a Celtic cross carved in the eighth century. It is unitive in composition, based as it is on Celtic spirituality. With the great O of creation at its centre, the crucifix imposed on and through it immediately allows the light of the four corners of the earth to shine through the darkness of the crucifixion. Thus the light and the dark are presented as the same reality. Humanity cannot have one without the other. Joy is not possible without suffering. Consciousness is not possible unless we become conscious of all the possibility for love and compassion residing inside of us.

Consciousness is possible at the precise intersection where the vertical and the horizontal meet. Humanity is the horizontal and God is the vertical. Humanity happens where the material and the immaterial meet consciously. Humanity is deified at this intersection. God comes alive in our universe to the extent that we cooperate and enact our capacity for love dwelling already inside us.

Should the symbolism of this icon cross be not enough to trigger our imagination, the figure of Jesus on the cross of crucifixion has been carved with his outstretched arms out of all proportion to the rest of his body. The art of this masterpiece from the eighth century still teaches conclusively that if we consciously seek the unitive field of consciousness, love will conquer even death.

The gospel of John differs from the other three canonical gospels in the fact that he calls Jesus "the only Begotten Son of God". Herein lies the human dilemma. Quantum physics teaches that consciousness is the basis of all humanity. In what way can Jesus as man be the whole and not but a part like the rest of us? Jesus as the only begotten Son of God in essence violates the totality of being which resides alone in the Creator of the universe. As Islam claims, "There is no God but God."

God of course resides as the whole in every cell of the human body, and therefore resided in the human body of Jesus as it does in all of humanity. But Jesus cannot be called the nonlocal Intelligence through which humanity was first created. The human body came into being as a consequence of the big bang. If we were predetermined, then God would have violated his own plan of creation. Jesus could only be born consequent to the big bang. His body could not precede matter.

The question is, was Jesus a man or God while he lived on earth among us? At the Council of Nicaea in AD 425, Jesus was doctrinally declared to be God incarnate. The church copper fastened this decision. Anyone who differed was considered a heretic and summarily excommunicated. The church, vested in its own self-interest, declared itself to be the only definitive authority on earth pertaining to the being of Jesus. Through political wrangling and debate, the hierarchy of the church under Constantine, the Roman emperor, established the gospels of Matthew, Mark, Luke, and John as the four acceptable accounts in the canon of the New Testament. Constantine, determined to bring centrality and control over his Roman Empire, joined political and religious sentiment together at the Council of Nicaea.

Many other narratives about Jesus of Nazareth existed at the same time as the Synoptic Gospels. Indeed there were many variants of Christianity at this time, all with their own followers. The Council of Nicaea, in the interest of centrality, declared all gospels apart from the Synoptic canon to be heretical. The church ordered them to be destroyed. From the time of Constantine until the twentieth century, the Synoptic Gospels were the only acceptable and widely known accounts of the Jesus story.

In 1945 a great new discovery of ancient texts was found in the Egyptian desert at Nag Hammadi. Among the manuscripts was the gospel of Thomas. This gospel, unlike the Synoptics, consists of 114 sayings of Jesus. It is one of the Gnostic gospels.

The Gnostics taught that any of us can have a personal relationship with God. We can have the very same relationship with the divine as Jesus did. We can have the same kind of oneness. The inner light of God dwells in each one of us. We can avail ourselves of this light on our own. No intermediary is necessary. We can be our own guides by staying in tune with our own consciousness.

IF you bring forth what is within you, what
you bring forth, will save you.
IF you do not bring forth what is within you, what
you do not bring forth will destroy you.

—Saying 70

We can readily see why the early church dismissed the gospel of Thomas as heretical. The idea that Jesus advocated for one's own inner light totally contradicted the power and control the church had invested in itself as the arbiter between man and God.

It should also be noted how spiritually consistent this saying of Jesus is with the findings of quantum physics. What is deepest about us is our spirit of interiority.

When you know yourself, then you will understand and know
that you are children of the living Father … If you do not know
yourself, you dwell in poverty, and it is you who are that poverty.

—Saying 3

The gospel of Thomas clearly indicates that the very Godhead dwells within us. God is there but for our effort to capitalize on our own divinity. The gospel of Thomas portrays Jesus as a human person like the rest of us. Jesus is a very approachable man. He is extraordinary in his ordinariness. He is truly one of us. He is wise simply because, like all of us, he has lived through the rubble of life's indifference and learned from it. There is nothing magical or supernatural about the Jesus of Thomas. If the early church had chosen the gospel of Thomas instead of John and inserted it in the canon, perhaps Christianity would be in a better state than it is today.

Instead, what Jesus preached, lived for, and died for was usurped and turned into a politicized message of indoctrination. The church's legislators, through their own interpretation, preached a message quite different than the one Jesus intended. The Christian church became a variant of the scribes and Pharisees—the whitened sepulchres of the New Testament. Law and dogma became more important than compassion and love. Morality became the church's own version of it. It dogmatized a message but never lived it.

Christ's message is very simple, but organized religion has complicated it. With all the infighting over the personhood of Jesus, the different sects still refuse to recognize the unity for which consciousness pleads. Consciousness is indifferent to the politicized theology of religion. All it asks is that we accept the oneness of the cosmos.

The Christian church of the West has ignored the simplicity of Jesus's radical message of love. Hypocritically, the US church prays for its own sons and daughter killed in war with no mention of the countless innocent people murdered by the nation's invading soldiers. Christian churches in the West are arrogant. They never admit that they assist the assassin more than the victim in their prayers. As Martin Luther said, "We now have guided missiles, but misguided men."

Jesus was surely one of us. He never claimed to be the Saviour. He realized what was deepest about his own being and became radially alive with the vibrations from God arising within him. He showed as an individual what one man can do.

The same divinity that existed within him also exists within each one of us. He invited us to become our own saviours by cooperating with the vibrational God living within us. Jesus said nothing about Adam and Eve and the pride they displayed in the garden of Eden. He never mentioned original sin and its impact on innocent lives. He never spoke of himself as a necessary atonement for the sin committed in the garden of Eden. All this theological thinking happened long after he had departed. If he were alive today, he would admonish the church of Rome for imposing such insinuations and limitations on his message of love.

There was nothing magical about Jesus. He literally lived an extraordinary life precisely through his ordinariness. The stories of the miracles surrounding him are a device used in literary form and are meant to give the message about his compassionate nature. They are statements of hyperbole, most likely. Miracles can only happen in accordance with the natural law.

The gospels are essentially poems of love, written by writers who were very impressed with the Jesus story. Inspired writers often exaggerate in trying to relate a message they passionately believe in. Sometimes lovers, even today, exaggerate the beloved's physical qualities: "You should see her eyes. They are the size of saucers."

Miracles add or detract nothing from the central message. Reporting of miracles was very common in the cultural milieu of the times. Ultimately it is the central message of the Christ story and not all the theological discourse and arguments which surround it that matters.

Fundamentalist Christians, who interpret scripture literally, not only insult human intelligence with their answers but also pour scorn on the beautiful, edifying life of Christ, his compassionate message of love, and its impact on an uninspired world. Fundamentalism always lacks imagination, and without imagination, great literature cannot be written.

I saw a stranger yestereen;
I put food in the eating place
music in the listening place
and in the blessed name of God
he blessed myself and my house
and the lark said in her song
often, often, often,
goes the Christ in the stranger's guise often, often, often

goes the Christ in the stranger's guise.
—Irish Rune

———————————————

Where there is consciousness, there is a continuous resurrection. Jesus lives today as much as yesterday. His message lives on in the consciousness of the universe. It is as available and alive today as it was in his preresurrection days. His spirit has not been transmuted nor transmorphed. He remains his consciousness as much today as he always was. Consciousness lives before and beyond our physicality. It has no need of resurrection. Consciousness has no beginning and no end. It is unsubstantiality which gives substance its foundation. Consciousness is eternal. To grapple with physical resurrection is merely an anthropomorphic concern.

The message of Jesus centres more on the metaphysical than the physical. His energy still runs with us everywhere and is capable of transforming and resurrecting us into a more advanced species. The higher part of his being lives with those who follow. There is no separation. The material world causes our illusory separation. "My God is me." It is the "I" behind the illusion that I am searching for. The best is yet to be. Jesus taught humanity this. Save the world with hugs and kisses.

———————————————

Our task must be to free ourselves from this self imposed prison, and through compassion to find the reality of ONENESS.
—Albert Einstein

———————————————

———————————————

No one can read the Gospels without feeling the actual presence of JESUS. His personality pulsates in every word. No myth is filled with such light.
His sayings are beautiful.
—Albert Einstein

———————————————

188

I am a Jew, but I am enthralled by the luminous figure
of the Nazarene ... No one can read the Gospels without
feeling the actual presence of Jesus. His personality pulsates
in every word. No myth is filled with such life.

—Albert Einstein

I believe in Christianity, as I believe the sun has risen,
not only because I believe it, but because by it,
I see everything else.

—Aleksandr Solzhenitsyn

If anyone among you should be called Christian
he should thank God for being named one.

—Aleksandr Solzhenitsyn

The story of Jesus cannot be fully appreciated without some knowledge of literary form, such as myth, metaphor, hyperbole, oxymoron, simile, symbolism, and paradox. One cannot fully appreciate the intent of the author who formulated this poem about a courageous man without an appreciation of the subtleties involved in creative writing.

Every narrative within the enclosure of the Jesus story has been filtered through a personality some fifty to one hundred years after Jesus died. Each of the writers of the Synoptic Gospels wrote the same story, but from their own perspective. The process of rendering or editing was necessarily involved in the final report on the Jesus story. The cultural milieu of the time was mainly auditory or by word of mouth. As in all stories, some of the details, when retold, would have been calcified with hyperbole and historical inaccuracies. This always happens when history is coloured by memory. No matter the narration, it is the central truth that matters.

Fundamentalist Christians do a terrible disservice to Christianity in their insistence that the New Testament must be understood literally. They remain closed, cold, and domineering in their appreciation. They are opposed to growth and discredit humanity for thinking intelligently. They pay attention to the words but squeeze all the music out of them. They support Israel as the Holy Land of the Chosen People, but forget the most central message of their leader, who hoarsely cried out to this world, "Do not murder." If Jesus were with us today, he would rage at Israel and cross over the apartheid wall to bring compassion and love to the Palestinian side.

Jesus was an iconic man. He became so in-cultured with the identity of the poor and the downtrodden that he took on the aura of the mythic and the mystic. His message of love lived on in their minds. No one had ever spoken to them like he did. His countercultural approach to life made such an impression that his followers felt compelled to write it down. They realized it had the potential to change the world. The story of Jesus, recounted through the imaginations of the Evangelists, became a heroic tale because of the memory and impression Jesus left behind him.

Jesus was a man of such magnificent proportion and magnitude that, like all artists, the authors of the Synoptic Gospels could not describe in prose the beauty, the purity, and the courageous truth of this countercultural man. Jesus represented to these writers a most awe-inspiring man who joined earth and heaven together. He showed them that even now, heaven and earth are one, held together through the invisible thread of consciousness.

Words are not adequate to describe the experience of an encounter with such a man. The Evangelists resorted to art in their attempt to praise and revere the goodness and the Godness in the heart of Jesus. Even though he never heard of quantum physics, Jesus joined the visible with the invisible. His mission was to turn humanity towards the invisibility of consciousness, which is the unifying, unitive field underlying all life.

We need to turn our gaze to the invisible in order to give meaning to the visible. The ego has no meaning or purpose unless it is connected to the vertical and the transcendent. To the extent we grow in consciousness, to that same extent will we and our world grow more integrated and holistic. Awareness is our first baby step on the ascending road of spirituality.

Unless we cooperate with the unitive flow of body and soul, we will not find a resolution for our deepest yearning. The more we actualize our spirituality, the more we grow peaceful and serene with our own centre. The more we ascend spiritually, the more we experience ecstasy.

Because atheism has severed the connection between body and spirit, it becomes a descending experience which only creates dissociation from what is deepest about our own being. We become a house divided against itself.

Atheistic materialism has been hugely successful in dumbing down the West into accepting a nihilistic conclusion for the human journey. It has conditioned the Christian West to erase the name of Christ from its nomenclature. Some atheistic writers have become insanely insistent that the story of Jesus is a huge lie. Jesus never existed historically, they claim.

It is true that there is little historical evidence for the person of Christ. He is mentioned, however, by the historian Josephus. It must be remembered that in the time of Jesus, there were few documents written, even about people who were politically more important. Add to this the countercultural message and lifestyle which Jesus lived and taught. He was so unique and different that his iconic lifestyle gave credence to his personhood. The message of this iconic man in itself is a proof of his authenticity. His message, even to our deadened ears, seems still to be the right one.

What Jesus said and did was beyond the bounds of acceptance in Semitic culture. Women were very much second-class citizens in his day. To chat with them in a public forum was unthinkable. Add to this that the woman at the well was a Samaritan. This happening was so unlikely that it makes the story of Jesus's conversation with her historically feasible. We know that this unusual story has a ring of truth to it, simply because it is so out of tune with the times in which it was situated.

The process of demythologizing the Bible is called *cultural anthropology.* It is a very important literary device used to discover historical truth. Stories live on in people's memories, and though the details of the story may vary, the message of the story remains the same.

Jesus was very good at storytelling. He created stories with paradoxical endings. He understood metaphor. Consider the parable of the Good Samaritan. The Samaritans were considered little more than terrorists in the time of Jesus. But as the story unfolds, the Samaritan turns out to be the true man of compassion, while the other highly respected citizens turn their backs and walk away.

The father in the parable of the Prodigal Son, instead of whipping and incarcerating his wayward child, embraces him, forgives him, and kisses him with unconditional love.

These stories carry profound messages and remain the greatest challenge to our own indifferent world. They promise, despite our dissolute living, that God will still be forgiving and unconditionally loving. "Let him who has not sinned, cast the first stone."

Even though the gospels were written fifty to a hundred years after the death of Christ, the stories from the oral tradition can be identified as having an historical foundation. This happens in all our stories. Despite the fact that they may be embellished and filtered through the personality of the storyteller, their central message always shines through.

The aphorisms of Christ are one-liners:

- Love one another as I have loved you.
- Turn the other cheek.
- Give him your coat as well.
- Blessed are the poor.

Aphorisms register very readily and stay on in the folk memory. Because of this, they should be considered historically true.

The message of Jesus, irrespective of our cultural religions, is perhaps the most inspiring and hopeful ever to be proclaimed to the ears of humanity. It is relevant to everyone. It is universal in its applicability. When it is understood as its author intended it to be, it remains unapologetically remarkable and inspiring. It is a message for all seasons.

Past religious conflicts have drawn a shroud over its curative and healing power. If the conflicting religions, instead of their own interest in indoctrination, allowed humanity free access to the purity and truth of the Jesus story, it would be understood more clearly and accepted as the greatest antidote to human misery.

Jesus came among us to teach that no visible power on earth has the right to control our invisible consciousness. It is up to each one of us to change the paradigm. We have that power within us. Jesus taught this: "The Kingdom of God is within you." When we know this, it is all we need to know. The message of Jesus is quite simple really.

It is difficult for interpreters of the Bible to reach its essential truth. It cannot be read literally because so many of the verses in it seem totally contra-dictionary. As the saying goes, "Anyone can quote scripture to suit his own purposes."

Through biblical scholarship, we now believe the Infancy Narratives do not represent historic truth. These stories surrounding the birth of Christ have their source in the Egyptian myth of Horus. Compositional creativity is involved in the Infancy Narratives. The retelling of the Horus story reflects the compositional creativity of its author, but cannot be used as an argument to destroy the whole Jesus story.

Horus was the Egyptian sun god. Without the sun, there cannot be light, and without light, there cannot be life. Horus, according to Egyptian mythology, is the sun who nurtures life.

The Evangelists turned sun into Son, thereby making Jesus into the new light and the way.

Horus, the Egyptian sun god was born on the twenty-fifth of December. He was born of a virgin. He had twelve disciples. He died and was resurrected three days later.

It seems historically certain that the Infancy Narratives in New Testament scripture were plagiarized from Egyptian mythology. This may be shocking to Christians who celebrate Christmas with fanfare and passion. It must be remembered, however—and this must be stressed over and over—that the details in the Christmas story do not disprove the whole story. The central message remains the same. Jesus came to tell us about God dwelling within us.

The human mind loves sensationalism. To this day we are more impressed by apparitions of the Virgin Mother than by the infinitely more miraculous experience of a perfectly formed baby appearing from the tomb of a mother's womb. We are surrounded by daily wonders, but we take little notice of them.

The author of an infancy narrative used an ordinary event and turned it into something sensational. This in truth is poetic license. It cannot be understood literally.

The same poetic license was most likely taken in reporting the sensational miracles of Jesus, such as changing water into wine. These sensational happenings should not be considered historically true. They were used as a device to elevate Jesus into the realm of the supernatural. Such is the power of poetry. Poetry can say things that are beyond reason and science.

Not everything has a name.
Somethings lead us into a realm beyond words.
—Aleksandr Solzhenitsyn

Miraculous happenings were very much accepted culturally in the time of Jesus. They are but details and, when demythologized, take nothing away from the central message of Christ, which proclaims that consciousness contains us.

Poetry can make the mind fly and see other
realities behind the veil of literal reality.
—Seamus Heaney

The notes in a symphony are but scribbles on a page when they remain written. Atheists look at the symphony of life as but scratches on a page. They observe the tree and fail to see the chlorophyll running through the leaves.

Poetry turns the murmur of prose into an unexplainable experience. We name it music. Without this mystical experience, a tree is but a lifeless enterprise and a symphony but random scratches on an uninspiring pamphlet.

If an atheist claims that they can appreciate the experience of music, then they have already crossed the threshold between matter and its continuum into spirituality. Experience denotes spirituality. It is the one great antidote to a nihilistic attitude.

Atheism is debilitating. It robs humanity of its appreciation for the one, the true, and the beautiful. Science is a futile enterprise unless it is interjected with spirituality.

Fathers and mothers cannot love and sacrifice for their children without self-abnegation. If we do not sacrifice for our children, then paradoxically we will sacrifice our children. The needs of the ego which materialistic atheism promote are antifamily to the core. Ego promotes selfishness to the detriment of self-giving. It stands in total opposition to the teachings of Jesus—that we receive by giving away.

It is only through the poetry of paradox that we can see what Seamus said, "other realities behind the veil of literal reality".

We remain too anthropocentric, convinced only by the obvious. Our language is arrogantly much too small. It fails to span itself with wider wings and take flight into higher spheres. Atheism likes this state of affairs, because it is precisely in such an atmosphere that atheism can best profit and sell its wares.

The human spirit, informed by a much more noble purpose and indeed by the accumulated wisdom of the ages, vociferously declares that atheism is the very antithesis of all that is beautiful, hopeful, and beneficial in our human enterprise. An inexhaustible Presence beyond our obvious manifestations declares itself in the mystery of our ordinary, everyday events, but we fail to notice it.

The cold mathematics of atheistic science refuse to accept this. Atheism is intolerant of imagination, and without imagination there can be no transcendence. That is why, in contemporary Western civilization, our utilitarian productions are our only trophies. We have lost our ability to value and create objects of beauty. Without spirituality there can be no creativity. Atheism has turned our world upside down.

The spiritual ignorance of the so-called enlightened ones is causing much more harm and pain in our troubled world than the superstitions of the unenlightened in the past ever did. Atheists remain dualistic and refuse to adapt to the more advanced vision of quantum physics, which is unitive. It is precisely because of this division, because of the bully tactics of an overarching atheism, that all the murder, crime, hatred, and corruption have entered into Western society. A rediscovery of the Jesus message is our only hope and antidote. The Christian world, like Christ, must disobey the lust of atheism and become countercultural. This is the way, the truth, and the life.

Jesus lived life in a very ordinary manner. He was no celebrity, nor did he ever claim fame. He is remembered today because he hammered out his consciousness on the anvil of his own personality. He invested his life in all the doubt, confusion, and suffering that human life brings with it. He told this world to endure it gladly because, in the end, it is only through one's spirituality that one can overcome the fear of death. All our fears are only temporary. It is through love and compassion for one another that suffering takes on meaning. We are heirs to an Eden that is eternal. Suffering is but an Olympian challenge. To be crude, it is the dung needed for our fertilization. It is but the tooling of creativity.

This is the essential truth contained in the Jesus story. This is still the message which our messed-up world must try to enshrine once again.

We cannot afford—irrespective of our cultural religious differences or the irrepressible urge of atheists—any longer to suppress Christ's central message, Consciousness implies doubt and search. Opposites are wrapped within it. The storm brings the rage of the rain, but it is through rain that new sprouts bring wisdom and manifestation. This is reality. We cannot escape it. The greatest wisdom is to accept and surrender to our insecurity. We are but a river run into an ineffable sea.

One does not have to convert from a cultural perspective to join the Jesus movement. The essence of his message is compassion, and we all can agree with that. The rest of the message is not essential. To live compassionately is to live consciously.

Jesus was very ordinary and one of us. He tells us simply that what he has done for us must now be done by us. We all live as one in the same nest of being.

Finally, there remains an interesting fact about Jesus the Nazarene. Of all the three great monolithic faiths in the West, Jesus was the only prophet who lived what he preached. It is precisely because of this actualization that he was crucified.

Christianity, through following the way of its founder in its purity, is caught rather than taught. It would be far more beneficial to the human race if the Christian church gave up on its dogmatic preaching and lived instead the central message of Jesus. Christianity becomes numinous and liberating to the extent that is lived. When the Christian world begins to recognize the cosmic Christ in all being, then this world will become whole instead of the shattered and splintered entity it is today. The cosmic Christ is nonsectarian and a respecter of all that is true and enduring in other cultural expressions.

What power-seeking men have done to the purity of the Christ message is a colossal lie. Interested in their own agenda, they preach his message but do not live it. We call this religion. Spirituality, on the other hand, concerns itself with the purity of Christ's message. It is caught. It cannot be taught. It cannot be objectified. It is a lived experience. It is conjunctive, joining heart to mind and not the other way around. Christianity cannot be preached without the preacher first living it.

Should atheists become too arrogant and haughty in their rejection of God and the teachings of Jesus Christ, they too must be castigated for their dismissal of divinity simply because of the way religion has lived it. Religion is much more about the political machinations of man than it is about an authentic living out of the Jesus message. The terrorism of absurdity which atheism teaches destroys not only what Christianity teaches, but the enlightenment which the message brings to the world.

The singularity of Christianity lies in the fact that it has been modelled by a living man, who walked among us and showed us how to live by his witness to his message.

It is easy to say we are courageous when our cowardice has never been tested. It is easy to say we believe when doubt has never smothered us. Suffering can never be understood unless we have first experienced it.

How can you expect someone who is warm
to understand someone who is cold
—Aleksandr Solzhenitsyn

Jesus understood human suffering. He lived the content of its context. Humans spend more time worrying about suffering than the endurance of it.

Fundamentalism, whether atheistic or religious, is very dangerous. It is those who feel cosy and well-off materially who preach and teach an uncompromising orthodoxy. Atheism finds its fertility among those who are already materially wealthy and have little concern or compassion for the incomprehensible suffering of the poor. The psychopathic lifestyle of the elites, be they of a royal Christian hierarchy or Zionist vintage, preaches a message which complements their vision for a new world order. Uninformed by the suffering of deprivation and devoid of a spiritual value system, they divide human beings into two categories, themselves as the masters and the rest as slaves to serve them.

Christianity as lived by Christ asks this world to rise up and in full-throated chorus to defy the creeping, encompassing, devouring crawl and sprawl of atheism, which will destroy all that is beautiful and good in this world.

Religion is more about man than it is about God. So too is scripture. To therefore deny both the falseness in religion and scripture, as atheists do, in order to debunk God is in reality to debunk man—including the elites.

EAST-WEST DIVIDE

astern thought in regard to the being of consciousness is almost the exact opposite of the Western approach. The way of Jesus the Nazarene is very Eastern. Had his story not been tampered with so much, the West would be peppered with living monasteries of deep thinking. Then Christianity would be far more vibrant and attractive. Western religion is in deep decline not only because of the onslaught of atheistic materialism, but also because of its disempowering indoctrination.

To the Eastern mind, there is a power beyond man and nature which penetrates humanity's existence. It is the real source of vitality in this world.

To the Eastern mind, God manifests himself in all the works of nature—in earth, fire, water, and air; in man, animal, and plant. Sex is sacred and considered a manifestation of divine power. It is considered a sacrament.

The East considers matter an illusion. The world is infused with and by consciousness. There is no reality outside of it. So we must detach from matter to find consciousness. If humanity could learn to live simply where bodily needs are met in a sustainable way, then, like the rest of the animal family, we would stay in harmony with the gravity of the universe.

The indoctrination of atheistic materialism in the West has dismissed subjectivity in the process of reasoning, thereby dismissing the reality of God. In the East, however, it is the subjective intuition of the investigator which leads to God. Intuition more than reason is the proof. It is the experience of surrendering to self-transcendence that renders intuitive recognition.

Objective, materialistic science does not give knowledge of reality as such but of reality filtered through a personality. When the subject is excluded, reason goes out the window. There can be no reasonable, objective truth without subjective interest. The West has dismissed transcendence precisely because it has dismissed subjective experience. In effect, the very evidence which has to be reasonable cannot be given when experience has been taken out of the equation. Without the subject, an object is but an illusion.

Atheistic, objective science had almost won the day in respect to enlightenment. But quantum physics put an end to its banter. We have arrived at the horizon of a new day. Object and subject must cooperate, each informing the other. Spirituality is as necessary to science as science is to spirituality. Only through both disciplines can we find unity.

In the East, the interpreted and the interpreter are one. We in the West have been indoctrinated to think scientific, mathematical language is true and mythological language is a lie. We think of myth as something superstitious, founded on ignorance, when in fact it is meant to elevate the human mind into a much higher appreciation. Myth, poetry, and symbolism are much closer to an intuitive and unitive acceptance of truth than the cold, abstract language of mathematics.

We must pass through the rationality of materialism to enter into the freedom which consciousness offers. The Western mind from the time of Plato and Socrates has been mechanical and mathematical. It is cold and abstract, too much head and too little heart. It tells us nothing about the experiences of joy, laughter, and appreciation. Human feelings are not considered.

The best things in life are felt
rather than seen.
—C. S. Lewis

You can have life
and still do not see.

—Aleksandr Solzhenitsyn

Because of the separation of body and spirit, Western society has become schizophrenic. It separates and concentrates on the ego, to the detriment of the spirit. The Eastern mind is unitive. It marries matter with idealism. The East recognizes consciousness as concrete, intuitive, and symbolic.

In the East, God is both father and mother, conscious and unconscious, physical and metaphysical, imminent and transcendental. In the West, apart from atheism, God is seen as the Father—unconscious, metaphysical, and transcendent. In general, the Western approach to God is spirit detached from body. Matter is considered inferior to spirit. This world is a vale of tears. Western religion is antibody.

Eastern religion joins body and spirit in the one continuum. It is through our bodies that we discover our souls. The Eastern approach to life is mystical and, without the baggage of Greek philosophy, is more constructive spiritually.

In the atheistic West we need a new paradigm which best befriends consciousness. The consciousness which quantum science declares as the bedrock of matter argues authoritatively that the invisibility and indivisibility of matter presents the possibility of a hereafter. It is now up to humanity to better understand that possibility.

Dare to Be Spiritual suggests an answer. It declares that God is the unifying Being and the ultimate source of all creation. The spirit of God runs through everything. Matter is holy. It reveals the same creative spirit which runs rampant in the conscious and the unconscious. The whole of creation is grounded in this one great nonlocal Intelligence. There is no separation between heaven and earth. Heaven is in one continuum with earth.

There is no dualism in Eastern theism. There is only oneness. The ascent to God is an ascent into higher consciousness. This higher consciousness dwells within the heart and soul of all humanity. It raises us up to the heights of supreme dignity. This enhancing source of energy enters not only into the soul of humanity, but also into the life of plants and animals. This all-encompassing energy is present everywhere and in everything, but it is still apart and greater than the sum of the parts. Humanity is a manifestation of the unmanifest.

All the world is pervaded with this mighty source of consciousness. All being resides in this great source of consciousness, but the parts do not summate the great Consciousness, which resides higher and outside of it. The true purpose of life is to climb higher and higher into the bliss which pure Consciousness offers.

To manifest the unmanifest is to detach from all attachments, consumed with the one desire to journey deeper into the inscape of pure being. All other desires only cause suffering. Life is a journey into what is already inside of us. When we ignore or deny the call of the spirit, we refuse to come home to the centre of our own consciousness. When we choose to remain spiritual illiterates, we make space for a spirit of victimhood, anxiety, stress, and insecurity to enter into our inner being of consciousness.

Consciousness asks for balance and the wisdom to learn what it means to keep divinity alive within us. The materialistic West has yet to internalize that hell is simply to separate ourselves from the one consciousness. In so doing, we lock ourselves into a state of being which will never know appeasement. By nature, there is an unquenchable longing stamped within each one of us. There remains an insufficiency with all that is available. We are never satisfied, no matter our wealth. Money brings with it a desire to control. The elites control those who have handed their spiritual freedom over to them. Without a soul, a nation becomes enslaved.

In our experience of material living, we remain in a state of disorder and dissatisfaction. We are a house divided. We never seem to have enough. We indebt ourselves to the bankers, which is exactly where they want us. Debt causes interest always to flow in one direction. We feel trapped and become frightened. We never seem able to cross the hurdles which the world of economics erects in front of us. We become slaves to a system which is man-made and forget the very call of our being towards a higher nobility of character.

If, however, we retain our self-esteem and acknowledge that it is divinity which defines us, then indeed we will realize that not even the powers of hell will conquer us. We will never allow the greed of the bankers to destroy us. With the practice of a living spirituality, we overcome not only our temporary worries, but even the fear of death itself.

Surrender your desire for the satisfaction which materiality temporarily answers, and replace it the desire which Consciousness offers eternally.

In the East, the created world is holy. One cannot reach heaven without it. The natural world is but a reflection of the uncreated, archetypal world of the great unconsciousness. In the East, all matter is interconnected with consciousness. It is a spiritual connection, making the trees, fields, seas, heavens, and all creatures living in them holy. Nature is not seen as something for humanity's use and exploitation, but as a strand in the nest of all being. When it is used for humanity's sustenance, then it must be done with reverence, sensitivity, and compassion.

The West has much to learn from the East. Had we followed this way rather than the logic of mathematics and objectivity, the planet would not be in the imbalanced state we find it. Terribly, though, the Western world still solely concerns itself with business and economics. The holy name of God is excluded in the enterprise of making money. To the enlightened man, surely the very unifying field holding all life together must be recognized in all just enterprises.

What remains most notable about the human enterprise is the absence of God from human deliberation. Until the one great Consciousness is recognized and brought into economic deliberations, the profits of corporations will remain imbalanced in favour of the few who own 98 per cent of the world's wealth.

The West has been so dumbed down spiritually that it scarcely relates to its all-embracing consciousness any more. Not only does the corporate world act atheistically, but the private lives of humanity have also removed the primacy of spirituality from their lives.

Truly our world is disordered. We are very sick. We know it from all the horror of war and cruelty erupting around us. We blame the foreigner over there, when in fact the West as the invader spreads its atheistic compulsion for profit.

We as individuals fake spirituality at the momentous moments of births, weddings, and deaths. The church hatches, matches, and dispatches. Attendance at church on such occasions is more ego-related than worshipful. It is more social than spiritual.

We have yet to learn that our spirit is the one spirit of consciousness which joins us all together as members of the same family. When we live consciously, there is no enemy. There is no foreigner. There is no "over there". There is only the inherence of our own bodies, which is the one Consciousness of all that exists.

The West, steeped as it is in having more than emptying, in doing more than being, cannot appreciate the act of surrender or acceptance. We substitute loudness and vulgarity for silence and a sense of interiority. The West is completely out of tune with the way the Creator intended life to become.

The East is mystical and far more connected to what is practical for the sustenance of our planet with humanity in it.

It is precisely because we have not been enlightened about the reality of our true spiritual identity that we look on consciousness as some kind of coercion or imposition. We identify our liturgies as boring because they have no bearing on our everyday experiences. Boring religion bears no semblance to the passion and vitality which an awakened spirituality brings with it.

Spirituality connects us to the world of reality, which is then connected and subsumed by the great Consciousness. All human acts become holy when we do them in the name of God. Even the simplest act becomes a sacred event when we connect it to God. When we take a walk in the woods or watch a beautiful sunset, we feel uplifted into a restoring experience. The thrill of a bird's song or the cries of wild geese passing in amazing formation across the sky can leave us breathless. Such an experience can make us sing out hosannas in praise of beauty.

Little does the West recognize that such an experience is the language of God talking to us. We have become so disconnected from the natural world that we only hear deadly loud language and never the music within silence. If we wish to live spiritually, then we must connect to the unifying field which holds both the material and the spiritual in continuous unity.

The East does this very beautifully. Its approach is mystical, whereas the West believes life is merely practical. Through the indoctrination of materialistic atheism, we are trained for a job but not for life. If we could only realize that the reality which is most practical in this world is to divinize ourselves with the truth of our own consciousness.

What remains primordial is that we connect with what is already inside of us. This is the way of redemption and salvation. We are our own saviours. God, through his evolutionary plan, ordained this way. We cannot become holy or spiritual if we want to do it our own way. We reach the peak of the evolutionary process together and not separately. The spiritual way is ultimately to reach our completion.

The spirituality of the East is holistic. Divinity enshrouds all life. The parts are not separated from the whole. Everything humanity does is infused by the spirit. The West compartmentalizes and refuses to see in a holographic way. Therefore the material world, instead of enabling us to transcend suffering, causes more disease. It is only when we choose to act holistically that we reach a peaceful and serene experience in this world.

We remain unrequited because our ego and our spirit are separated. It is this separation which causes a sense of alienation from ourselves. We no longer appreciate the bliss which is within us. It is the one being who sees and hears and knows.

The consciousness in you and me is the same consciousness that pervades everywhere. There is not a particle of matter, a grain of sand, a bird a butterfly, a leaf, an animal a human being which is not grounded in the unified field of consciousness.

The West's problem is a spiritual one. Reason must marry intuition if a spiritual new world order is to be enshrined. The Western mind has been tooled to think only in terms of the object. It has canonized the conclusion that objective reason is the only way to find truth. In doing this, the body and spirit become separated. Atheism consequently leaves no room for intuitive thinking, which is a higher way to appreciate the invisibility of our consciousness.

Atheism masquerades under the banner of liberating humanity from the oppression of organized religion. Organized religion nonetheless does present hope, insofar as it advocates belief in some marvellous Presence who operates with incredible order and precision in the universe.

The incalculable error of atheism is not its attack on religion, but its dismissal of a cosmic Intelligence. Atheism removes matter from its ultimate conclusion. It makes the minor into the major. Its scrutiny is exercised in a special location but demands a nonlocal Intelligence to give evidence of its presence in its investigation. Atheistic scientists seem to forget that the evidence lies within themselves much more than in the object they are scrutinizing.

Never before in the evolution of humanity has the possibility of total annihilation faced us. Our nuclear age, if it does not destroy us, should and must compel us to make a choice between good and evil. Never before has the deceit of atheism so confronted the human race. Through its abhorrent claim that no intelligence greater than our own is in charge of the universe, we move more and more away from our mooring. We become the mongrelized captains of all we survey. More and more we realize something has gone terribly wrong with modern society, but as individuals, we have little courage to challenge the immorality of the system.

Actions necessarily are followed by reaction. If the human race does not resist the fundamentalist teachings of atheistic materialism, then the stultifying plan of a genocidal brotherhood called the illuminati will culminate in the abolishment of Christendom.

Throughout the ages there has always been human outreach towards the transcendent. This outreach, stamped by nature within us, has always played a role in the guidance of our affairs, usually for the betterment of our tribal affiliation. Our reactions have not always been chivalrous nor honestly appreciative of the other—sometimes built on horrendous ignorance and unenlightenment, sometimes prejudiced and superstitious. However, one constant has been always present, and that is humanity's belief in some great Intelligence beyond the power and control of man.

This was the prevailing system of thought until the overpowering, interpenetrating influence of atheistic mind control became pervasive. So subtle and covert has this thief in the night been in entering the premises of our presence that we have almost totally replaced our gratitude for the privilege of living with a sense of entitlement. Atheism has robbed from us an appreciation of our higher selves. It appeals to the proximate and immediate needs of our stomachs without ever mentioning the vomiting and excessive excrement which follow.

The West has become the message of its atheistic media. The modern Christian world, in forgetting all the beauty of its civilized past, has sold out its excellence for a fistful of kitsch. Our new scripture has been written by atheistic evangelists, and we accept it as lustily as the fundamentalist no-Godness men have written it. We now treasure deals instead of the ideal.

Brothers, I have the very warmest love for the Jews and
I pray to God for them to be saved. I can swear to their
fervor for God, but their zeal is misguided.
Failing to recognize the righteousness that comes from God, they
try to promote their own idea of it, but now the law has come to an
end with Christ and everyone who had faith may be Justified.

—Romans 10:3–5

Religion as much as atheism restricts itself through its own level of systematic thinking. It canonizes itself as the only truth, thereby closing itself off from the unifying reality of the one consciousness which pervades everything. It is time atheism and organized religion sought reconciliation and turned back to the discovery of the one consciousness which permeates all reality.

The elites of organized religion and the political, secular, atheistic establishment work hand in hand to suppress the growing, agitated, frustrated search of the masses for their own truth and dignity. Elitism among the religious and secular hierarchical classes cause nothing but social unrest and inequality.

Organized religion and secular, atheistic elitism—which, to the passive, indoctrinated mind, seem to be arch-enemies—are in fact singing the same hymn of power and control to frustrate the dreams and the hope of the human prospect.

A church which is only interested in its own preservation and enrichment, legalistically deprives not only its faithful followers of a sense of their true identity, but also exploits the message in the name of a man who lived, with every fibre of his being, a life of compassionate love and understanding. If saints and scholars appear to arise from a hypocritical institution, then be sure it is not because of the saint's adherence or obedience to the established way. Saints and artists are carved from their own individual courage to see and live life differently. They are most surely counterculture heroes who reincarnate Jesus in a gentle and compassionate way. They reject the conventionality of the prevailing mob mentality in a transcendent way.

The world may be impressed by a saint like Mother Teresa of Calcutta. But contrary to the propaganda which the church uses to canonize her, she became a holy person not through the dogmas of the church, but through her conviction and living out of the Jesus message. She lived her life totally contrary to either the secular or religious elitist paradigm. A corrupt organization can never be the cause of holiness, nor does it have the authority to canonize it.

This planet is facing an axial turn. The choice is ours. Atheistic materialists must begin to recognize there is an unquenchable longing in every soul for something more. The longing itself is the proof. It is unquenchable. No gadget or toy can ever fully satisfy us. We are doomed to be spiritual. It is an inescapable reality. Our very consciousness tells us this. It would be an unbearable torture if this unquenchable longing could never have a resolution. Atheistic materialism is wreaking horrendous damage on the human spirit in its promotion of the material as the only solution to the human dilemma. Humanity's needs are best requited through the affairs of the heart, not the belly.

It is a perversion to use the unquenchable longing written into our interior by directing it solely towards the needs of the ego. It destroys the continuum, the togetherness of the here and now into the hereafter which consciousness prescribes. The cosmos is one.

Some-thing-ness is always preceded by a cause. Even in the scientific understanding of quantum, the no-thing of consciousness is what upholds some-thing-ness (the atom). While we may not be capable of giving evidence of God in the rational, objective sense, to claim as atheists do that there is no God is a contradiction even on the rational level.

Contraries are complementary, but in our contemporary engineering of the social fabric, the balance is so out of kilter between the here and the hereafter that atheists have managed to manufacture a God who best suits their purposes. Their god does not like the God of the natural world. They erect barbed wire all around divinity.

Atheism has pulled a blind over the tiny spectrum of light presently available to us. Sight deprived as we already are, atheism wants to blind us completely. It systematically teaches that life has come about by mere chance. There is no afterlife. There is no God. Through its arrogant claim to enlightenment, atheism vests itself with infallibility. Haughtily it proclaims its denial of God is the only illuminated, sophisticated answer to life's fundamental question. The affairs of the body alone in our material world are all that matter. The human brain as the dynamo for mind energy is meant to serve only the needs of the body. It has no other purpose. After the total disintegration of the atom, there is nothing more. If we claim that there is, atheism demands evidence, missing the proof that the something of their located study limits the infinity of the nonlocal Intelligence and measurement.

Atheism has invaded the unquestioning mind of the Christian West. It gnaws parasitically in such a covert, devouring way that soon there will be no Christian West left. Even now the Christian countries of Europe, through the spread of Islam, sense a massive threat to their identity. Indeed it seems quite likely that the West's magnificent cathedrals will one day be turned into mosques.

Even now, our planet's greatest architectural achievements have become cobwebbed tombs of emptiness instead of centres of praise and worship. This is not due to the aggressive spread of Islam, but to the indifference of Christianity. Atheism has so enslaved the Christian West that it has closed down our great cathedral doors to worshippers, replacing them with hordes of museum gawkers who have lost the sense of their own spirituality and the passion of the artists who built these treasures.

Atheism, like a crawling pack of wolves, is stalking the perimeters of our holdings. We are daily bombarded by messages, methods, and means which totally pervert our heritage. Dumbed down by the sophisticated barrage of the atheistic onslaught, we no longer have the wisdom or enlightenment with which to defend ourselves. We have become so mind-controlled that it is now more acceptable to profess atheism than a belief in transcendency. To be a Christian is not cool anymore.

If the West is to lose its grand heritage of Christianity, it will not happen because of the immediate spread of Islam, but through the insidious, incremental covering of an asphyxiating atheism. The signs are already with us.

For evil to triumph, all that is necessary,
is for good men to do nothing.
—Edmund Burke

People will not look forward to posterity
who never look backward to their ancestors.
—Edmund Burke

Silence in the face of evil
is evil itself.
—Bonhoeffer

Atheism, for the sake of its self-interest, destroys the truth. It does not provide a moral compass. It leaves the human race rudderless. The Christian West has usually sought moral guidance from the church, but even organized religion in contemporary society has been co-opted and infiltrated by atheism.

Money can buy even religion and turn it into a warped morality. The atheistic elites have become the new hierarchy of religious doctrine.

Atheism, in its global agenda to destroy the order of a spiritually balanced planet, has almost totally succeeded in robbing the holistic purpose from life.

The time has come for all the unawakened Christians of this world to jump off their delusional couches. In the interest of posterity, we must pick up our shovels, retrench, turn off the switches on our mind-conditioning programs, and furiously declare to the atheistic elites that we have finally become aware of their ultimate plan to murder most of us.

The elites are psychopaths. We have given our power and control over to them. They have coaxed us into their snare with the insidious and incremental lure of catering to our egos. Edward Bernays capitalized on our unquenchable longing for something transcendent and replaced it with a placation of egotistical desires. Economy became the content of the West's value system.

Throughout the West's social engineering since the sixteenth century, there has scarcely been an area of study where our experimentation or investigation regarding social concern has been approached in a holistic way. The idea of humanity's spirituality has been totally expunged from our scientific studies. The parts are studied as though the whole were not present.

Atheistic doctors treat the human body as though it were just a machine with no demonstrable energy running through it. When all life has disappeared from the body and relatives grieve around the corpse, atheists in the medical profession have no compassionate words to offer. The moment compassion is shown, atheism flies out the window. When compassion is present, so also is divinity.

Atheism has invaded modern Western society to such a degree that it reigns supreme in all the vital areas of life. It controls the economy, medicine, education, and mass media. As though such a nefarious infiltration were not enough, atheism even now is convulsed in the act of destroying the value system of the Christian family. The aim of atheism is to homogenize all the sustaining principles of life into the gruel of their own pernicious thinking. An ever-growing degeneracy in family living and relationships has turned indecency into a laughable comedy. The more vulgar and crass we become, the more hilariously society applauds our degeneracy.

Everybody blames the Jews for killing Christ
and then the Jews try to pass it off on the Romans

I am one of the few people
who believe it was the Blacks.

I hope the Jews did kill Christ
I would do it again
I would fucking do it again
if I got a chance.

—Sarah Silverman

<hr>

Atheism is unnoticeably blinding us. Only a resurgence of our inbred spirituality will save us.

The atheistic vision which the new world order covertly promulgates is to rid the planet of religious cultural differences. Its aims to homogenize the human race into one bland hegemony. It purposely appeals to our lower instincts and offers a quick fix to our egos. Violence, crudeness, and irreverence are promoted as cool in our mass media. Vulgarity has become our greatest achievement in the art of communication. We settle for the superficial. Mindless entertainment has smothered our need for meaning and purpose.

We must reclaim our dignity. We are not just cogs in the whirring machinery of atheism. Children in our educational system must again be prepared for life, not just a job. The atheistic agenda treats children as product more than as human persons, capable of thinking. Public education is turning out trained seals who repeat what atheism has indoctrinated them with. There is little originality or newness coming out of their interiors.

One of the main reasons public education is so biased in favour of the atheistic agenda is that the elites who own 98 per cent of the world's wealth endow public schools to teach the atheistic rendition of patriotism. A festival of ignorance prevails not only in the marketplace of our world, but also in our schools of learning. Children's minds are indoctrinated to become cogs in the wheel of the atheistic agenda. Dumbed down through cognitive laziness, they become dependent on a government that controls their minds. They emerge as products, devoid of originality and individuality, on the assembly line of corporate, atheistic factories. Young people are trained to sell their souls for a place in the sun.

Such programming promotes a herd mentality. A child must never grow into an individual because that way he or she becomes more difficult to control. To change this deceptive perception, one must change the information frequency. This cannot be accomplished without a value system to interpret it.

Students in the public education system are trained to be more like Pavlovian dogs than individuals who think with moral consciences. The purpose of integral education is to tease out the originality and imagination with which each individual child is blessed. Instead, the atheistic agenda pumps its own nefarious value system into them.

The enlightenment which the atheistic elites propose is global in design. It is meant to control us in every aspect of our humanity. It involves itself in every sphere of local and national politics. That is the reason money, profit, and balancing the budget are of supreme importance to politicians. When the Christian West begins to recognize that self-transcendence rather than self-actualization is the primary drive in our lives, will we incarnate social justice and equality in our world? The global design which atheism promotes will only bequeath more inequality.

To even mention the holy name of God on Wall Street is a total taboo. Schools produce machine-like processors which spit out the answers of a split personality. Students in the public education system of the West appear on their graduation day to the applause and approval of family and friends. Little does society recognize that the youth who stands before them has been transhumanised into a half person attached to a cyborg. Of such is the atheistic vision intended for future graduates.

Atheism cries out for the separation of church and state, and rightly so. But morality and ethics demanded by the unified field of consciousness is not the same thing as the separation of religious cultural traditions from the state. Morality stems from a person's conscience. It is a universal endowment and of absolute critical importance in a student's formation.

Education, irrespective of religious cultural differences should be allowed to encourage ethical and moral behaviour. It is an integral part of the building up of a society which is substantiated by what is good and noble about the human condition.

Under prevailing circumstances, the religion of atheism is allowed to indoctrinate the minds of children, to the exclusion of a value clarification course which teaches moral behaviour. A basic understanding of ethics and morality is absolutely necessary for the integration of the whole person. It is a nonthreatening exercise.

If the West is to survive and become integrated, then the elitist monopoly, whether it be religious or atheist, will be forced into a new world paradigm. Contrary to the enslaving tactics of the elites and their atheistic new world order agenda, we need a different paradigm based on the indelible rights of one's conscience.

To the psychopathic elitist mind, the rest of us are but animals with a herd mentality. Pushing their agenda to its ultimate conclusion, they envision one world religion in the new world order. At first glance, this vision seems utterly acceptable, in the sense that it would end all the conflicting arguments between organized religions. When taken literally, this vision seems consistent with the unifying field of consciousness.

The elites of both the secular and religious orders want one world religion, but instead of freeing humanity from the curse of division, they both intend to subjugate the human race into a state of slavery which best supports their own selfish strategy. Atheistic elites have become so successful in their will to dominate the world chambers of debate that they have now infiltrated even the Vatican. Unbelievable as it may sound, such is the power of the elites' corruption that that atheism and religion now sing from the same hymnal.

The atheistic elites believe that they are the highest evolved species on earth. Their thesis is that the whole evolutionary process of natural selection has ended with them. They alone are the enlightened ones. They believe in their own superiority.

Although they believe in a steady state of reality, they maintain that even if the big bang occurred, it did so only to have its process end with them. They alone are entitled to become the illuminati or enlightened elite of the species. The rest of humanity has not been engendered with the same energy or vitality. The illuminati claim to know what is best for humanity, and because of this claim, their aim is to rule the world. Even morality and ethics can be bought when enough money is exchanged in the transaction. When the ideas of God and morality are thrown out the window, corruption rushes in to usurp their space.

This is why the Western world is in such turmoil. The evil which atheism brings with it is devouring us. The terrible tragedy in Western society is not that God is missing, but that we, its citizens, do not miss him.

A nation without God is not a nation.

—Dostoyevsky

The atheistic elites live at the top of the pyramid. Through an upwardly mobile defence system, they render themselves untouchable and invisible. The rest of humanity—dumbed down, entertained, distracted, and ignorant—is there for their system's usage. Most are but useless eaters to be eliminated. Whoever is left will be kept as a slave.

We have become so intimidated by the loud-mouthed harangues of atheism that we lie low and scarcely murmur a disagreement with their indoctrination. We buy into their vulgarity and sometimes even seem to enjoy it. We have been brainwashed to such a degree that our only concern is the needs of our ego. We think we are entitled to all the surplus cheap goods which China makes for us, without ever reminding ourselves that our acquisitions are polluting the Yellow River—not only with chemicals, but also with the sweat and tears of the gentle little slaves who attend to our demanding and exaggerated needs.

Have we ever considered that the shirt or blouse we are wearing might well have been the very last piece of cloth a poor Bangladeshi girl touched before she was burned to death in a hell-hole factory? So insidious is the evil which atheism promotes that the very clothes we wear are stamped with its nomenclature. Distance creates indifference. Injustice is acceptable so long as we don't see it or run into it.

Atheism is a great deceiver. We scarcely detect its enterprise running in disguise in the knickers and underwear we use to cover our private parts.

Atheistic materialists scream offensively, "If God exists, give me the evidence!" Instead of defending ourselves from their slam, our touchdown will occur when we shout back at them, even more loudly, "Give me the evidence to the contrary!"

Intuition is far more convincing than evidence. God is understood culturally in different ways, but underneath all cultural differences, each culture, in its own original way, expresses a universal outreach of the human spirit towards the transcendent. Every culture on earth, since the appearance of the humanoid, has expressed an unquenchable longing for something more.

The reaching out of the human mind and heart towards something greater arrives from that same sense of incompleteness which creates the illusion that we are separate from one another. We are all stamped with the same unresolved longing. This yearning is itself proof of our cosmic consciousness. There has to be a reason for our unresolved longing. Nature teaches this.

A new spiritual paradigm is needed. A greater recognition of the common bond of our spirituality, which unites rather than separates us, must be integrated with our daily experience. It is time to chant a consistent message that atheistic elitism is an abominable sin against humanity. We have much more in common with each other than that which separates us. Despite our cultural differences, the vast majority of people outside the atheistic construct of the West believe in the same life force which the East calls a cosmotheandric God. This understanding alone unites us on a level higher than our cultural differences.

Atheism and the future it attempts to push us into is degrading and frightening. Like organized religion, it is not relevant to the needs of a holistic world.

Both organized religion and atheism are dualistic. They separate instead of understanding matter and spirit as one continuum. We are all one under the same God. There will never be wholeness on the planet unless we once again unite mind and spirit. It is time to turn our bombs and bullets into butterballs.

To the so-called sophisticated, scientific mind of the West, culturally Indian expression, when properly understood, is by far the most hopeful and socially engaging theology ever carved out by humanity's search for significance and truth. All sentient matter is holy to the Hindu mind and invaded by divinity. Different aspects of the one God, Brahman, appear in the form of various animals. When connected to each other, they represent the one God and humanity's search for the one great Consciousness. The East treasures transcendency. It is saturated by myth and metaphor. To the Western mind, however, the sight of sacred cows walking the streets of Delhi is incomprehensible.

Humanity, when confronted by ineffable mystery, resorts to myth or metaphor to point towards a higher meaning. Myth is a mask, as it were. What we see is the image which covers the face. It is only when the mask is taken away that we can behold the face.

To the Western mind, indoctrinated through the medium of mathematics, we can only tolerate cold facts as believable. We think myths are a lie. Because of our limitation, we miss the music in everything. Atheistic materialism has done this to us. We can no longer appreciate myth or poetry. The East has managed until quite recently to hold on to their mythology, which accounts for their far greater ability to express the divine running and living rampantly in the midst of the ordinary.

Unfortunately, the East is losing its grip on what is essential in this world. It is losing its ability to cradle the insubstantial, the invisible, and the ineffable in a world which is starving for it. The encroachment of Western atheistic materialism is destroying their more enlightened culture.

We are at a crisis point in the history of our evolutionary life. A stark choice now faces humanity. Atheistic science, instead of turning towards the unitive field of consciousness, hubristically refuses to accept the evolutionary push of the human prospect into something greater. It much prefers, for the sake of profit and exploitation, to kill off five billion human beings from the face of the earth, leaving the rest to live as slaves, merely to serve those who believe this world belongs to them. This world is their paradise. Their psychopathic minds have turned this world upside down.

Organized religion, instead of providing humanity with a moral compass, has disengaged us from what consciousness demands be our primary focus. Religion concentrates on its own egoic indoctrination much more than on the liberation which a compassionate Consciousness offers humanity.

The organized doctrine of the church proclaims Christ as a divine ransom to appease his Father. Jesus became the scapegoat for the sins of humanity. The Father objectified him by turning him into a suffering servant who took away the sins of the world. The Father has been so offended by humanity that the only reconciliation possible with his Godhead is divine retribution through the suffering of Jesus, his only begotten Son.

In that one act, God, it seems, would have taken the steam out of the evolutionary push by changing his purpose in midstream. Instead of allowing humanity to sin through its own free will, God became enraged with the evolutionary plan that had been operating quite nicely from the time of the big bang until man began to challenge the process. Instead of suffering through natural selection to a higher level, our process from stardust into a greater refinement needed to be suddenly interrupted. Did God not know from the beginning that it is saints and devils together who push forward the evolutionary plan? Surely Yahweh knew. Why then did he have to send Jesus to violate it?

It would seem organized religion has delivered the wrong message. Not only has it violated the evolutionary process by placing Jesus in the middle of it instead of at the end, but even more shamefully, it has turned God into a monster who ordered the murder of his only begotten Son as a fitting retribution for his offended majesty.

We in the West have almost exclusively turned our backs on what is deepest about us—namely our own spirituality. Our minds have been turned into sponges which only absorb atheistic propaganda. The idea of possibility has been squeezed out of our lexicon. Our culture is colourless. When the imagination is missing, beauty and wonder fly away. The stars no longer tantalize us, and our environment becomes slate grey. It is time for us to wake up and reorientate our gaze in the opposite direction.

Scientific, atheistic conclusions, bereft of the involvement of a higher Intelligence, will inevitably one day end up in bankruptcy. Our so-called sophisticated enlightenment will be recognized as stupidification. Whether we believe it or not life is meaningless without an absolute. We are doomed to be spiritual.

"Our main problem is spiritual." Tell this to the politicians or organized church leaders and they will either feign interest or laugh at you. There is huge indifference or intolerance for transcendent values in the forums of Western power any more. Atheism has reduced humanity to the cyborg state of automatons without a heart. When the heart is missing, life loses its mystery. It becomes totally utilitarian. The human person is no longer necessary simply because he or she can be replaced by robots who will work more precisely and efficiently. The vast majority of the human race will be considered by the shadow hand of the new world order as "useless eaters", only worthy of extermination. *Illuminati* and *elimination* are synonymous words. They contradict the very illumination of their representation.

We in the West, who have been so propagandized to only accept truth in terms of evidence, yet seem to dismiss the findings of quantum physics in respect to consciousness as the groundswell and insubstantial support for all things substantial. Quantum physics, for the first time in human history, provides us with the possibility, without defining it, of a spiritual destiny. Never before in the expansion of human knowledge have science and spirituality been so connected. The very idea of atheism, apart from all of its destructive values, is henceforth challenged to the very core of its principles. Atheism no longer makes sense even on the purely secular level. Quantum physics reintroduces the worthiness of imagination and wonder back into the human equation. Quantum physics is tolerant of conjecture and agnosticism, but never atheism.

The secular science of quantum physics has paved the way for investigation of the invisible as the construct of the visible. A new day is here for the possibility of a realm which exists beyond the grasp of our anthropologically obsessed minds.

The day Science begins to study non physical phenomena
it will make more progress in one decade
than in all the previous centuries
of our existence.

—Nicola Tesla

Modern Western governments, either through atheism or intimidation, are coerced into ignoring the great All existing behind and in human intelligence. Call it, what we will, the fact remains that it is consciousness which substantiates all human existence. There is no escape from this fact. So why do we continue to substantiate and make laws which prostitute this most basic of all tenets?

It is only through the forfeiture of the ego to its continuum into the transcendence that love can be treasured and existentialized on the face of our planet.

Divinity is always involved in just laws and equality. It is the overarching embrace of humanity. Without it, we lose our self-respect, our worth, and our dignity. It is time that Western culture replace its grasping and pushing for the snuff of stuff with a more enlightened grasp of invisibleness, intangibility, abandonment, surrender, and nothingness. The work of spirituality is to make the unmanifest, manifest.

We in the West have become so misinformed that we spend our drugged-out existence in torpor. The corrupt messages with which mass media mind-controls us infects us like a virus. We carry an archon with us and treasure it. It has become our identity and authenticity.

We have forgotten our true heritage and sold it out for twenty pieces of silver. Atheism, Judas-like, has kissed us. We are so impregnated with its infection that we are incapable of understanding it as a wolf in sheep's clothing. Atheism is the most dangerous of all humanity's diseases. It is the primary heart attack. It destroys our interiority.

Atheistic materialism has so swamped the information waves of Western culture that its occupation is on the brink of devastating the human enterprise. We already sense it in the atmosphere. Family life is constantly eroded. The air trumpets fear and strife. The low vibrational spectrum of stress and struggle smother our sanity. We live in a madhouse where the criminals run free while the good are incarcerated. Atheism is terrified that humanity should seek its true identity and self-worth. It recognizes that truth shall set the prisoner free. Its main aim is to keep the human race in ignorance and slavery.

This is where we are right now
No one is left out of the loop.
We are experiencing a reality based on a thin veneer of lies.
A world where greed is our god and wisdom is a sin.

Where division is key and unity is fantasy,
where ego driven cleverness of the mind is praised
rather than the intelligence of the heart.

—Bill Hicks

Without God as our ultimate, humanity is reduced to a state of helplessness. It behoves the West, for the sake of its culture and identity, to wake up. Not only must we deprogram ourselves from our choking atheism, but we must reorientate ourselves towards wonder, appreciation, and prayer if we are to live fully. Man without prayer and appreciation becomes a monster.

My brain is only a receiver.
In the universe there is a core
from which we obtain knowledge strength and inspiration.
I have not penetrated into the secrets of this core,
but I know it exists.

—Nikola Tesla

Atheism has so deadened us that we no longer can decipher the mystery of our ordinary lives as a harbinger of light extraordinary. As we see things with and through the limits of our five senses, we consider life as ordinary, monotonous, and tedious. It seems to lack delight for most of us.

Quantum physics points to a deeper dimension. It proclaims consciousness as the root of all reality. Consciousness envelops all there is. It is infinite and eternal. It carries on after our bodies have turned to dust. We are in this field of consciousness even now as we exist in this state, shackled as we are by matter. In and through our bodily death, consciousness remains unhampered by any obstacle. We enter another realm.

Spirit cannot be measured through a microscope or telescope. It cannot be tried by acid. It dwells in a different realm, beyond human scientific measurement. It has become one with the one, the true, and the beautiful. We can only intuit it through our imagination. On earth, we can appreciate faint smacks of it through our experiences of compassion and the music which emanates from humanity's artistic endeavour. Such experiences are but echoes from the great concentric centre of creativity which is our origin and our destiny.

If the doors of perception were cleansed,
everything would appear to man
as it really is! Infinite!
—William Blake

Our senses betray us. We see, touch, hear, taste, and smell, but dimly. If we could pull back the curtain of our limitations, we would understand life from a totally different perspective. The glory and the pity of our existence is that we take so much of it for granted. We seldom appreciate it for its miraculousness. We have the power within us to turn our lives into an exciting tour of eternity or a drowning journey to the bottom of the sea. No matter our perspective, though, the laws of nature and the conditions of spirituality remain ever constant.

Not only must the vast majority of the Christian West deprogram itself from atheism, but it must be enlightened enough to distance itself from illusion.

Nature loves the game of hide and seek. There is always a little child ready to jump out from every twist and bend on the crooked road to surprise us.

We see less than 1 per cent of the electronic spectrum which surrounds us. A fish eagle sees far more accurately than we do. We hear less than 1 per cent of the auditory spectrum which surrounds us. An owl can hear a mouse scratching over a mile away. We smell less than 1 per cent of the odour spectrum which surrounds us. Dogs amaze us with their ability to trace a smell back to its source many miles away. In comparison to these birds and animals, our senses are indeed limited.

Obviously, we determine our perception by the way we sense it. But life becomes much more obvious when we attempt to understand it on a different or higher frequency. To really appreciate life, we must grow ever more spiritual.

The human eye is but a receptor. What we interpret as real is but an image registered upside down on the photoreceptor of the human eye. Without even batting an eyelid, the brain turns the image in the reverse position so that we can interpret it intelligently.

We decipher light, when fractured by a rain shower, as a rainbow. We do not recognize that all light is white and composed of all the spectrum of colours we see in the rainbow. The fact is that rainbows are an illusion. There is just white light. Animals that do not possess a receptor cone can never see a rainbow. It is our illusion alone. Reality on the purely human level is not really what it seems at all.

Our consciousness interacts with another dimension
Our physical sensors only show us a three dimensional universe.
What exists in the higher dimensions
are entities we cannot touch with our physical sensors.

—Bernard Carr

Even now we are traveling at 220 kilometres across the galaxy of the Milky Way. However, we perceive ourselves as stationary. Not only is it imperative that we wake up from the deceitful propaganda with which material atheism has filled us, but we must rekindle a sense of our spirituality in order to perceive reality as it really is. It is our only way forward.

A transhuman world is determined to end our capacity to perceive beyond the seeming. It is a rogue informer, robbing us of our ability to become spiritual. Atheism is the world's greatest misdirector and deceiver.

It programs us to see the smallest availability of light. It blinds the mind. It is cannibalistic in nature.

It is difficult for the human mind to fully appreciate the fact that life, as our senses decipher it in a three-dimensional way, is an illusion. Our senses seem to trick us. We decipher the information our senses give us as solid. But with an appreciation which probes ever deeper, we realize that the material world is mostly empty space. If all of the heavy matter in the world were squeezed together, it would fit into the palm of a hand. The atom, which is the building block of the material world, is 99.99999999 per cent empty space.

There is an indecipherable space between oneself and the other. The cosmos is one, and consciousness is the unifying field of our reality. We are not separate from one another. This fact alone demands that we must live compassionately with one another. We touch ourselves when we touch another.

Learn to see
realize that everything connects to everything else.
—Leonardo da Vinci

The bellicose, atheist West, with its lust for occupation and murder, needs to learn that all invasions are essentially a plundering journey into one's own territory. To murder and maim is to wage the greatest evil against consciousness. When we kill foreigners, we massacre our own citizens.

Atheistic materialism disorders us. It turns us into an enemy of the universe. Atheistic materialism has robbed us of our possibility. It has hijacked us from our sense of responsibility and dignity. It is the arch-enemy of the human prospect and the destroyer of human decency.

We need a new paradigm. Jesus never saw himself as a pawn in the evolutionary game. He was much too preoccupied living the life of consciousness within him.

What the Christian church teaches as dogma is that the Creator of the universe did violence to his own omniscience. It is as if the whole process of consciousness was a mistake. Man should never have been given the free will to love or sin, according to this interpretation. Jesus thereby becomes the substitute for the sin and errors of all other human beings. The human race can only be saved by him. Humanity's cooperation and obligation has therefore been erased from the picture.

It is written that Jesus said, "I am the way, the truth and the Life." Since the Christian church obtained the copyright to this claim, it has twisted it to mean that it is only through the church's own dispensation that we can find salvation. This hubristic claim is as intellectually insulting as the nihilism of atheism.

What Jesus meant when he said "I am the way, the truth and the life" is literally, poetically, and metaphorically correct. No matter how we twist this aphorism, it remains exactly the same. "I am the way the truth and the life." The only difference is in the interpretation of it.

Jesus never meant this claim to apply to himself only. He meant it to apply universally. The kingdom of heaven lies within each one of us. To the extent that humanity attempts to actualize it, each one of us becomes the way, the truth, and the life. You are the way, I am the way, and we are the way together. Just as Jesus showed the way, so the human race collectively must become the way, the truth, and the life.

We become the way through our compassion for the earth and all of God's creatures featured in it. "As the father has sent me, so now I am sending you." Jesus came to teach us how to live compassionately with one another. He spoke about the interconnection of all living things, one with the other. He spoke about consciousness as the groundswell for human existence, long before quantum physics.

He learned his lessons by remaining close to the inconspicuous truths of the natural world. His inspirational teachings erupted within him in a metaphorical way. "Learn your lessons from the lilies of the field." The kingdom he came to preach was essentially one of the human heart. He measured the insights which he learned from the peasantry of his rural environment. Birth, death, joy, and suffering were everyday experiences learned from his simple surroundings. There were no great tomes of literature available to him in those less enlightened days, and yet not even once did his inspiring teachings ever lead a single follower astray. Even to this day, despite what atheistic men say, his testament remains the one great constant of wisdom which dares humanity to grow in the direction which nature imposes. The soil of the earth fertilized his unique mind. He prefigured the highest and most enlightened way for civilized living.

He never tired from inspiring his followers to seek their higher selves. Where there was hatred, he preached love. Where there was arrogance, he preached humility. Where there was hurt and intransigence, he preached forgiveness. He interpenetrated life with his own magnanimous insight in such a way that even the most ignorant and unenlightened felt uplifted by his compassion and understanding.

The New Testament, although incomplete as a full portrait of his singular character, still reverberates with this message of compassion. We deduce all we need to know about him from his parables and aphorisms. These literary devices resonate with the main implications of his central message.

The remaining parts of the story are considered by many as hyperbole. Whether they are considered historically accurate or not, the fact remains that the centrality of Christ's message remains the same with or without a fanciful language.

Christ did not leave huge tomes of intellectual content for his followers to decipher. Unlike the enfeebling distinctions and answers which organized religion teaches, Jesus was a man of utter simplicity who spoke from his heart through the wisdom he garnered. Even today, he is truly a teacher urgently needed in a world gone mad with dehumanizing intentions.

The end product of transhumanism is to turn us into subhumans. Transhumanism twists evolution into involution. Contrary to the natural law, it is the inverse of what consciousness intends for humanity. To the gurus of the new world order, the transformation which transgenetics and transhumanism engender is considered progress. To arrive at such a state is considered by the atheistic materialists to become superhuman, when in fact, through nanotechnology, it turns the human person into a synthetic replica. Unless we humans put a stop to our heroin-addicted digitalization, we too, because of our arrogance, will be kicked out of the garden of Eden like Adam and Eve.

Nature will only take so much before answering back with a ferocious whiplash. Atheistic materialism and its prodigious machinery can never solve humanity's deepest problems. Transhumanism leads to indentured servitude. We have no need of it. It contradicts the very nature of our evolutionary process. It leads us backward rather than towards the future. The only way forward is to grow into consciousness. We need heart more than head. Jesus lived and modelled this message for us. The truth of his wisdom will heal us. Without the spiritual language of the heart, we become straw men in a wasteland. Our heartbeat alone is our most exultant song.

Every day, the human heart beats two hundred thousand times. It pumps almost a thousand gallons of liquid and travels a thousand miles through our veins and arteries, silent, unnoticed, and unassisted by an individual. The human heart is the most powerful electronic field. The heart has brain cells.

Atheism and organized religion are all head with no heart. No wonder they have such a deleterious effect on the human condition. They separate rather than connect—as it was in the beginning, is now, and ever shall be!

This is the refrain of consciousness. Jesus recognized the eternity of consciousness coupling heart and head together. In the time of the Egyptian pharaohs, the transmigratory passage from the underworld to the outer world, according to the Book of the Dead, was always judged by the balance of the human heart with a feather. Jesus seemed to know this. He balanced human heart and head together. As in the Book of the Dead, Jesus realized the central part played by the human heart in matters both physical and spiritual.

The future of our planet needs the same balance. This is the equation of equality. It is the only access to the eternal. Atheistic materialism, bereft of the human heart, truncates and disintegrates. It is destructive of destiny. Devoid of consciousness, it only touches but never experiences. Through its insistence on form, it misinforms. It relates only to locality, and excludes the bird's song unless it beholds the thrush that is singing it.

There is new data suggesting that the heart's field is directly involved in intuitive perception through its coupling with an energetic information field outside the bounds of space and time.

—Institute of Heart Math

If Western society is ever to escape the madhouse in which atheistic materialism has incarcerated us, then our system of education must become more inclusive and less prejudiced. Science and spirituality must be twinned, one to the other. An integrated education requires the interpenetration and application of spiritual values to our overexercised and exaggerated egotistical needs. As things now stand, we have become a truncated people, incomplete, with a fierce yearning in our hearts for something more. Satisfaction and resolution escape us when we have neglected our consciousness.

Atheistic materialism holds us in limitation to servitude and illusion. If we do not journey beyond our five-sensory perception, we will never learn what lies beyond the seeming. We will remain in the madhouse of our present reality, enslaved and indentured through the power and control of the elites. This is where the gurus of atheistic materialism wish to permanently locate us. Robbed of our self-esteem and worth, we become manipulated to address the needs of our psychopathic overlords. Only consciousness will liberate us. Our spirituality is the only way possible to free ourselves from our manacled sense of solidity. There is much more to life than the feeble human eye can ever see. But the elites do not want us to know this. Atheistic materialism desperately requires that we stay on the surface of seeming.

Atheism abhors and ignores the universal reality of consciousness, which when embraced will liberate us to see more clearly. Atheism is anticonsciousness. It is a total contradiction of infinite awareness. Despite its mind control and propaganda, it is doomed to failure because our yearning remains our one great reality. Atheistic materialism does not address our uneasiness and remains the root cause of all our frustration. When we search and become more aware of the interconnectedness and interrelationship of all life in the natural world, we discover we cannot be apart or outside of it. We are not separate.

What lies between us and the rest of what is, which we consider outside of us, is but an illusion. Empty space makes us a part of the one hologram. This understanding, through which science and spirituality complement each other, must become the bedrock and foundational support of our educational system. Without this approach, information only leads to a doomsday scenario.

Spirituality is interdenominational. It is nonsectarian. It does not threaten any cultural belief system. It belongs to our human collectivity and has universal application.

A holistic educational approach is possible. It is nonthreatening and avoids the prejudices which cultural religious differences introduce. Our spirituality, in the fullest sense of human consciousness, defines us. It is in our very rootedness and inheritance. Nature dooms us to be spiritual. Spirituality is indelibly stamped on our essence.

Any educational system which neglects the registration of spirituality in its curriculum will manufacture a product bereft of compassion. A society without a heart will live for work instead of life. This is precisely the present state of our education system. Our children, dumbed down to a purely animalistic level without a spiritual dimension, will one day stampede as beasts of burden. Deprived of the sense of a discriminate conscience, our progeny will gore the human race to death.

On the other hand, when spirituality is infused with all the unfolding discoveries of science, wonder and awe will erupt and give us reason for celebration. It is precisely because both organized religion and atheistic science have preached dualism instead of unity and integration that this world has become a madhouse. Our spirituality comes from the interconnection between immanence and transcendence. All is one cosmologically.

The Christian church especially, as the renowned interpreter of the Christian way, has adopted a lifestyle in total contradiction to the simplicity of the Nazarene. Its promulgations are all head with no heart. Its liturgies have lost their mystery, and its celebrations are a test in endurance and mortification. It has crowned itself with croziers, mitres, and all the trappings of control and might.

Just like the control of the fascist, atheistic media, the church has burned the life-enhancing message of the Nazarene into a charred loft with no one singing in it. It has invaded that sacred private space where consciousness lives in each individual. It has rewritten the story and told God that its recounting of the Jesus message is better than the original.

Like atheism, organized religion has made a mess of things. Like atheism, it has turned everything inside out. The message of Jesus Christ can be summed up in one word: compassion. But like every other institution, Western religion organized itself into a corporation. With the support of the Emperor Constantine, it became a political institution. From that time forward, it editorialized the message of its founder to suit its own agenda.

If organized religion is ever to become relevant in this world, then it will have to redeem itself and remain true to the central message of Jesus. In an atheistic world which denies supernatural intervention in human affairs, the miracles which surround the life of Jesus must be seen as an expression in literary form, used merely to enhance the remarkableness of this unique man. They are meant as a device to express the character of his singularity.

The message of Jesus as Redeemer and Saviour, according to natural law, makes no earthly sense today. The clash of opposites, such as good and evil, light and dark, and agony and ecstasy, are fundamental to the natural law. Opposing possibilities are written into the very process needed for new life. In order that Jesus become our Saviour and Redeemer, we must be redeemed from something evil. But good and evil are inseparable. One cannot come into being without the other. This clash happens inside of each one of us. It is not outside the self but within.

If that is the unitive law of the natural world, then it is impossible for God to interfere with it. To do so would be a violation of what the Creator established from the beginning.

Organized religion has avoided the logical sequence of this argument by turning Jesus into a scapegoat. The problem of sin in this world cannot be solved by an external, scapegoat saviour. This work must be carved out by our individual selves alone. Sin and evil are not dualistic. They are unitive along with everything else that exists in this world.

If there is no sickness, then there is no need for a cure. Evil in this world arises accumulatively because we as individuals have not done our homework in bringing a balance to the warring opposites within ourselves. That is why we as individuals, just like Jesus, must come home to our own centres and battle courageously between the forces of good and evil which exists within each one of us. The elites of this world, be they secular or religious, want to control our God-given individual choice concerning our own individual reality. Organized religion tells us, in effect, that we do not have the power within our being to be our own saviours and redeemers.

Jesus did not come to suspend or upset the natural law with any sort of sensational miracles. He lived his life so compassionately and with such intensity that two thousand years later, the world is still impressed by his goodness and reverence. He disclosed the inner, unifying world of consciousness by teaching humanity that our vertical search for God must be lived horizontally. We become our own saviours and redeemers to the extent we become other-centred.

The cosmos is one. Consciousness is the unifying field of all reality. Consciousness lives invisibly. It lives through and passes away from materiality. When matter morphs into immateriality, it exists in a sphere where the microscope and the telescope are no longer necessary.

Objective, rational science has nothing to tell us about an afterlife except to point out its miraculousness. Atheism dabbles with theism without first learning its alphabet. It has no competence to preach metaphysics. It knows nothing of ontology and yet arrogantly proclaims its message as though it were the expert in all these disciplines. It opens its mouth much too widely and selfishly. It wants to gobble up everything.

It is only when this world begins to realize that consciousness runs through everything that we will begin to reverence and respect it as the one great energy which will engender humanity. Only those who attempt to live spiritually can direct humanity to a higher rung on the evolutionary ladder. The appalling sickness we perceive extant in contemporary society is due to the lack of a cultivated spiritual consciousness. Organized religion is greatly to blame for this state of affairs.

Atheism thrives to the extent that a true cultivation of spirituality is not modelled by the church hierarchy. Still arrogantly standing on the rock of its foundation, it has aborted its meaning. Power corrupts.

Even rocks, however, are full of empty space. They need to be, or else they will collapse into a lump of heavy matter. Everything that lives must be porous and allow fresh air to filter its lungs. To live is to change constantly. An institution which stands still goes nowhere. It needs fresh air. It is only Christ's central message of compassion that matters. The rest is fluff. An institution built on fluff has no foundation. The rock and the mission which Jesus talked about will only appear when his followers live out his message in the real world. The rock which the ecclesiastical elites stand on is as equally closed or open to evil as the church of atheism.

Spirituality cannot be legislated nor mediated by anyone. It has to be cultivated in the garden of one's own soul. Any institution which canonizes itself as a mediator in the dispensation of the spiritual experience, through its hubristic egoism, makes a god out of itself. As the gospel of Thomas says, we are guided through the inspiration of our own inner light. Organized religion, for its own benefit, expatriates humanity from the original ground which Jesus spent his life proclaiming. Spirituality is caught. It cannot be taught!

The real God is so big that there are as many approaches to divinity as there are individuals. The way that the Nazarene lived is the process the unified field of consciousness invites us to follow. The message is simple, despite the church's efforts to complicate it. Love your neighbour as yourself. Do unto others as you would have them do unto you. This is a unitive call. It is about relationship. This is all we need to know. It teaches us how we must live in our contemporary matrix.

Quantum physics teaches us that there is no matter as such. Our all is our nothingness.

All matter originates and exists only by virtue of a force
which brings the particle of an atom to vibration and
holds this minute solar system of the atom together.
We must assume behind this force the existence
of a conscious and intelligent mind.
This mind is the matrix of all matter.

—Max Planck

Only a conscious spirituality can turn things around and bring balance to the planet.

The Creator, from the moment of the big bang, has filled us with a divine energy and creativity. In our contemporary Frankenstein world of fear and corruption, we need the attention of a benign Creator to set all our crooked ways straight.

We have arrived at an axial point in our planet's history and formation. Our future lies in the realm of a more developed consciousness. We grow in compassion to the degree that we inform ourselves with divine consciousness.

The key to growth is the introduction of a higher dimension of consciousness into our awareness.

—Lao Tzu

We live in a world which has become expert in the covert subtlety of mind control and propaganda. The madhouse which modern society now lives in is completely inverted. Compassion and the intelligence of the human heart are considered naive and stupid. Materialism teaches that profit, no matter the animalistic goring we undertake to get there, is the only way forward for humanity. "Cooperation" has been degraded to spell "corporation". As Shakespeare said, "There is something wrong in the state of Denmark."

Thousands of children at this moment are starving to death in Yemen. Last night two hundred more refugees were drowned at sea off the coast of Libya. Thousands of our fellow human beings are freezing and dying in the thinly covered camps of Lebanon, Greece, and Turkey. Palestinians are daily tortured and murdered through the brutal dictatorship of the Israeli government. Western civilization refuses to cry out in unison against such cruelty.

We use science to confirm our atheism when it suits our purposes. At the same time, it is science which confirms, through quantum physics, that all life on earth is one. But we do not like the findings of science when they do not solidify our own prejudices. The fact remains that when we expand our minds to travel beyond the illusory, we are all one to one another. Jesus has told us this in his parables. Hinduism tells us, "Thou art that." And St Catherine said, "My me is God."

Every human person is constructed from the same blueprint of creation. We are one as the cosmos is one. We are in one another. Quantum physics confirms our spirituality. Atheistic, materialistic science is very selective when it comes to this evidential truth. It dismisses consciousness because consciousness is so contrary to its own thesis. With the understanding given to us by quantum physics, spirituality and materiality, immanence and transcendence are joined together as one. Truly we become each other's brothers and sisters.

When we allow this understanding to take possession of the very core of our being, this planet will no longer experience division. There will never be a foreigner or a slave among us any more. As the Irish rune says, "There goes Christ in the guise of the stranger."

We will go on expressing our cultural differences, of course, and find beauty and reverence in their difference. But never more shall we raise a hand in violence against a foreigner who in reality is our sister or brother. This is the possibility given to us through an intelligent understanding of our spirituality. The consciousness of our spirituality will liberate us from hostility. There are no lines of delineation or containment on God's map of creation. Passports and national boundaries are of man's creation and invention.

Western civilization has been covertly choked to such an extent that it no longer makes the connection between all the war machinery, the bombs, the guns, and the bullets which it sells to poorer countries and the innocent children, women, and men its profitable sales leave screaming in death pains behind them. The Zionist illuminati who live in the top tier of the command post are removed from the carnage of human suffering they have caused. Even if they were to walk among the corpses left behind by their murderous ways, their hearts would remain psychopathic because of their preoccupation with money and profit.

There is an elephant in the room of Western psychopathic behaviour, but the political establishment refuses to acknowledge its presence. A shadow government controls the Western world. Shills do all the dirty work for them. We think our votes make a difference, but the winners in our elections are selected long before our ballots are counted. Ninety-eight per cent of the world's wealth lies in the control of the Zionist illuminati. With the obscenity of such unimaginable wealth, the destiny of the Western world can be bought or sold according to the dictates of the few, leaving the rest of the human race in penury and poverty.

The Federal Reserve of the United States is the reserve bank into which most of the money in the West flows. Even the federal government of the United States has to borrow its money with interest from it. This swindle alone is the greatest hoax in the history of the United States. The wealthy few who control this bank are indirectly involved in the deterioration and destruction of Christian values in the West.

The power and control of the Zionist illuminati is so infectious and destructive that even now the very Constitution of the United States, crafted so carefully, is being torn to shreds.

I want to tell you something very clear.
Don't worry about American pressure on Israel,
we, the Jewish people control America
and the Americans know it.
—Ariel Sharon

Once we squeeze all we can out of the United States,
it can dry up and blow away.
—Benjamin Netanyahu

The West has become so intimidated that unless we stay with the orthodoxy and doctrine of the Zionist illuminati, we are considered a threat to homeland security. To condemn Israel for its Nazi-like persecution of the Palestinians is now considered anti-Semitism. The West is not even allowed to discuss it without being accused of a hate crime. We become terrorists merely by challenging what is considered politically correct.

We skirt the truth at all costs, never giving even remote recognition to the elephant in the room. We make detours and relentlessly drive up dead-end streets; we chat and politicize endlessly, accomplishing nothing, because we are too afraid to admit and confront the cancer that is stealing the centrality of the human heart, which is unavoidably necessary in all human deliberations.

The consensus of Christians in the United States, although mostly articulated behind closed doors, is that Jews, who represent only 2 per cent of the population, influence America's policies to a degree far in excess of their representations. Zionists not only control the Federal Reserve and the banking cartel, but also the legal, medical, and educational systems. Hollywood is Zionist controlled and owned, as are all the main channels of broadband communication. So powerful have these tiny elites become that they have even infiltrated the Supreme Court.

Christian values, so clearly evident in the shaping of the United States Constitution, are slowly being eroded and replaced by the values of Zionism, which are defined as the final solution to the planet's problems on the Atlanta Guide Stone. Brain bashing of the Christian value system in America is now so prevalent that it has become unnoticed, while anti-Semitism is considered a mortal sin. Christian politicians, bought by Zionist money, never mention the presence of the elephant in the room. They argue ad nauseum about injustice and inequality without ever naming its nemesis.

Fundamentalist Christians, through ignorance and literalism, invert the meaning of the Jesus story. They substantiate the Zionist apparatus of lies and power. They promote the boundaries and control of the Holy Land as the rightful inheritance of the Zionists, thereby continuing the slaughter of innocent Palestinians. Christian fundamentalists treat Zionists as though they are the Chosen People. The Old Testament God of the Zionism may address their bloodcurdling need for lust, jealousy, and murder, but the New Testament God of Jesus totally contradicts the new world order of Zionism.

Fundamentalist Christians are blind to the fact that Christ did not die as a rebel out of a commitment to a territory or a boundary. He gave his life in compassion for the downtrodden. Moreover he called the scribes and the Pharisees of his own day whitened sepulchres, and whipped the Zionist moneylenders out of the synagogue. Christian fundamentalists fail to make the connection between the scribes, the Pharisees, and present-day Zionism.

Zionism is European in origin. It has no claim to the Semitism of Palestine. It has come out of the Caucasus, and its adherents, the Ashkenazis, are converts to Judaism. They are not Semites. Anti-Semitism is a misnomer. But it has been used as ploy to suppress criticism. To paraphrase Voltaire, truth is what you are not allowed to discuss. The power and control of Zionism is never mentioned in the halls of officialdom. Zionism is expert in propaganda and mind control—so much so that the vast majority of innocent Jews do not even realize the con job Zionism has been operating on them as well as the Gentile world. The vast majority of Jews, like the rest of our brothers and sisters, are good hard-working people. They struggle to pay their bills and put food on their tables. They love and take care of their families just like the rest of humanity. They do not feel chosen nor set apart. They live perfectly ordinary lives.

However, Zionism is an archon on their backs. It has hijacked their identity, just as it has hijacked the Christian identity of the United States. If Zionism continues on its backward push to natural selection, it will inevitably cause a bloodbath upon the planet. When a people claim specialness, superiority, or supremacy and attempt to control the masses, conflict is born. For the second time there will be a Holocaust, and innocence will once again be the victim.

In order to stop this from happening, the Christian West must become heroic and courageous enough to recreate the principles of its identity. Compassion, which is an affair of the heart, is sadly lacking in a world which is evolving into a future head-only society. It is an atheistic brave new world which Zionism envisions. As Christians, we cannot allow this to happen. But we must protest nonviolently.

For a start, we can renounce its propaganda and learn to source our information from alternative media. We should become suspicious of politicians who support the murderous tactics of the Israeli government. We can assume that they have been bought off through the endless supply of corrupt money which Zionism is steeped in. We must revert to our Christian heritage and learn to be as Jesus lived. Having material stuff did not register highly in his message.

Christ's story is the most universal and tolerant of all messages. It is nondiscriminatory. It applies to the East and to the West. It is relevant to Black and White, Jew and Christian alike. It is the highest achievement in the story of our evolutionary process. This is the energy which will push us into a higher reality.

Compassion invites, but it does not compel. It calls us to a recognition of the truth. It confronts evil and calls it by its name. It does not detour or drive up endless dead-end streets. It does not avoid nor imply. Its only brutality is its honesty. It is the most necessary of all qualities in our political interchanges. It looks in the eye of the elephant in the room and pronounces its identity. It gives us the courage necessary to tell the Zionist illuminati that, contrary to the consciousness which binds us one to the other, atheism has inflicted the greatest wound on human process and progress. It is the very antithesis of human dignity and divinity's intention.

Compassion must be centrally involved in all our political endeavours. It applies to Black and White alike. It applies to Jew and Christian alike. There is no overtone of supremacy or superiority in its application. It refuses to divide us into the few and the many. It avails itself even to the enemy and answers all applications, no matter the complication of the petitioner. It is the ointment of consciousness which grows us all together in the one tree of many branches. It roots us together in the one wellspring of sustenance. Its greatest ache is that we avail ourselves of it or invoke it so infrequently in our political undertakings and dialogue. It is the most curative of all medicines and bandages the wounds of everyone.

This world, despite our cultural religious differences, needs the central message of the Christ-man to guide and save it from destruction. His message of compassionate love is the most soothing ever to register on the human ear. The application of his message, through its faithfulness to all that is natural, will catapult the human race into a balanced reconstruction.

This world has not been created to be millionaire-driven. Its radial force invites us upward and not downward. Economy is not our true purpose. Quantum physics teaches that we are at heart all a part of the one universal Consciousness. The cosmos is one. Nature demands that we share rather than spare.

The ego becomes an empire of selfishness when denied its future flight in outwardness. Atheistic materialism, for the sake of profit, destroys the purpose for community building. The one, the true, and the beautiful, without the photosynthesis of compassion, becomes as dead as a doornail.

We cannot grow or be sustained through inward selfishness. Only some dynamo outside our egoic selves can bring us enlightenment.

Atheism puts an end to this essential flow. Despite its clever answers, it steeps the world in darkness. Isness already surrounds us. It does not need rational proof or evidence. To require evidence is akin to asking a fish to identify the immensity of all the moving waters of the world. The evidence which an atheist demands reflects more the ignorance of its questioning author than the sublimity and wisdom involved in the answer.

Atheistic materialism centres totally on the product without ever making a connection to the producer. The ultimate tragedy of atheism is its forgetfulness. It throws the human race out of balance. The new world order which the atheistic agenda has imposed on our already broken and fractured world gathers nothing but money into jars. It expects the rest of humanity to pick up the shards from the jars in which it has imported its stolen spoils.

We have once more reached a defining moment, such as the jump from an ape to a human person. Now that we have made that leap into a consciousness of being conscious, the same radial pull tugs at our consciousness once again. Survival of the fittest again presents itself. Do we stand still on the level of natural selection, or do we process into an experience outside of space and time? Atheism wants us to stand still. Its atheistic gurus tell us, "This material world and its experience is all there is. Evolution is over and done with. Be happy with your accumulation of material goods! Only science will save you." Jesus teaches the exact opposite.

In the words of Russia's great writer Aleksandr Solzhenitsyn, "The meaning of earthly existence, lies not, as we have been used to thinking, in prospering but in the development of the soul."

Compassion is always other-related. God enters into our human reality the minute we practise it. A compassionate atheist is an oxymoron! The moment he or she displays compassion, atheism flies out the window, despite any reasonable argument to the contrary.

The new world order which atheism imposes on us is totally destructive because, in debunking spirituality, it takes all human dignity and hope with it. A new world order of spirituality, on the other hand, brings with it a restorative justice. It returns to each human person his or her dignity and uniqueness. It does not divide and conquer, as atheism does. It unifies. Atheism not only divides and conquers in foreign lands, as the West has done in the Middle East, but it also wages war on its own citizens. It destroys the moral structure whenever and wherever it is allowed to blossom.

Atheism hates and seeks to destroy the unifying field of consciousness. The natural law demands that the onward push of global consciousness must be respected. If the United Nations does not obey this, it becomes instead an assistant to the powerful, atheistic, controlling countries of the West. As Dietrich Bonhoeffer, the inspiring German martyr, said, "Silence in the face of evil, is itself evil."

A new world order with the central message of Christ stamped upon it will heal the earth from the devastating conclusion which atheism offers. When the holy name of God's assistance is called upon in our political arena, a greater Intelligence than our own will guide us. The way may be painful, but the result will always be a peaceful solution.

A baby aborted in midstream has only experienced darkness. That is precisely where the atheistic evolutionary story has placed us. The full experience of daylight can be only enjoyed through a passionate struggle and acquiescence to darkness.

How can the human race ever become enlightened unless its journey of complexity consciousness is not energized by some great, radial Intelligence? God must be central in all our human deliberations.

Quantum physics teaches that the atom, as the base of materiality, is 99.99999999 per cent empty space. This means that we humans are almost devoid of matter, so there is truly no fixed material world. The material world, as we think we see it, is an illusion. Our minds convert reality in a three-dimensional way; they cloak consciousness with matter. Solidity is all in the mind.

All we see is a representation of reality and not its essence. If we could really appreciate consciousness in its full purity, then this world would know that you are part of me and I am part of you, because we are all aspects of the same infinite consciousness we call God. Because the mind reflects but a tiny vibration of pure consciousness, most of the divine energy within us lies untapped, undiscovered, and unappreciated. To change this world, we must tap into consciousness.

Money, profit, economy, cultural tribalism, materialistic atheism, banks, war, murder, and the spoliation of the planet for the sake of egoic greed are destructive. They send out a negative vibration which destroys creativity.

Be the change you want to see in the world.

—Gandhi

There once lived among us a unique man who understood the indivisibility of a higher consciousness from the inhabited planet which divinity created. Jesus lived his life in total humility and in alignment with his Creator. His story is unique. The courage and the passion with which he lived and died still stand as the most awe-inspiring life ever lived. The revolutionary impact of a compassionate lived experience still has the power to impress even atheists. No one has made such an intense impression as he. He shunned the trappings of an egotistical, materialistic world. His sayings remain the groundswell for a civilized society. His compassionate understanding of the unifying connection between body and spirit still holds out the best hope for humanity's integration and destiny.

In this corrosive age, when so much ugliness and egoic materialism are swamping our world with negativity, perhaps for the first time we might begin to integrate Christ's message of love and compassion into contemporary living. Neither the religious nor the secular authorities of the West have ever seriously tried to incorporate Jesus's nonpartisan approach in solving the problems of life on this planet. The secular, materialistic, driven world considers his message naive and even stupid. The West is full of brawn and little spirit. We need the gentle message of Jesus to bring balance back into our sensate world.

Religion has imprisoned Christ's central message in its own self-interested propaganda. Had his message been allowed to fully impregnate the human spirit, we would know we are citizens of a heavenly kingdom, a people of a royal court, and a nation set apart. Instead, politicized religion has moved Christ's centrality to the periphery.

The Western world has morally fallen apart because all the passionate dancing and singing of celebration has been squeezed out of the Jesus message. The church itself is responsible for this.

Nature is intolerant of a vacuum. With the leader missing, scouts with ulterior motives infiltrate and misdirect the mission, to such an extent that direct opposites become bedfellows propelled by diabolical intentions. If the Christian West is ever to rediscover its heritage, then not only its secular institutions must change, but also the constitution of the church.

We need a new understanding of the Christ message applied in an interpenetrating way. The promulgations beamed out by grey-haired arrogant patriarchs has little meaning or relevance in our confused world any more. We have lost our moral compass, and the church has missed the opportunity to save us from atheism.

Our contemporary understanding of God is but a set of commandments and illusory doctrines which have no relevance in a world set ablaze by the promise of science and technology. Science and technology have brought us many wonderful inventions which can be constructive when used sensitively. Their one great flaw is that they separate us from one another more than they bring us together. The more we enter the world of virtual addiction, the more we remove ourselves from our interconnection and interrelationship with our own ground and the soil of nature. Materialistic atheism alienates us from the lessons which nature teaches.

Whether we live in huge cities or the fruitfulness of the countryside, we all have the same dependency on the offerings of the natural, selfless earth. We are all the same when it comes to sustainability. We become disjointed spiritually when we eat the food which nourishes us without giving recognition and reverence to the source of our nourishment.

Organized religion has been more caught up in human sexuality than it has in ecology. Our greatest sin is the prophylactics we wear to smother the birth of divinity in our psyches. The human mind has been atheistic and religiously plundered to such a degree that we no longer recognize the interconnection between spirit and matter. God forbid organized religion should ever promote recognition of the same consciousness running through matter, the way they proclaim it in sacramental theology. Organized religion, just like atheism, removes us from an appreciation of the sacred in all created reality.

Sometimes an appreciative walk in the woods or a stroll by the seashore can give us a sense of integration and transcendence far greater than what we get by obeying the compulsory mandate to worship on a Sunday morning.

Organized religion has made such a mess out of its mission that for the most part it has done more harm than good in explaining an understanding of spirituality. It has disconnected humanity from its original ground and replaced that ground with obedience to the laws of its own making. Along with atheism, it has inculcated spiritual illiteracy in Western society. Ignorance and fear are the main tools used by elites to keep the masses under control. Constantine used these tactics at Nicaea in AD 425. The atheistic elites use the same techniques today in their terror-laden propaganda.

It is spirituality alone which teaches us how to discriminate between good and evil. Without it, we allow forces outside ourselves to determine us.

A huge task awaits the incarnation of a new world order. It is absolutely necessary that the new world order of atheism be toppled. This can only be done through the spirituality of disobedience. Each individual must, through an integral choice, give his or her own witness. We must learn the lessons of our new alphabet to fully establish our new world order. The letters A-B-C are no longer enough.

The mission confronting us is tough. Spirituality cannot be explained. It must be lived. There is no other way to eradicate atheism. It can never be accomplished through violence. The compassionate way of Christ is our only answer.

The Christian story must be recreated with the excitement, passion, and courage of its author. Once again it must centre on the authenticity and physicality of a man who recognized his commonality with suffering and confused humanity. Christ was a torn and tattered man like most of us, but, true to his own dignity and integrity, he shaped the edifice of his God consciousness to such a degree that, two thousand years later, his name is even recalled in a lot of our curses!

The paradox is that humanity, with all of its profanity, is really crying out for some kind of sanity to prevail in a world that has been turned upside down. Our sin becomes our very cry for salvation. Absence carries with it a profound message. Violence and corruption are our cry for a moral compass which will save us. Most of us hear the cry. We recognize our woundedness. But we have yet to learn the presence of God in absence. It is we who are the absence. The hope remains that, one day soon, our terror and sin will bring us to our knees.

The crassness and profanity of modern society are a paradoxical attempt to scream out at God for his absence, when it is we who are the absent ones.

While atheism dismisses God, organized religion teaches that God exists. However, organized religion has relegated divinity to a space which is the antithesis of hell on earth. But if God is not involved with us in our hell on earth, then there is no need for the divine to exist at all. A God who is absent from the here will never be found in the hereafter.

We are God's experiment with divinity. Our cooperation is needed for a proper solution. The central message of Jesus revolves around an earth tested by the realities of both heaven and hell. Jesus did not come to redeem humanity from governance by the natural law. He learned through his own struggle that life erupts with joy when lived in a spirit of self-forgetfulness. Humanity redeems itself through selflessness. This is the message of Jesus.

He hammered out God on the anvil of his own personality. He let the light of divinity shine out from his own interior. He pleaded from the mountaintop of his own experience that we awaken to the one God living inside of us. Without this relationship, divorce will be our only marriage.

Few, if any, have ever reached such an intimacy with divinity as Jesus did. Through his own process of courageous refinement, he gave astonishing witness to the God within each one of us. His accomplishment has been an inspiration to those who follow him. Compassion is his one sacrament. This is the one mark he demanded for ordination. All else is but hubristic adornment. Medieval vestments, mitres, and croziers are mere theatre, bereft of pedagogy. A tattered cloak and a pair of wooden shoes might better be used to capture his spirit. Such symbols would enact a more searing impact on an audience searching for a moral compass and leadership. Golden croziers and diamond rings symbolize snobbery and are the very antithesis of the Jesus message.

The usurpation of power and control changes lies into seeming truth. We have reached an axial point in the development of Western civilization.

We must retrench and recover the power which the atheistic agenda has stolen from us—or else we destroy ourselves.

A singularity does indeed confront us. However, it is the singularity of Christ's central message, which this world must follow if the human potential for oneness is ever to be realized. The singularity of transhuman technology which atheism proposes is in total opposition to all that is natural. It will only destroy us. Far better to live with the accumulated wisdom of the ages and human intuition. To go forward, we must sometimes retreat to recover balance.

We do not need the Atlanta Guide Stone to show us the way into the future. Jesus has already done that for us. In the name of this heroic man, in the hope for a future cosmotheandric world, and for the sake of peace and unity on earth, might we unite and say together, the prayer he taught us two thousand years ago:

Our Father, you live in heaven.

You are the Holy One.

May we realize daily that you live within us.

Through our complexity consciousness, may we cooperate with your plan and bring the unity of consciousness, which you will, into fruition, here on earth as it is in heaven.

We ask you to nourish our spiritual illiteracy and be our moral compass in all our choices.

Give us the courage to forgive others as you so compassionately love and forgive us.

May we realize the insufficiency of all material goods, so available but never fully satisfactory.

We recognize within our being an unquenchable longing for something more.

We petition your attention to our spiritual hunger.

Through our search, in the inevitable exchange of faith and doubt, no matter the circumstance, stay with us on our incredible evolutionary journey.

And never allow us lose sight of the fact that we are your cocreators. Amen.